NATIONAL CAMERA

University of Minnesota Press / Minneapolis London

NATIONAL CAMERA

Photography and Mexico's Image Environment

Roberto Tejada

Roberto Tejada

Tucson April 25, 2013

Portions of chapter 1 were previously published in *CR: The New Centennial Review* 4, no. 2 (2004): 1–31. Early portions of chapter 3 appeared in *In Focus: Manuel Álvarez Bravo* (Los Angeles: Getty Publications, 2001), in *Manuel Álvarez Bravo: Parábolas ópticas* (Mexico City: Museo Nacional de Arte, 2002), and in *Mexico/New York: Photographs by Álvarez Bravo, Cartier-Bresson, and Walker Evans* (New York: D.A.P., 2003).

Published by the University of Minnesota Press
111 Third Avenue South, Suite 290
Minneapolis, MN 55401-2520
http://www.upress.umn.edu

Library of Congress Cataloging-in-Publication Data

Tejada, Roberto.
National camera : photography and Mexico's image environment / Roberto Tejada.
p. cm.
Includes bibliographical references and index.
ISBN 978-0-8166-6081-0 (hc : alk. paper)
ISBN 978-0-8166-6082-7 (pb : alk. paper)
1. Photography—Mexico—History. 2. Mexico—History—Pictorial works.
3. Photography—Social aspects—Mexico. I. Title.
TR28.T45 2009
770.972—dc22

2008039250

Printed in the United States of America on acid-free paper

16 15 14 13 12 11 10 09   10 9 8 7 6 5 4 3 2 1

for Susana Tejada, *dans les archives*

Contents

Itinerary: Travels in the Image Environment

> History comes to a head in a moment of disaster, in the time of the disaster that structures the danger of history. In the almost-no-time of this breakdown, thinking comes to a standstill. It experiences itself as interruption. . . .
>
> One can no more escape this obligation to think than one can escape the obligation to act. And what must be thought and acted upon, under the illumination or darkness of these questions, is the possible convergence of photography and history.
>
> **—Eduardo Cadava, *Words of Light: Theses on the Photography of History***

On October 16, 1909, presidents William Howard Taft of the United States and Porfirio Díaz of Mexico convened for a meeting in the borderland cities of El Paso, Texas, and Ciudad Juárez, Chihuahua. A first for the two dignitaries, the encounter was marked with no small measure of official ceremony and speculation as rendered newsworthy, at least in part, by the mass circulation press of the day.[1] A series of information service photographs comprise a document of that diplomatic occasion, and, together, they configure a narrative trope relevant to a larger historical and theoretical picture I draw in this book. Because there is evidence of Díaz's neighborly performance documented in these images as a means to secure his failing despotic position, these photographs should reveal the political uses of image technologies and the social investments they were thought to render profitable. At that pause in the pageantry of ribbons, flags, and national anthems, captured by the photographic moment of the Taft–Díaz encounter—between the solemnities of epaulets, coaches, crested helmets, and top hats on the 1909 borderlands of El Paso and Ciudad Juárez—these images trace not only the complex political and historic wagers between Mexico and the United States, a troubled history preceding the occasions they represent and predisposing in part those that followed, but also the kinds of representational interactions that surfaced and developed in the image environment later distributed between the two nations, a handful of which are the subject of this study.

It begins with a photograph of Díaz rendered in confident midstride down an infantry-lined street of Ciudad Juárez, surrounded by an entourage of cabinet members and military staff (Figure 1). He is shown heading toward the cameraman, presumably toward the U.S.–Mexico International Bridge that he is to cross—his straight-on gaze conveniently in the area of the photographic vanishing point. On the other side of the Río Bravo, the camera—substituting here for Díaz and his diplomatic corps—faces the Nineteenth Infantry Battalion, headed, we are told in a caption, by General Franklin Bell (Figure 2). The Mexican commander in chief and his officials are greeted at the dividing line by the relevant North American authorities (Figure 3), then led away in a carriage and by an equestrian retinue shown parading through a street of El Paso—whose building facades are lined with American flags folded into fans framing head-shot images of Taft. En route to the determined meeting place (not insignificantly, El Paso's chamber of commerce), crested military riders in formation are rendered the instant they

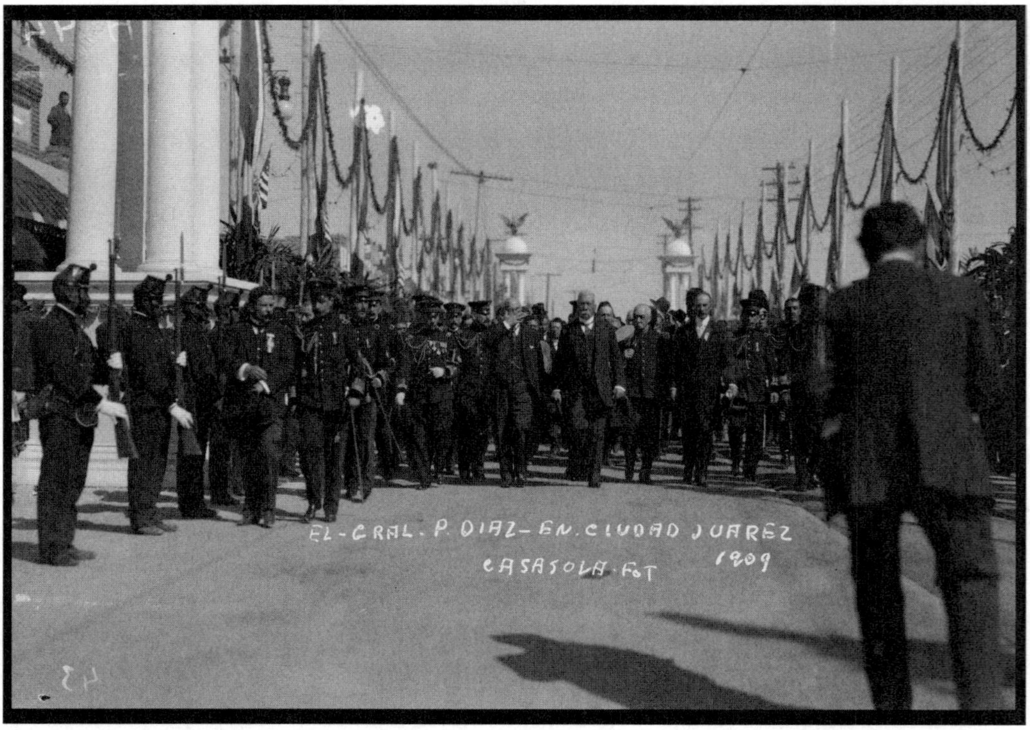

Figure 1. Porfirio Díaz and military staff, Ciudad Juárez, 1909. Casasola Archive. Copyright SINAFO–Fototeca Nacional.

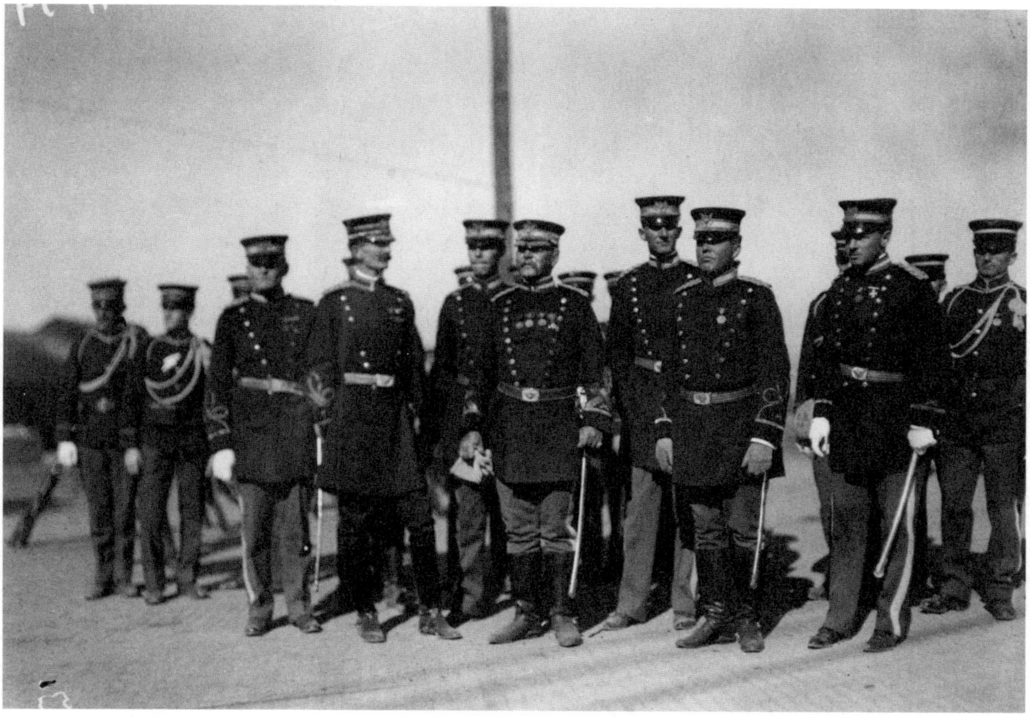

Figure 2. Nineteenth Infantry Battalion, headed by General Franklin Bell, 1909. Casasola Archive. Copyright SINAFO–Fototeca Nacional.

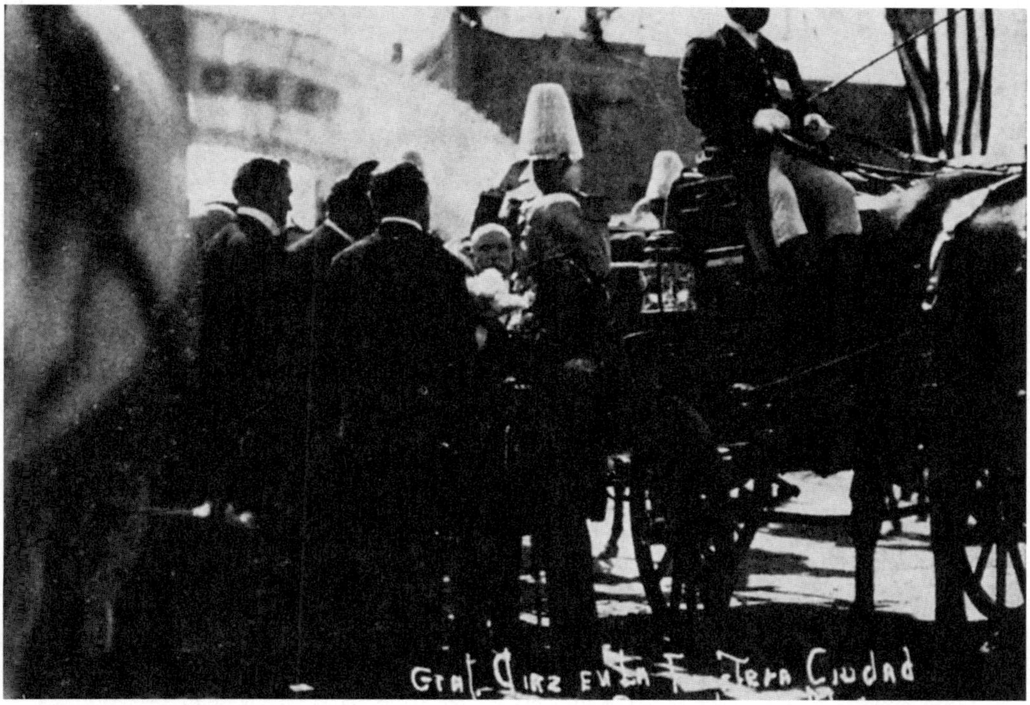

Figure 3. Porfirio Díaz greeted by North American authorities, El Paso, Texas, 1909. Casasola Archive. Copyright SINAFO–Fototeca Nacional.

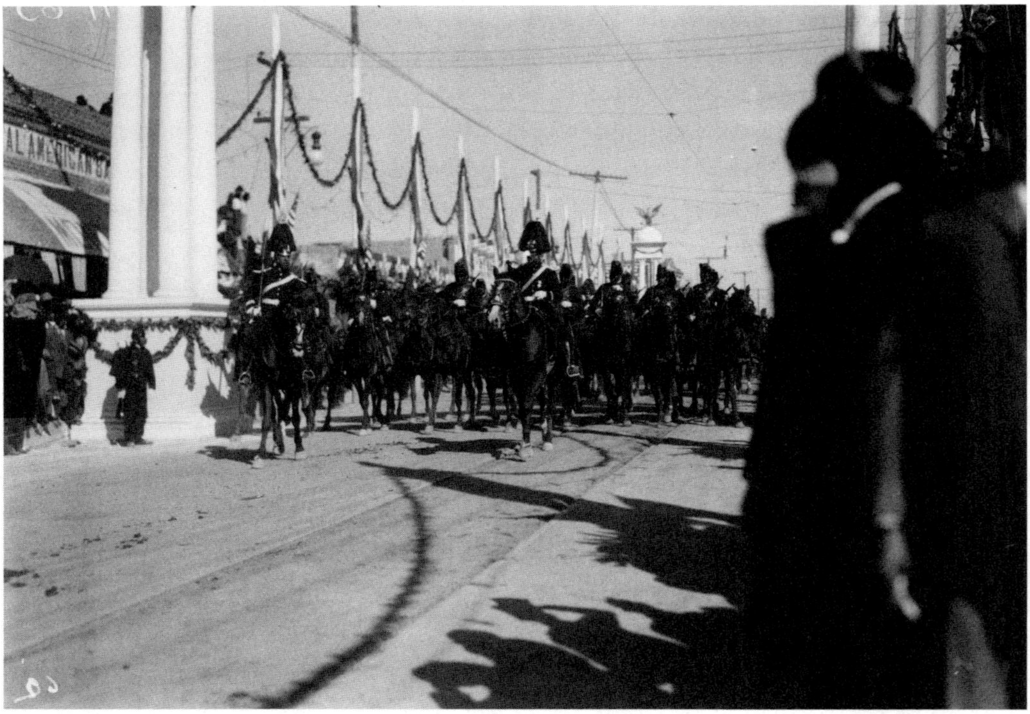

Figure 4. Military procession with American flags, El Paso, Texas, 1909. Casasola Archive. Copyright SINAFO–Fototeca Nacional.

advance to safeguard the horse-drawn carriage in which Díaz—beyond the photograph's frame—is now invisible to the image itself (Figure 4).

There appears in this succession no photograph of the presidential handshake that followed in El Paso, but press reports claim the private interview lasted only a few minutes and that, thereby, glasses were raised cordially to the bordering nations. This is followed by another sequence: a sidelong view of Taft in a horse-drawn coach as it rushes now to Ciudad Juárez—his shadowed profile barely discernible in the quadrille he forms with the officials riding in his party (Figure 5). Then comes an official press photograph of Taft and Díaz, standing side by side, each stiffly posed in a hall of the Ciudad Juárez customhouse, and each flanked by his particular representative of the national defense (a caption refers to Captain Butt, on the left, and Coronel Pablo Escandón, on the right) (Figure 6). Now encircled by crested officers, with raised bayonets lining the edge of the frame, the two presidents exchange a final handshake to bid farewell on the steps of the customhouse (Figure 7).

Across the historical distance, and lacking the intention of the photographs' maker(s), one is left to conjecture at various levels—not the least of which is the potentially calculated or accidental nature of the final image in this sequence (Figure 8). As President Taft finally walks away with his back turned to the ceremonial aftermath and its symbols of office, his arms swinging at his side, the

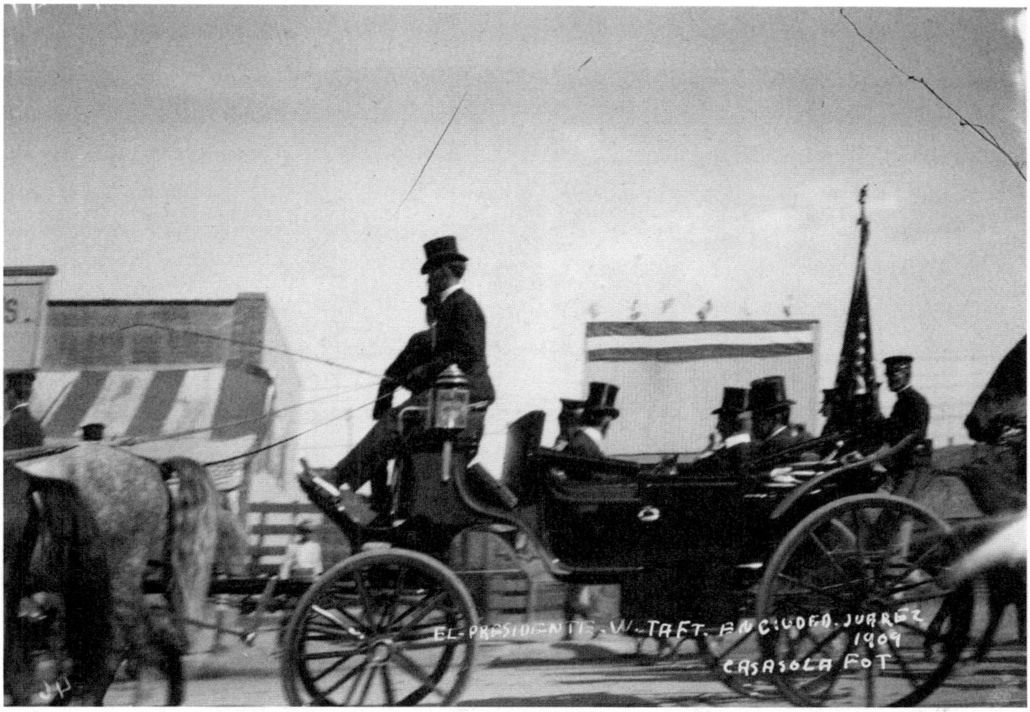

Figure 5. President Taft in horse-drawn carriage, en route to Ciudad Juárez, Sonora, 1909. Casasola Archive. Copyright SINAFO–Fototeca Nacional.

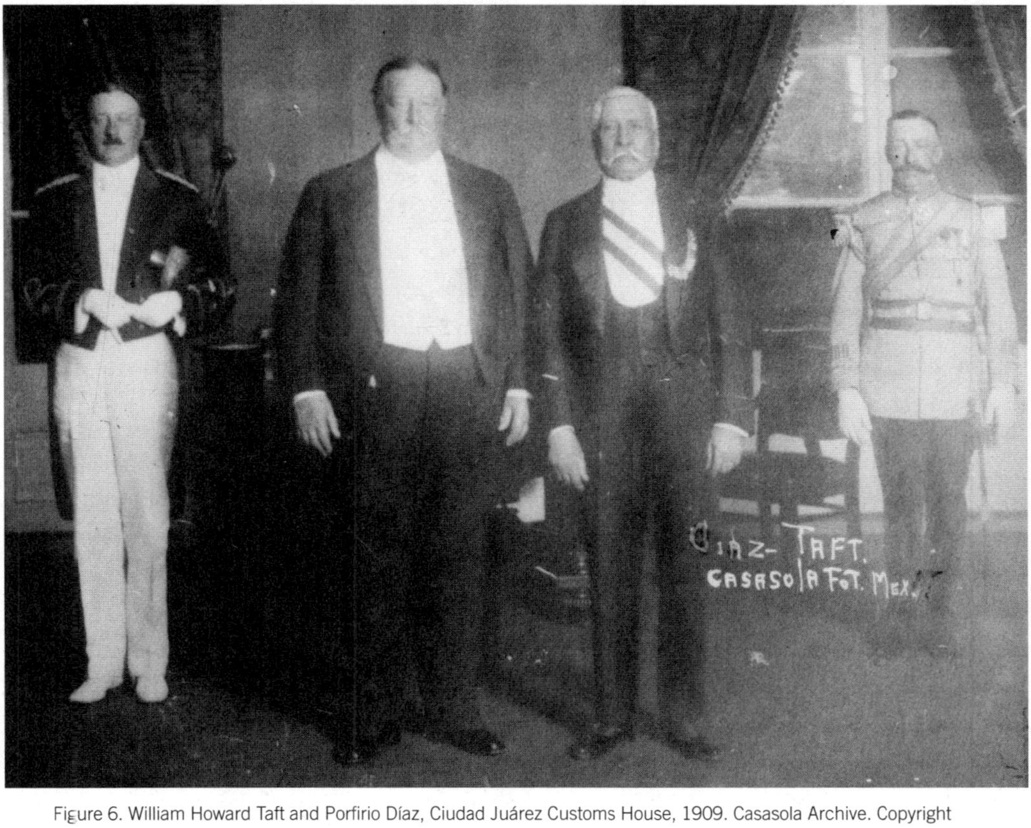

Figure 6. William Howard Taft and Porfirio Díaz, Ciudad Juárez Customs House, 1909. Casasola Archive. Copyright SINAFO–Fototeca Nacional.

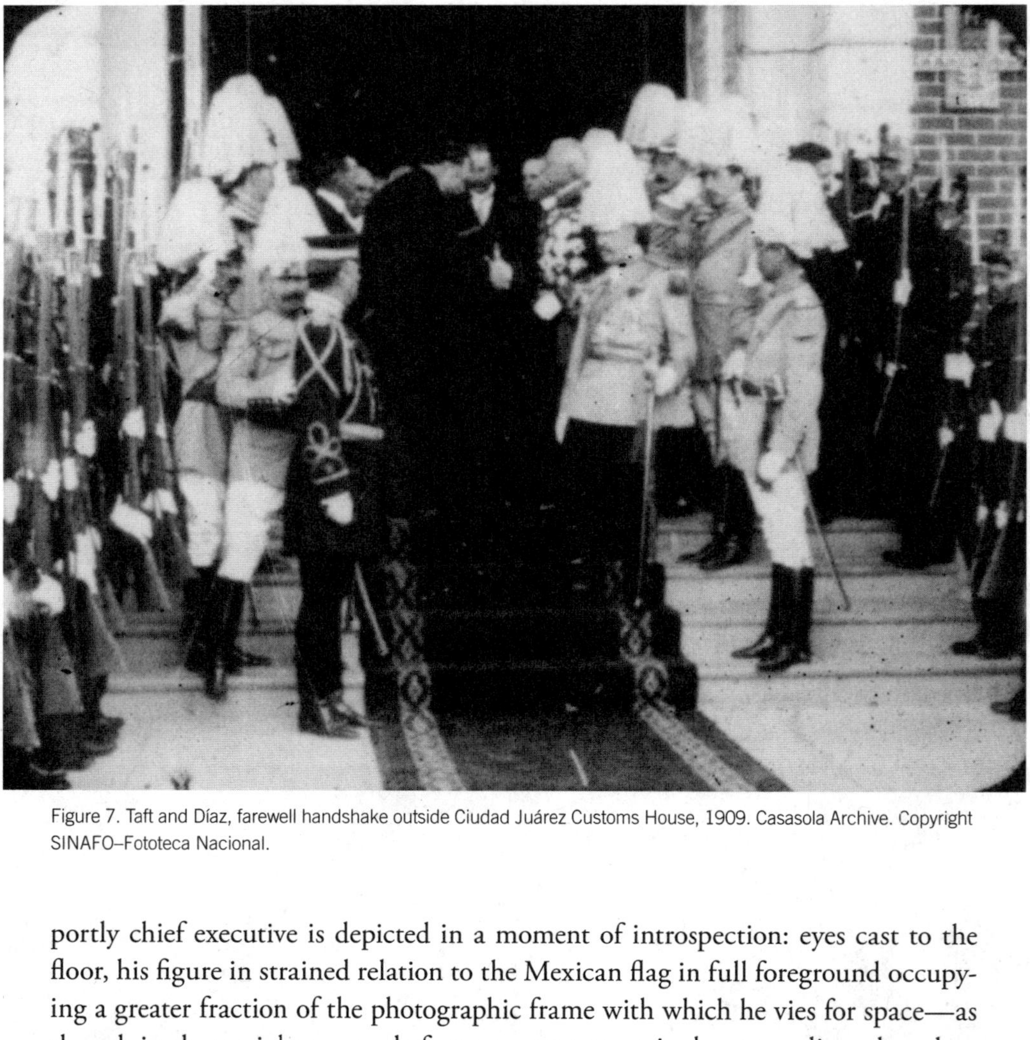

Figure 7. Taft and Díaz, farewell handshake outside Ciudad Juárez Customs House, 1909. Casasola Archive. Copyright SINAFO–Fototeca Nacional.

portly chief executive is depicted in a moment of introspection: eyes cast to the floor, his figure in strained relation to the Mexican flag in full foreground occupying a greater fraction of the photographic frame with which he vies for space—as though in that weighty pause before one component is about to eclipse the other.

President Taft reflected on the occasion in a letter to his wife, Helen, perhaps an afterthought—the biographies are unclear—or in advance of El Paso on the train from Los Angeles, via Albuquerque:

> There is a great fear, and I am afraid a well-founded fear, that should [Díaz] die, there will be a revolution growing out of the selection of his successor. As Americans have about $2,000,000 *[sic]* of capital invested in the country, it is inevitable that in case of a revolution or internecine strife we should interfere, and I sincerely hope that the old man's official life will extend beyond mine, for that trouble would present a problem of the utmost difficulty. I am not quite sure at whose instance the meeting was had, but I do know I had received the communication, perhaps directly from the old man, of an informal character, saying how glad he would be to have such a meeting brought about. He thinks, and I believe rightly, that the knowledge throughout his country of the friendship

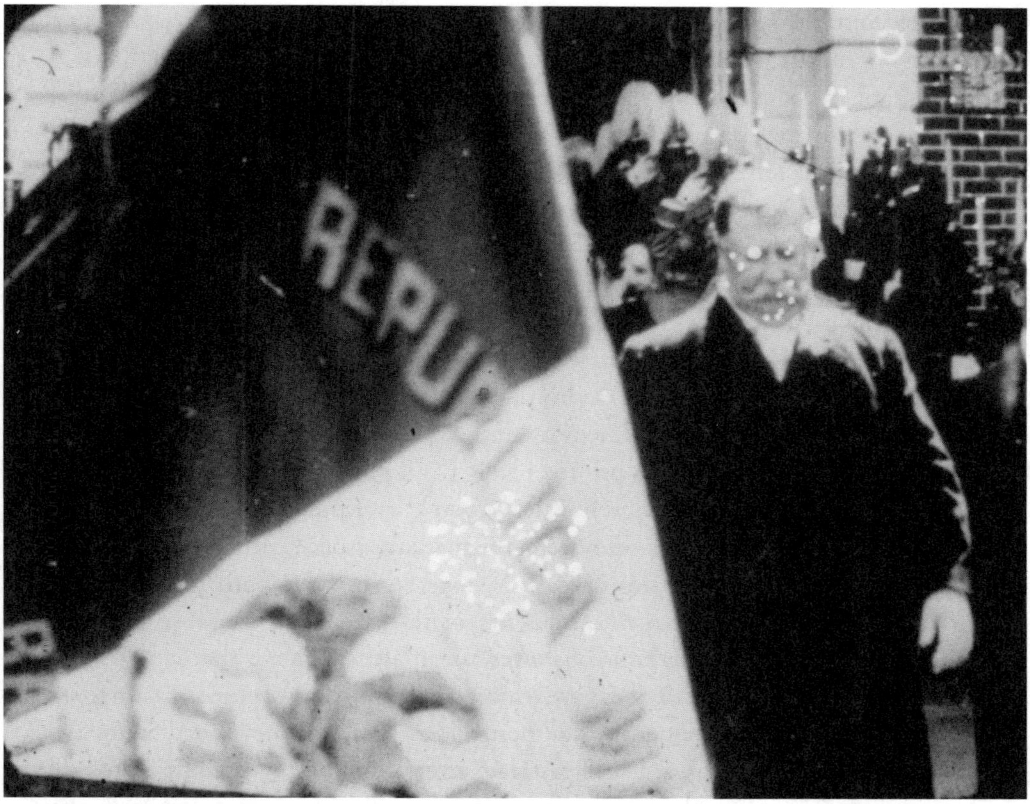

Figure 8. President William Howard Taft and Mexican flag, 1909. Casasola Archive. Copyright SINAFO–Fototeca Nacional.

> of the United States for him and his Government will strengthen him with his own people, and tend to discourage revolutionists' efforts to establish a different government.[2]

In fact, as the actual historic episodes transpired—I later evoke these in full—a year and a half later Díaz's "official life" came to an end, insofar as he was compelled to resign and flee into exile on account of the revolutionary forces previously feared by Taft and the U.S. American interests Díaz was eager to safeguard. On May 10, 1911, insurgent strikes on the federal garrison in Ciudad Juárez, and the city's eventual fall to a recalcitrant division of the Maderista movement, played a decisive role in Díaz's capitulation and departure two weeks later, further underscoring the strategic and symbolic importance of the setting here. (The book's very last rehearsal again takes place, as with the Díaz–Taft meeting, on the actual geopolitical dividing line between the two nations during the 1970s; these bookend examples, while they are not simultaneous in time, speak across a distance, about discontinuous patterns of situation and place.)

Perhaps self-evident, a vital sign motivates the foregoing and so much of what follows. Those episodes that are the incidence of the United States in Mexico, and of Mexico in the United States, cannot be evenly separated into positive parts pertaining to mutually exclusive historic narratives. In the punitive intervention that gave shape to the national sidelines of the existing political map, as well as in the latter-day blurring of those boundaries, there are less tangible involvements to be examined at the level of symbolic representation. These events and their visualities remind insofar as they remain, sometimes manifest, other times dormant, but each time suggestive of descriptions to be accounted for in joint or twofold effects.

The political contour between Mexico and the United States can be measured in part by the meetings that take place in the time zone of relation I call the "shared image environment." Both the product and cause of a convergence, this common scene, or image environment, is staged in terms that address the overlapping spheres of countermemory and aesthetics—and more specific to my purposes here, as deployed in printed records and photographic renderings. This actual and virtual contact zone has deep-rooted investments, therefore, in various borderlines—differences or movements that are at once theoretical, practical, and political. These properties have come together in ways both troubling and revealing, especially in the visual culture of the twentieth century, and they create, through visible relations of power, an image exchange that is not blind to discrepancies—rather, very often creative of them—and otherwise alert to an intertwining history of modernity and postmodernity across the United States and Mexico. It is a surplus I want to investigate after weighing the encounter in such a visual relation by which the contiguous terms are indebted on some level, and at varying degrees of intensity, to the other. In the intervals and pauses afforded by scrutiny, my aim is not to deny the fact of historical inheritances but to point, perhaps optimistically, to present uses and future tenses in which that weight can be transvaluated.

Insofar as the visual–cultural studies project is invested in the politics of representation—as Stuart Hall and others have inaugurated—it associates with such disparate disciplines as media criticism, art history, studies in colonialism, literary theory, ethnography, and philosophy. One could argue that such an interdisciplinary approach implies an ethical task as well, with an interest in cultures *other* to the dominant visual regime, and with an imperative to denaturalize the image, which is constitutive of perceived societal patterns and cultural prejudices. In the image environment made available today by global high-speed communication—a mediated sphere wherein the algorithmic unfolding of life establishes touch with the sciences of calculation—physical bodies make actual and virtual contact with the sensorium of alphanumeric signs and sound bites coming over the work station monitor and speaker.[3] If the realm of politics is ever more interior to the drone and drab—in a rhetoric of equal liberties and the so-called values of public life—then word-glut and image-blitz are as habitual to the psychosocial pathology of our wired existence and as natural as a starry night . . . at least its electronic screen-saver surrogate glowing red and green across the invisible geography of the digital West.[4] If cultural citizenship and the politics of representation seem everyday more restricted to a sameness of practicable form, and public culture continuous with the semblance of message and media, then the task of interpretation across disciplines is to question the overarching assumptions, not exclusive of the foregoing discursive effects, with regard to visual practice.

The following accounts look to photography in Mexico for arguments about the technology of the image, about the structure of history, about the state of bordering nations, and about the body as a site for the subject effects of social exchange. This book is art historical in the broadest sense: the photographic medium implies a development internal to its form and method, but so external to the story of itself as to perform the go-between for ideological and cultural amendments. Despite the tendency of much art historical interpretation to gesture toward a necessary account, be it formal or thematic, photographs nevertheless invite unforeseen associations, and these effects surface in a double writing when composition and cultural descriptions labor jointly to be productive of subject matter. This is not to submit that laws of history exist prior to an outcome or that history is a template prior to events but to wager that a photograph is meaningful only insofar as it is part of an organized but always nascent image sphere.

Readers of photographic history and theory will notice a relative paucity of reference to Walter Benjamin in the rehearsals that follow. His writings, however, along with those of discerning and sensitive observers like Eduardo Cadava, squarely inform my views on the optical, especially in what concerns the image environment. Benjamin's remarkable insight drew an intimate and imposing relation between social formations, visual purpose, and language difference—the secret kinship between variety and vision. If the printed word in translation was at one time the most effective and enduring process for tracing cultural description and difference over time and geography, this translation effect soon surrendered aspects of its sway and creative force to the representative claims of photography—even as the former nonetheless made gain of certain residues derived from the latter. That is, photography and translation can be viewed in so many ways internal to one another, as the technology of the image and the afterlife of written meanings assemble to expand the imaginative and political reaches of what there is in the world and how we come to know it.

This is especially evident in Benjamin's writings from the early to mid-1920s. Although his direct references and research into the relevance of the camera and photography did not appear until the 1930s, in his lengthy study of Goethe's *Elective Affinities* Benjamin elaborated a theory of the artwork and its implications for photographic image making. In one suggestive passage on Goethe's literary text, Benjamin claims: "The novella is comparable to an image in the darkness of a cathedral—an image which portrays the cathedral itself and so in the midst of the interior communicates a view of the place that is not otherwise available. In this way it brings inside at the same time a reflection of the bright, indeed sober day."[5]

A metaphoric interplay around optical technologies can hardly be gratuitous, given the significant references, in the second part of Goethe's novella, to the camera obscura.[6] There are several underlying syllogisms at work in Benjamin's terminology of this period, and elective affinities between "photography," "translation," "afterlife," "optic unconscious," "semblance," and the "expressionless," or that which is irreducible to its content. In "Surrealism: The Last Snapshot of the European Intelligentsia," Benjamin evokes a violent struggle between the world of concrete particulars, the fact of advancing events, and the preterits of a history wherein bodies of men and women assume a singular and collective sense. Through technology, bodies and images "so interpenetrate" as to summon a somatic cataclysm after which "no limb remains unrent," no matter how prepared for sweeping changes in the public arena. Benjamin nominates the "image sphere" to serve as an ambit for bodies that image technology can submit to illumination, and it was the genius of surrealist technique to have suggested the time zone of relation that opens between one-to-one identity and the point farther—that is, between "the play of human features" and the "face of an alarm clock."[7]

Because the body continues to be a forceful and prevalent shape for the imagery of thought in modern systems of representation, we can locate somatic concerns at the axis of thinking about art and politics from the viewpoint of sexual difference, that is, at the interstice between aesthetics and anaesthetics. If we equate the nervous system with the social order, in that they both seek "at every point to resist stimulation and change, to avoid pain (or pleasure), to remain in equilibrium," then "the aesthetic is by definition a threat to this equilibrium." In his very suggestive argument, the art critic David Levi Strauss suggests that the space between the anaesthetic and the aesthetic is inhabited by power and desire, in that "the aesthetic is all questions, disequilibrium, and disturbance [whereas] the anaesthetic only masks symptoms; it does nothing to treat the root causes of pain, to trace it back to its source, give it meaning, or counter it with pleasure."[8]

The somatic activates foundational contributions to feminist film writing and visual studies that form the backdrop to this book, beginning with Laura Mulvey's essay "Visual Pleasure and Narrative Cinema" (1973). To identify the "scopophilic" symptom of imperious or dominant (male) image making and viewer practices, Mulvey engages the technology of the moving image and the industry of desire that is Hollywood's "illusionistic narrative film." With a political understanding of psychoanalysis, she famously locates looking itself as a form of pleasure and unpleasure that hovers between "maternal plenitude and memory of lack." In this dynamic, woman is defined as a "bearer of meaning, not a maker of meaning";

looking is always lopsided in that the "determining" male gaze is ever active while women are consigned to be passive objects, represented figures ever "looked at and displayed." In sum, "Woman displayed as sexual object is the leitmotiv of erotic spectacle."[9]

Similarly, John Berger's *Ways of Seeing* (1975) contributed to thinking about the institution in Western art history that is the "female nude." Nakedness, writes Berger, is a condition of self-revealing, whereas nudity is an imposed requisite of display by male surveyors over women surveyed and represented. Berger asks the very suggestive question: Does nakedness have a positive value in its own right? If to be naked is to "be without disguise" and if nudity is "a form of dress," what is implicated in the static image of sexual nakedness if the subject is a woman, transgendered subject, or a queer person of color? The nude, be it painterly or photographic, so generalizes sight itself as to erode the links between "imaginative states" so that sexuality, now devoid of specificity, exchanges desire for fantasy.[10] (The foregoing articulations were published in the 1970s. That decade inaugurated the intellectual capital of photographic theorizing, as it also gave way, and not by accident, to the cultural speculation embodied in the two archives that frame this study.)

"Sexuality in the Field of Vision" (1984–85) adds to this line of questioning. Jacqueline Rose complicated any monolithic understanding of the "male gaze" by recognizing that absolute sexual difference, "the limiting opposition [in the visual realm] of male and female," maintains a forceful determination, an "economy of vision" projected onto "the human body by the [presumably male] eye." Rose identifies a double movement: women are depicted in an idealized form ("the nude," for example) in order to compensate, in the face of sexual difference, for male anxiety confronting the insufficiency that psychoanalysis frames as the fear of castration. This leads to the prospect of viewing against the grain of an image and the ideology out of which it was produced. To view visual space as a solid mass with no end points—those points of contact that constitute subject and objects—is to obscure the "form of resistance" that activates forms of address "*on this side of* (rather than beyond) the world against which it protests."[11]

Sidelines are constitutive of photographer and subject and, equally, of an image and its viewer. In her essay "Sexual Difference: Both Sides of the Camera" (1988), Abigail Solomon-Godeau cautions against "any too easy conflation of the fact of sexual difference on one side of the camera with the representation of sexual difference on the other." In the face of much criticism, which considers the analogic reality of the photograph to be a one-directional enterprise in what regards sexuality and visual representation—but equally so for cultural renderings of difference—Solomon-Godeau provides a counterreading that accounts for the active production of meaning as performed by the sexed viewer despite the presumed intentionality of the image. Sexual difference imbricates three different sites: gender identification of the photographer, the sexed subject positions "within photographic representation, and . . . the unstable and subjective nature of . . . the sexed spectator—the site where photographic meanings are equally produced."[12]

National Camera is beholden to the lens onto visual culture that feminism and cultural studies make available, and I rehearse that avowal in various ways throughout the book. My trope of the shared image environment also is indebted to the work of José Limón, especially *American Encounters: Greater Mexico, the United States, and the Erotics of Culture.* In this impressive rehearsal, Limón refigures the borders of the hemisphere and its disparate modernity as an intricate series of what he calls "unsuspected relationships." These interactions range from the double movement of immigration and modernist exile to the actual or symbolic mistranslations that are the "psychological patterns" of colonialism, especially those that press against the historically charged confines of the actual geopolitical dividing line between the United States and Mexico. Despite "the undeniable relationship of social inequality and domination," Limón is resolved to explore those twin presences that activate cultural articulation "in idioms of sexuality, eroticism and desire," hence allowing us "to envision and experience alternative" models of the association in what he locates as between "Greater Mexico and the United States."[13]

The drive that animates this book finds its form therefore in travel—between visual analysis and cultural theory, for instance—as it locates and dislocates the transnational magnitude of image exchange: in the manufacture and consumption of camera-generated images between Mexico and the United States, and in the kinds of writing this vast horizon activates. Attentive to cultural difference, but seeking to account as well for the global flows of visual culture, I acknowledge that images and their makers are prone to traversing national boundaries, even as they compel an understanding of historical and cultural specificity.

In the process, I do not mean to diminish important contributions made to photographic theory by many authors whose work I do not develop. However, in my interest to engage cultural and intellectual exchanges negotiated across the U.S.–Mexico borderlands, and across the lines of art and photography, politics and sexuality, I turn to an idiosyncratic range of photographic thinkers. My goal is to cover an important historical period, providing a view of the development of photography and the theoretical concerns the medium encouraged throughout the twentieth century. I look, therefore, at cultural sharing between Mexico and the United States, as transnational and rhetorical "border cultures" that extend throughout both countries. I move between several fields within photographic theory, including feminism, psychoanalysis, Marxist cultural critique, and visual studies. In this respect, my hope is to reflect the current trials and purposes of theoretical writing and to insist not on any overriding or uniform theory that serves as a conclusive description but on the wager of theoretical thinking within an interdisciplinary methodology.

To identify the photographic image as an untold authority is to say that it is unimaginable to recount or account for its ubiquity in modern life. Despite the now pervasive nature of the cinematic or digital image, or maybe on account of it, media interface is so much "inside photography" that many still pictures may so elude us as to be "invisible," considered self-evident or, on the contrary, viewed with the automatic suspicion prompted by a medium that already undermines so many assumptions about analogous objectivity, resemblance, and representation. I submit that this dissemination has made the "image environment" a privileged locus of late modern and contemporary culture—for it is equally inclusive of representation and political geographies, and of visual and discursive distributions.

Despite the new media, still photography continues to pose a problem, and it never ceases to waver between valuations as a fine art and mere mechanical reproduction, as a medium with aesthetic ambitions and social aspirations. Because of its widespread availability and its manifold cultural, commercial, and art-related uses, it is, at most and at least, what Pierre Bourdieu defines as "a middle-brow art."[14] Much of the vital work furthered in cultural studies has been resolved to legitimate the pedigree of the "popular" among the hierarchies of cultural artifacts. Indeed, in the realm of photography, this has often given rise to an important reconsideration of certain genres that had been hitherto relegated to a lesser standing. Fashion photography, the snap-shot print, vernacular studio portraiture, photojournalism, advertising product-shots, and other commercial and scientific forms of photography have undergone, in varying degrees, an "upward" process of "solemnification" as they are reified into objects deemed worthy of serious viewing.[15] Furthermore, this development has radically influenced the way we conceive of a "history of photography."

That neither a linear history of its material objects nor a summation of its various uses has the power to institute, establish, or enact an identity for "photography as such" is an argument convincingly made by critics from Jonathan Tagg and Allan Sekula to Victor Burgin. As well, Geoffrey Batchen, in *Burning with Desire: The Conception of Photography,* sets out to unsettle the "origin stories" claimed for the technical device and its system of effects, as he theorizes the conception of the medium and the environments it incites as a differential series whose history can never give rise to a unity. Batchen argues that because "photographic meaning is entirely mutable and contingent . . . the medium can have no autonomous history or fixed identity. . . . there can be no such thing as a singular photography at all, only discontinuous, myriad photographies."[16]

The assumption of this study is that there can be no origin, autonomous history, or fixed identity to photography—as practiced in Mexico and elsewhere during the momentous social transition in that country at the beginning of the last century. This is the crux of what follows, since the general subject I address is very much about the discontinuous scenes, situations, or episodes in the imbrication of art and photography, and the limit-case environments emerging from the radical gap that separates the visual and rhetorical regimes. It is for this reason that this survey brings together such seemingly disparate material. This study is also intended as a provisional attempt to underscore the reach and boundaries—indeed, the present-day predicaments and compromises—established between photography and other signifying practices and their methodologies.

Insofar as the camera is a powerful tool for recording the social history and everyday life of a place and its peoples, camera culture is shorthand for the multiple ways that picture making shapes our knowledge of a region activated between Mexico, the United States, and well beyond. This study explores the relations between visual documents and local identities, and how Mexican, U.S., and U.S. Latino cultures are reflected and transformed—that is, developed—in photographic images. From the Mexican Revolution of 1910–20 to the U.S.–Mexico borderlands of today, a transnational camera frames questions of history, territory, ethnic association, sexuality, and representation, asking us to look more closely at the built environment, social relations, and the different cultural roles of men and women. Insofar as it repeatedly presses against the written record—especially in the complex terms of cultural or sexual difference—photography is a problem that activates a series of what I call "shared image environments." What follows are episodes to inaugurate that history, insofar as a cross-cultural image environment is able to disrupt our conventional habits of discussing the photographic image. Photography is not a method for instantiating history; rather, it gives way to a philosophy of history in that it asks the questions, where is history in the structure of photography, and what is the place of photography in the structure of history?

The first of the following travels takes place in the years of transition from the unswerving Díaz government to the tumultuous regime changes of the Mexican Revolution—as per the periodic convention, between 1910 and 1920. As I address a handful of photographs from a vast collection known as the Casasola Archive—the source of the Taft–Díaz photo sequence above—the focus of the essay turns first to the theoretical and ideological underpinnings concerned with representation in the early philosophical writings of Antonio Caso. I then move beyond the geographic and political boundary of Mexico's still-emergent nation, in order to join aspects of what Caso aimed to articulate with the nascent modernist aesthetics that was simultaneously surfacing in the New York art journal *Camera Work: A Photographic Quarterly*. I am concerned, too, with the art criticism written in English by the Mexican artist and theorist Marius de Zayas. The discussion compels historic events and their actors, in the political transformations during those first two decades in Mexico, especially as suggested by the aforementioned archive of images amassed by the journalist and chronicler Agustín Víctor Casasola. The discussion also considers the photograph as a model for perception in the philosophy of Henri Bergson, as significant to the writings of Caso—indeed, to the general intellectual climate of Mexico—as it was to the *Camera Work* project. Thus the image environment that emerged in Mexico during the Revolution of 1910–20 was not cut off from foreign sources in the United States and Europe. Even during this period of intense cultural nationalism, the "foreign" element (Bergson, for instance) formed part of Mexico's philosophic tradition from the beginning, and it reappears at various junctures in what follows. Photography, then, is the connecting thread that joins three seemingly unrelated contributors to Mexican and U.S. American intellectual and material production: an image maker (Casasola), a philosopher (Caso), and an artist–theorist (de Zayas). Their work is linked by speculation on "the photographic" in the actual and virtual zones of politics and representation that opened up between the United States and Mexico, prior to and during the Mexican Revolution.

If this first account charts the "double writing" or "split vision" that occurred at the moment photography was prepared to upset the relation of succession and resemblance, the following episode relates sexual difference to the notion of photography as a "hybrid practice" in the work of Tina Modotti. To this end, I look at contributions to Modotti scholarship and feminist theory that allow me to build in several directions. I employ strategies to locate sexual difference in the visual field by addressing migratory structures and hybrid effects even in the fixity of the so-called heterosexual male gaze as per Edward Weston's *Daybooks* and photographic work. I look to the writings of Joan Copjec in *Imagine There's No Woman* for her insight into vision and sexual difference in terms of the psychoanalytic concept of drive and sublimation. I relate "On Photography," the sole artist statement Modotti wrote for her 1929 exhibition at Mexico City's National Library, to photographic modernism and Modotti's familiarity with the writings of Friedrich Nietzsche, chiefly *Beyond Good and Evil.* With this, I briefly examine the implications of a 1929 series of photographs at odds with the claims of Modotti's manifesto, and I look to the analyses of Elizabeth Grosz and others on sexual, cultural, and photographic difference through a concomitant cultural category: *translation.* A migratory practice for sidelong observers such as Modotti and Weston, who took part in its artistic and social cross-purposes, symbolic translation of Mexico's cultural differences can be viewed as generating a twin representative effect. By pointing to the folk and its traditions to symbolize a collective social purpose within the photographic frame of modernity, a translation or time lag took place: a no-less-powerful, but only partial, function linked to the representative whole.[17] My concern with sexuality and sexual difference begins in this second chapter and is linked across historical time, even as it borders the framework of this book, to the final chapter on the Boystown archive. To this end, a movement emerges to link sexuality in its reversible sidelines to photography's hybrid effects, from *figure* to *flesh* as it were—twin terms I examine.

In between, another account establishes the importance of Mexico City to photography in general and to the work of Manuel Álvarez Bravo in particular.

His photography can be seen to function as a site of contestation in ways that illuminate the complexities of the built environment, material culture, and urban social relations. These sidelines between representation and metropolitan space compel a brief discussion of the political–cultural climate just prior to, and continuous with, the years that Álvarez Bravo came into his own as a photographer, by way of what the critic Raymond Williams has identified generally as the systematic link between "metropolitan perceptions and the emergence of modernism."[18] From the interplay of photography and municipal patterns of relation, Álvarez Bravo developed his singular style of the 1930s and 1940s by framing the contradictions of Mexico's urban and rural life into social statements with a distinct lyric vision. Moreover, a shared image environment opens up between Mexican modernism, European surrealism, and American cultural entrepreneurship through the figure of Julien Levy on the occasion of a 1935 exhibition at the Julien Levy Gallery, "Documentary and Anti-Graphic Photographs by Henri Cartier-Bresson, Walker Evans and Manuel Alvarez Bravo." This transnational attention to art and culture is fundamental to understanding the separate components of an environmental whole, insofar as to bring these elements into focus is to inaugurate a cultural scene of travel whose matter is the "unnatural coupling" of photography and surrealism. To this end, I examine how "lifeless" or "anesthetized" renderings of the female body ensue from a dialectics proper to surrealism as offered by Rosalind Krauss. Photographs by Álvarez Bravo make discernible the imposing spaces between the figure as concept or object and the political uses of the flesh as sociosexual matter in transformation; they are connected to images in adjacent chapters as between the surface of appearance and the less visible workings of sexed perception. A significant aim of the book is, precisely, to think through that difference—parallel lines in a perspective appearing to touch. That real or imaginary place of convergence constitutes the "shared image environment."

The final episode travels radically forward in time to bring us back to the U.S.–Mexico borderlands, to the city of Nuevo Laredo of the mid-1970s, to a photographic archive that refers to the compound of brothels known as Boystown, and to lines drawn by deep-rooted habits of viewing. The chapter establishes a meaningful juxtaposition between photography as "social documentation" in light of contemporary art practice and postmodern photographic discourse. I begin by looking at archival photographs collected with an alleged aim for posterity that in fact serves the purposes of visually colonizing a social reality, and I relate it to latter-day practices. Such patriarchal or colonial fixity is necessarily resignified by photo-based, identity-driven feminist art that accounts for meanings within the photographic medium with greater or lesser degrees of negotiation, as image making, interference, intervention, and material alteration. What connects that archive to contemporary practice are bodily representations and feminist corporeal theories of vision, especially in a turn to the writings of Maurice Merleau-

Ponty, the relevance of whose category "flesh" I discuss at length. Art and image making, in and out of Mexico, underwent a significant change in the 1980s and 1990s, whereby uncontested immediacy is denaturalized into political "mediacy." This is what a former *New York Times* photography critic called "the crisis of the real." Andy Grundberg also submits that postmodern art takes up photography "because [it] is an explicitly reproducible medium, because it is the common coin of cultural image interchange and because it avoids the aura of authorship that post-structuralist thought calls into question—or at least it avoids that aura to a greater extent than do paintings and sculpture."[19]

The arbitrary nature of the photographic image belies the common wisdom that seeing is believing, and one premise of the art we call postmodernist is its compulsion to demonstrate the impossibility of ever representing pure unmediated meaning or experience. The contrast between the 1974–75 Boystown archive and the work made by contemporary U.S. Latina image makers is meant to draw the lines of that movement, even as it further seeks to lay bare the conception that the ground to any starting point is as unsteady as its terminus is open to productive unease.[20]

This book explores the relation between visual documents and local identities to show how Mexican and U.S. cultures have been reflected and transformed through photographic images. From the Mexican Revolution to the U.S.–Mexico borderlands of today, photography invites us to look "otherwise" at embodiment, image technology, and state citizenship. *National Camera* is a reflection on twentieth-century visual links between Mexico and the United States, between objects of photographic history and the structures that bring them into visibility (both social and descriptive). I seek to account for functions that allow us to reconfigure a theory of modernism proper to the cultural archive produced between bordering systems. These metaphors link the "tenures of land and light" to the nation-state, and "experiments in related form" to sexual difference. I connect "metropolitan matters" to cultural citizenship and the transnational capital of a nascent photographic art-market, and I associate "figures" or "flesh" to questions of posterity when the archive, like a body, becomes a site of uncertain knowledge. By engaging cultural production in this alternate arena, we can lay claim to a theory of modernism structured not as a second-order content applied at the periphery to first-order metropolitan forms; instead, we can expand the meanings of modernism by situating its fundamental energies in an image environment fueled by positive reminders of the colonial experience. To make mutual the "national" and "foreign" is to foreground the question of locality over a national framework for the production of art, its potential meanings, and representational effects. I suspect the image environment is a critical opportunity to so compel transnational politics and the economies of labor and image exchange, constitutive of a citizenry, as to possibly override our various social and aesthetic identities.

The objects of art history and visual studies turn jointly to that place whose attributes are to the urgency by which we represent the world in images and language, what a political standpoint is to representation and its decisive power to judge what we do and do not value. It is at the interstice of two distinct but analogous kinds of knowing—logical and sensory thinking—that photographic histories can gain a partial glimpse into the uncertain places that bring objects of inquiry into visibility.

1. Tenures of Land and Light: Casasola, Revolution, and Archive

There is something superior to the *spectacular sense* of the aesthetes, and it is the *life sense [sentido vital]* of the moralists who know the world is still in the making, that we are involved in the manufacture, and it is in perfecting it that we should spend our faith and breathing.

—**Antonio Caso, *Problemas filosóficos* (1915)**

By 1909, President Porfirio Díaz, at the autumnal age of seventy-nine, had governed Mexico like "the stern wise parent of his people" for more than thirty years, with one brief interim.[1] In the years leading to his encounter with Taft, opposition had begun to pose serious threats to his administration. A seasoned general, Díaz had had twenty years of military experience when he revolted against the Republic under Benito Juárez in 1871. Having gained the power of the presidency in 1877 and consolidated it by 1884, he certified his position, term after consecutive term, thanks not only to shady balloting practices and a loophole in the 1857 Constitution but by dint of rhetorical ploys and repeated retractions of his reelection promises.

To perpetuate his power, Díaz had surrounded himself with an influential group of experts in finance and public administration. Commanded by his secretary of the treasury, José Yves Limantour, this collective ruling elite came to be christened, derisively, as "los científicos." In a land ravaged by extreme indigence, rampant illiteracy, and visible racial disparity—tenacious residues of the colonial experience—these men of affairs were, under the banner of scientific advancement, privileging material progress and technological modernization. In the hands of *los científicos,* public policy increasingly reflected the questionable progressive aims for societal evolution as determined by a privileged class invested in the principles of European positivism. Peace and order were established through social repression, surveillance of the press, ineffective suffrage, and a mollification of the Catholic Church.

A thirty-year period in which the country's populace doubled to fifteen million, the Díaz regime also fostered remarkable material and technological expansion. Vast railway systems were constructed to transport passengers and freight domestically and internationally. Foreign companies like U.S. Standard Oil and the British-owned Huasteca Petroleum Company first drilled for, then readily industrialized and traded in, the coveted merchandise of energy. Mexico City was rapidly modernized: horse-drawn streetcars were replaced by automobiles and trolleys lining the avenues and plazas (Figure 9). Tobacco factories, textile mills, and bottling plants—to name only a few—were built, prompting immigration from the urban outskirts and rural provinces (Figure 10). French-inspired structural redesign of the city center created an urban space that formed at once a contrast and continuum with the colonial built environment and the vernacular architecture of the outlying neighborhoods (Figure 11). Because Mexico City was notoriously prone to floods, large-scale public works included a massive drainage system, in addition to monuments raised along the Paseo de la Reforma,[2] and a highly visible penitentiary whose punitive meanings were in no way inconspicuous.

Commonly referred to as the "Strong Man of the Americas," Díaz and his *científicos* produced an image of Mexico as a site of unwavering progress and a dependable place to do business. Foreign investment swelled, especially from the United States—but as more than one observer has remarked, not entirely free of patriotic scrutiny.[3] The Díaz administration upheld economic growth with politics that inspired both promise and apprehension in its national subjects, 90 percent of whom, at the poverty level, were deprived of the privileges of citizenry. "Interested persons and the contemporary American press assigned a value of $1 billion to American interests in Mexico."[4] From the powerful and vaguely distant place that was the United States, William Randolph Hearst owned hundreds of thousands of acres of Mexican land. Other speculators and landed families (or hacendados) owned mines, smelters, and plantations whose production was indebted to rural campesino labor. The Cananea Consolidated Copper Company in Sonora, owned by U.S. American investors, became the stage on which wage inequities between Mexican and U.S. American laborers led to a bloodshed often cited as the episode that effected the mobilization that led to the Mexican Revolution. Below I review this historical sequence as assembled into a photographic essay by George R. Leighton and Anita Brenner in *The Wind That Swept Mexico*. To accompany these images, Brenner's scathing words inflect signs of the social and economic rifts that were visible everywhere:

> In the passage of time the ancient communal lands of the villages were swallowed up, the peasants harnessed to the factories—herded to work, sometimes by a rider with a carbine.

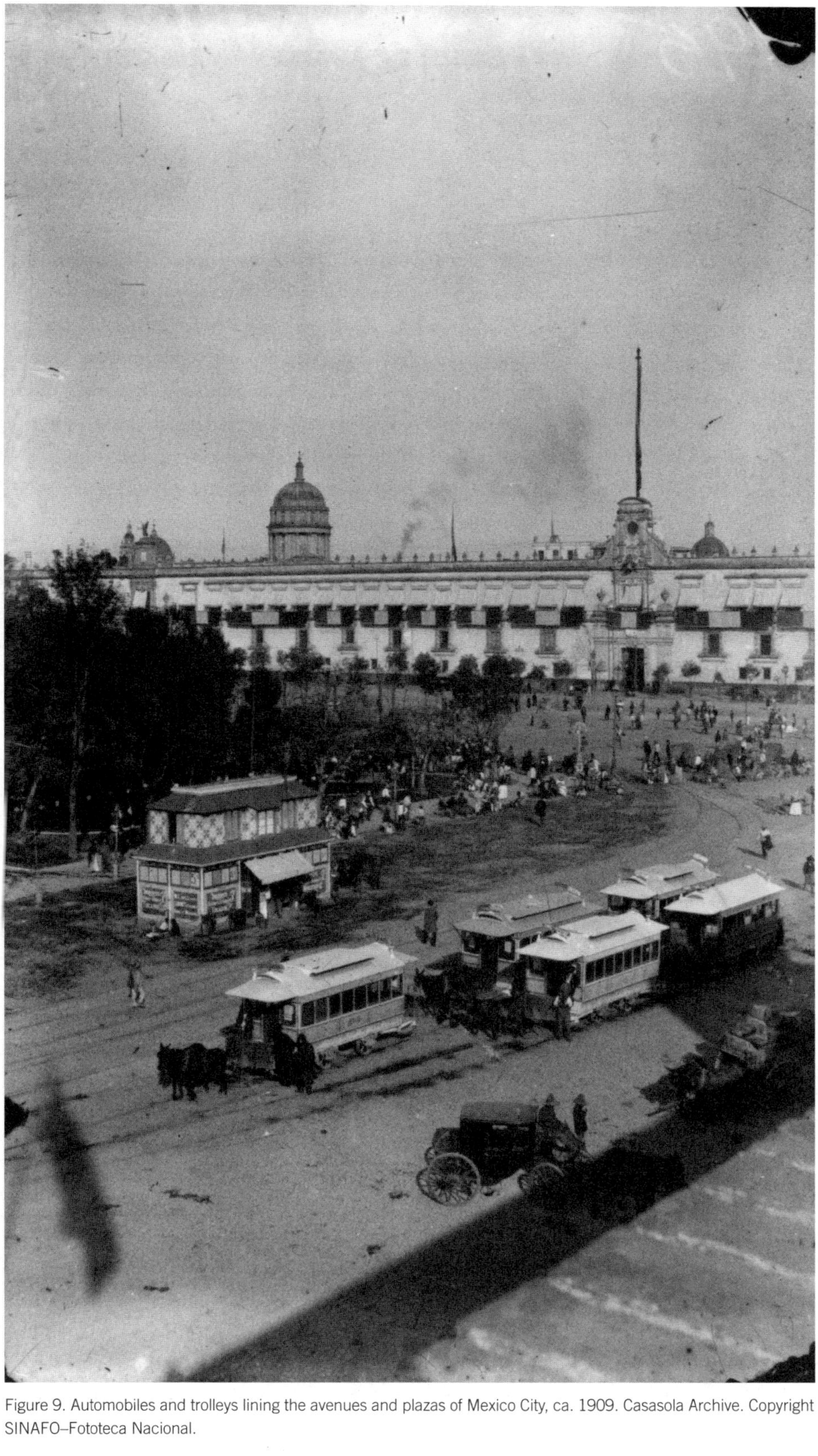

Figure 9. Automobiles and trolleys lining the avenues and plazas of Mexico City, ca. 1909. Casasola Archive. Copyright SINAFO–Fototeca Nacional.

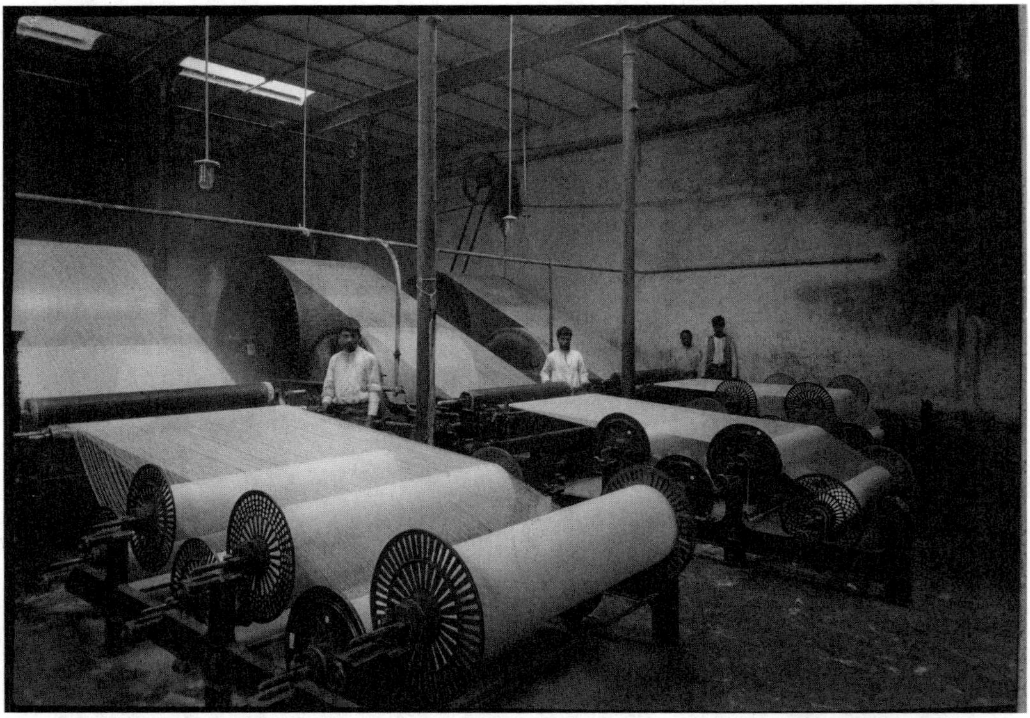

Figure 10. Textile mill and laborers, Mexico, ca. 1908. Casasola Archive. Copyright SINAFO–Fototeca Nacional.

There had been rebellions, strikes, attacks in newspapers. Troops put down the strikers, the rurales smothered the little rebellions, indiscreet newspapermen had time in the dungeon to think it over.

It seemed as though the regime, in its golden splendor of prosperity, was impregnable. Even though the anger and the hatred of centuries smoldered in the minds of the Indians, even though Mexicans sweated to belong to a middle class that scarcely existed, the government's bonds were at a premium on every exchange in the world. Few of the bondholders ever noticed that year by year the wealth was being concentrated in fewer hands. The bulk of the wealth was in the hands of less than one per cent of the people and most of that belonged to foreign investors . . . absentees.[5]

"Remarkable Exhibition"

Despite claims by Brenner and others about the "swallowing up" of villages,[6] in the waning years of the Díaz administration, certain native communities did organize to make legal demands. This led to staged uprisings that were repeatedly suppressed by shows of federal strength, including those that came to a violent pitch in the early 1900s in military campaigns against the Mayan indigenous peoples of the Yucatán Peninsula, and the Yaqui and Mayo of Sonora. These disturbances

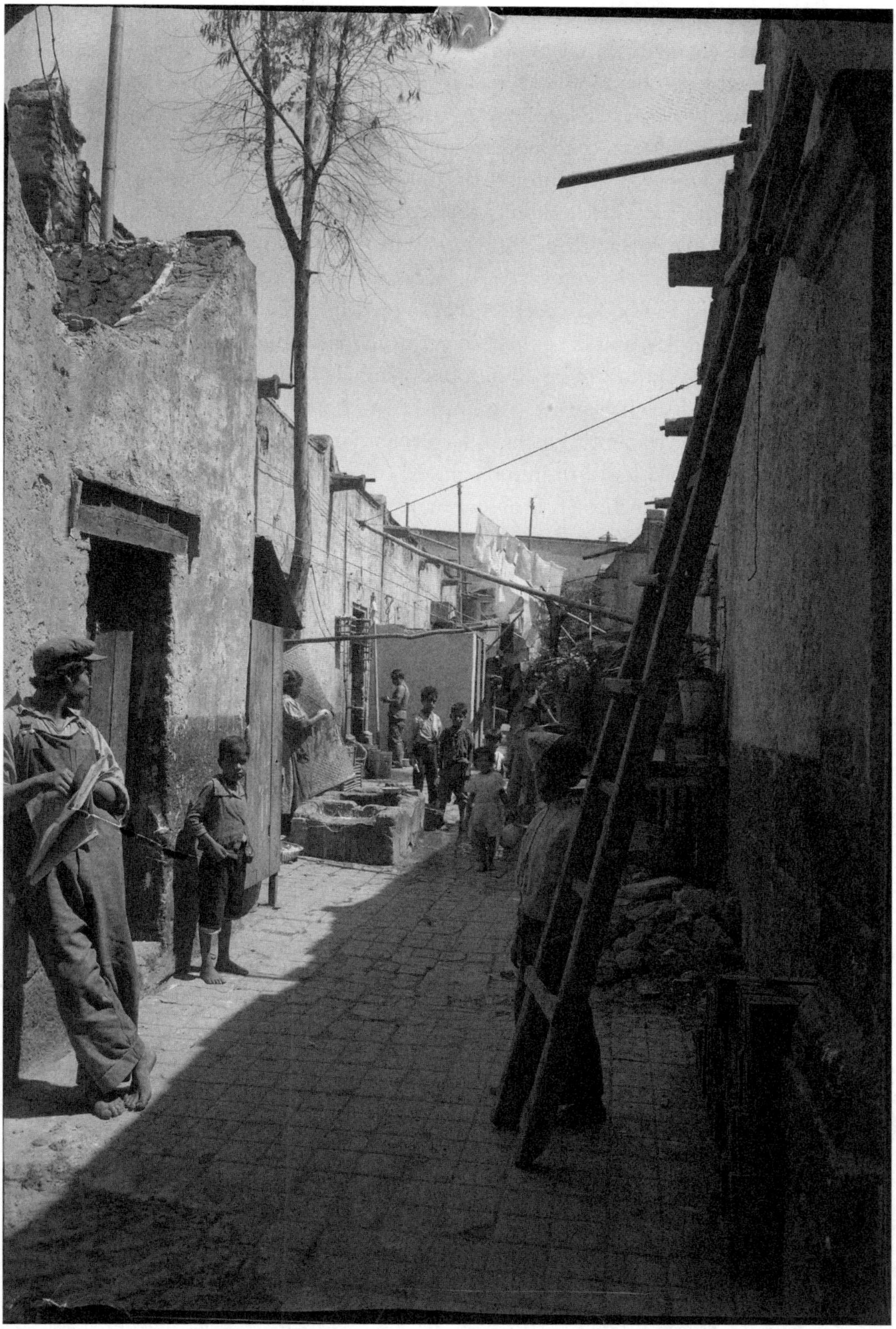

Figure 11. Mexico City neighborhood or *vecindad*, 1900. Casasola Archive. Copyright SINAFO–Fototeca Nacional.

betrayed the degree to which the nation's demographic realities were at odds with the modernizing social project as staged from Mexico's political center. Mexican natives—objects of a knowledge and practice that came to be known as *indigenismo*—served as a legitimating alibi at the national symbolic level while being treated as a hindrance to modernization.

Another photograph (Figure 12), an image alternately dated 1905 or 1922—a difference whose relevance should not be underestimated—clearly enacts the troublesome visual rehearsals of *indigenismo*.[7] Any descriptive time lag would invariably fail to deflect the immediate impact on first viewing the picture—a combination of looks and bodily cadences that suggest the relish, panic, and humiliation of public display, and the enhanced performativity prompted by the camera's presence. At what appears to be a fairground sideshow somewhere in Mexico (possibly the capital itself) there are two impresarios, both of whom, directly or indirectly, welcome the photographer. A larger man on the left sports a moustache, a porkpie hat, a collarless shirt in some muted color, and a tousled vested suit. He motions gleefully with his left arm and hand, his finger pointing to the human spectacle he and his lanky collaborator comprise, as the latter makes the actual or simulated gesture of hawking through a megaphone.

A man and a woman dressed in pseudonative attire have been posed on a bench for view. Turkey feathers protrude from the man's headband lined with shells and

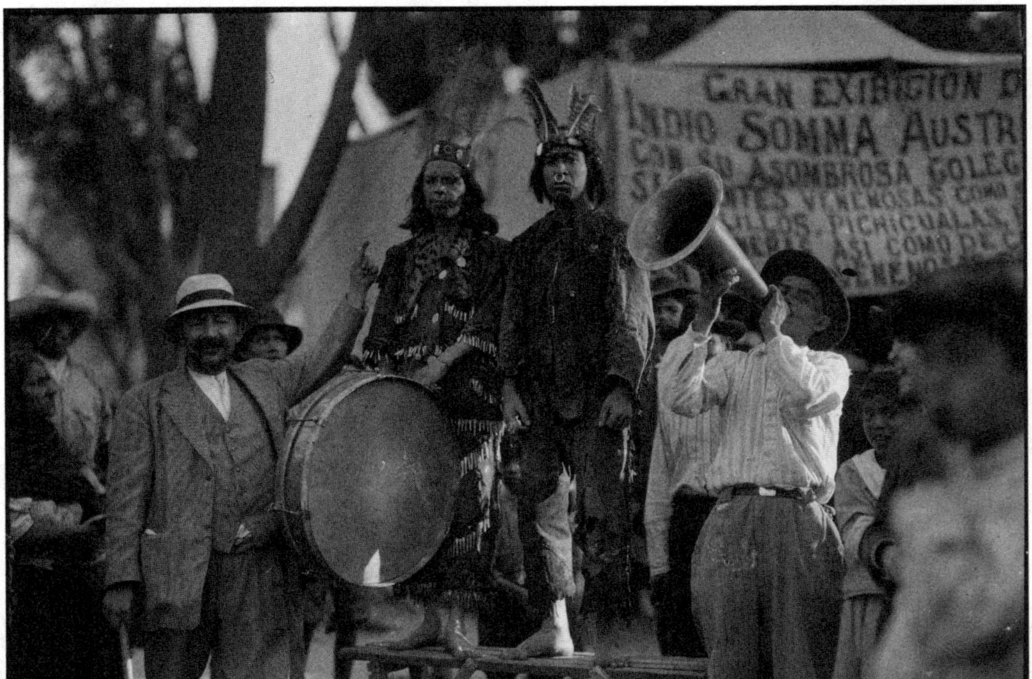

Figure 12. "Remarkable Exhibition," 1905 or 1922. Casasola Archive. Copyright SINAFO–Fototeca Nacional.

beads, and safety pins appear to hold together his leather jacket, fringed around the collar and sleeves, one of which comes to an end at a loosely clenched fist. These, together with his chopped hair, nose ring, and tattered pants, are the various signifying marks of primitivist visual discourses whose object is the "savage."[8] With a similar headband, the woman's dress is jingled all over with tiny metal pieces, pelted at the collar and sleeves, her hands supporting a drum specific to the European bandstand. Proper to the subjects themselves and to the disturbing weather of the scene—betraying affliction and defiance at once—are the downturned mouths, lips pressed in the withheld emotion of acquiescence, a chin on the verge of a quiver, the shadow of their brows blurring the direction of their gazes that nevertheless confront the viewer point-blank. In the banner behind the scene, we can barely discern the following phrases: "Remarkable Exhibition . . . Indian . . . with Astounding . . . venomous snakes." There is visual evidence to suggest that this image depicts a man and a woman not at all but two men in such an indigenous masquerade as to make one more deliberately "feminized" than the other. How we make those assumptions is the subject of a further rehearsal in the pages that follow.

Sexual identification notwithstanding, the image is memorable on many accounts, particularly the way it portends the nationhood relationship as one defined by an ethnocommunal imaginary. A postcolonial view, especially that of Homi Bhabha, is useful here in that his writing addresses the historically *uncertain* and unsettled nature of the term *nation,* which is a palpable form of living the locality of culture.[9] Because "nationness" can be regarded as the visual appearance of social affiliation, there is an emphasis on the dimension of time and history, for "the language of culture and community is poised on the fissures of the present becoming the rhetorical figures of a national past."[10] Insofar as a nation's visual presence is the effect of a narrative struggle, the production of a nation is therefore split, on the one hand, as a "lesson plan"—or the means by which the historical past is applied as an inheritance—and, on the other, as a staged event, that is, the far-reaching performance of an identification. It's a disjunctive time because "the people" are not simply tableaux but actors in a complex theater of history with scenes of social reference.

Therefore space is also relevant—as this photograph betrays so glaringly—for the people are located at neither the beginning nor the end of the national narrative but, again with Bhabha, along the "cutting edge" between the "social" as a leveling "community of consensus" and "the forces that signify a more specific address to contentious, unequal interests and identities within the population."[11] Nation turns from being a symbol of modern life to becoming instead the symptom of an ethnography that seeks to account for the "contemporary" within modern culture. What takes place in this photograph is a double vision made available by an everyday spectacle that performs anxieties about Mexico's sense of nationhood. In a practice that was likely not specific to this occasion, native peoples were grossly generalized in such a way as to be made monstrous, even as they embodied a "historical presence" or symbolized an object of knowledge for edification—its most extreme version being this public degradation. The twin vision activated in this performance is continuous with Bhabha's idea of a "double writing," in that the subject is intelligible only in the passage between displayer and displayed, between a present juncture and somewhere else, and "in this double scene the very condition of cultural knowledge is the alienation of the subject."[12] While the space of Mexican nationhood was delimited by a foreign exchange—both economic and symbolic—with the United States in particular, this potential menace to its sovereignty was balanced by Mexico's official ethnographic claim to be simultaneously "within" and "without" a culture. So the threat of cultural difference was no longer simply a problem of "other people." It became a question of that distance effect, an arrest or estrangement or internal remove, in viewing the "people-as-one." What this photograph demonstrates is that the technology of the image had the capacity to betray the space of the nation as being a visual landscape discontinuous with the historical institution of the state. There is additional evidence of these blind spots at the meeting place where a collective self-image encounters the logic that governs an archive. The scene involves an outsider in the precincts of power.

In 1908 the North American newswriter James Creelman traveled to Mexico where he interviewed Díaz, a landmark encounter published in an issue of *Pearson's Magazine*. The exchange gained greater notoriety on account of Díaz's sweeping claim that he would not seek reelection.[13] But the journalist also questioned Díaz as to whether he thought the vast indigenous population of Mexico was capable of "intellectual development." In his response, Díaz—himself of Mixtec ethnicity—revealed the following view, held broadly in the system of values known as integrationist *indigenismo*:

> To be sure, Indians are docile and grateful; all of them, with the exception of the Yaqui and some Mayans. They possess traditions of ancient civilizations that are proper to them. Among them you will find lawyers, engineers, physicians, military officers and other professionals.[14]

The uncertain science of *indigenismo*—with its debt to crude social evolutionism—sought the amalgamation of indigenous peoples into Mexico's national life and into its rhetorical and visual representations, which advanced a mestizo identity.[15] Because it viewed native communities as objects of study, not as autonomous subjects of history—even as it enunciated those internal cultural differences that problematize the binaries of past–present, or those of tradition–modernity—*indigenismo* staged the problem of how, at the beginning of modernity in Mexico, "something comes to be repeated, relocated and translated in the name of tradition, in the guise of pastness that is not necessarily a faithful sign of historical memory but a strategy of representing *authority* in terms of the artifice of the archaic."[16] The authoritarian claims made by Díaz—that "they are docile and grateful," that "they possess traditions of ancient civilizations that are proper to them"—join with this photograph to make palpable two occasions of *indigenismo,* when a scene in the official representations descending from power "above" meets an everyday set of tactics ascending from "below," to produce a split measure of time—that is, an image environment—by which a "metaphysics comes face to face with sociology."[17]

With a view to the discrepancies held together by the so-called Pax Porfiriana, most of the historical accounts of the causes that led to the Mexican Revolution can be separated into more or less distinct lines of perspective. These lines point to a dominant source possessing a specific identity to explain the Revolution's transformative social effects. Whether deemed an antiforeign movement, a legitimate popular rebellion, or the result of cultural contradictions that had reached a breaking point,[18] these histories follow patterns whose concentrations are invested in the crisis of sovereignty, the crisis of ethnicity and the internal social order, and, ultimately, a more overarching crisis of representation, in term of artifice and subject formation. It was by this measure of material and technological progress in Mexico during the Díaz regime—one that included the powerful advances in the technologies of the image by way of photomechanical reproduction and its circulation in the print media—that photographs can now tell the symbolic history of a national culture and will have been described in the strange temporality of the future perfect.

This "remarkable" photographic display questions the teleological command of past and present, and the historicist sensibility of the archaic and the modern that were the crisis points of the transition from the Díaz administration to the countermovements that led to the modern Mexican state. This photograph of a social spectacle obliges us to conceive of a picture as something identical and foreign to itself, and to question whether it is possible to signify community and visual communication in a photograph without resorting to a discourse of transcendence. It suggests the imperative to think image making and photographic representation simultaneously as something attendant to and replaced within the frame, as well as without.[19] What this means is best illustrated by a time lapse in the dates attributed to the picture.

Let us assume that the photograph was in fact obtained in 1922—and not as it is listed in an earlier publication, in 1905. What the picture belies in terms of the "national community as the 'many as one'" thereby spans the supposed furrow or dividing line of the histories that trace the transition from *porfirismo* to the post-Revolutionary years. What the photograph represents, suspended in this way between the temporal undecidability of those two dates, is the possible repetition of a missing passage in the origin story that is the Mexican Revolution. As I demonstrate below, this performative display and others like it constitute the part that gets carried over from one regime to the next. The photograph—in keeping with the spectacle of the Díaz period—constitutes an exhibition of itself ("remarkable" in a very different sense) insofar as the politics of the appearance it seeks to corroborate cannot serve as the metaphor of nationhood in the seemingly irreducible empty time of the photograph. If we call to mind the words of Díaz ("They possess traditions of ancient civilizations that are proper to them"), the picture signifies a symptom. It betrays the social residues of domination and a cautionary display from a colonial past repeated in the name of a future totality displaced in time. The photograph resembles a promissory note—reflected as well in the verbal portrait of Díaz with Creelman—in that it bears a signature whose identity is manifold, at once foreign and self-identical.

Casasola's Signature

There is a common provenance that unites the photographs considered up to this point. The Taft–Díaz images, those displaying the material culture of Mexico's belle epoque, and the carnival ethnography of the "Remarkable Exhibition" are all part of the Casasola Archive collection. Widely recognized in Mexico, the Casasola Archive is a vast resource of prints and negatives amassed by Agustín Víctor Casasola (1874–1938), his brother Miguel, and sons Ismael and Gustavo. The archive is presently housed under conservation in the city of Pachuca at the Sistema Nacional de Fototecas (SINAFO, National Institute of Photography Collections) headquarters. In the mid-1970s the resource was deposited as a gift to the Mexican state by the collection's steward, Gustavo Casasola, and since that time a number of publications and exhibitions have drawn from this trove of over thirty thousand photographs, whose value is not only archival but aesthetic as well.

The photography historian Olivier Debroise reminds us that in 1910, at the age of thirty-five, and at the outbreak of the Mexican Revolution, Agustín Víctor Casasola had already worked for sixteen years in the print professions—first as a typographer, then as a writer of copy for the news-daily sports pages. Having purchased his first camera in 1900, Casasola began to illustrate articles he was writing with photographs of his own, and he soon established a name for himself among his cameramen colleagues and amid the elite classes so often depicted in the society pages—often the foremost section—of newspapers like *El Liberal, El Popular,* and especially *El Imparcial.* Possessing something akin to what Friedrich Nietzsche christened the "historical sense" of modern man, Casasola began also to collect and meticulously preserve the photographs he and his brother made. But his collection was also to contain countless images obtained by other photojournalists, many of whom have since been consigned to anonymity.[20] Casasola found eventual employment at the Catholic newspaper *El Tiempo,* and then at *El Imparcial,* which betrayed consistent signs of *porfirista* partiality.[21] Flora Lara

Klahr has demonstrated how the photographic and information industries were mutually enabling advocates of each other. Newspapers and magazines featured publicity for picture-taking equipment next to "notes and reports on the latest advances in photography."

> In the Sunday sections of El Imparcial articles appeared from Mexican and foreign contributors on technical points ("Photographs Without a Lens. Surprising Developments"; "The Photographic Rifle"; "Landscape Photography"); on its applications to war ("The Use of Telephotography in Logistics"); on its use in medicine ("Radiography, A Photographic Proof of the Illness You Are Suffering From") and on its application in publicity.[22]

We are indebted to the Casasola Archive for visual knowledge of the figures and events that unfolded in public space and as official spectacle during the Porfiriato. The examples examined herein are a mere handful of the countless official pictures of the Mexican despot taking a moment away from his political goings-on and civic life to pose for the various cameras that rendered him timeless. One important aspect of the Casasola Archive—prior to 1911—is precisely an ambivalent but compelling pull between the *authority* of Díaz and the sometimes-unstable *authorship* of his image. In one anonymous photograph from the archive, Casasola himself is shown standing at the right-hand edge of the frame, his face close up and exacting at the bellow-type viewfinder of the large-format camera he steadies with both hands. He frames a picture within the photograph—of Díaz, who, on September 23, 1910, signs an official declaration to be deposited in a niche of the foundation stone to the Federal Legislative Palace under construction (Figure 13). A fortunate visual loop or chiasmus, the inverted relationship between two political constituents, is set in motion in this particular image. As Lara Klahr succinctly observed, the "photographic industry consolidated the power of the image and made it a natural medium for the image of power."[23]

Cognizant of their role in image manufacture, the brothers Casasola made photographs and collected others that—in various degrees of detachment and disclosure—report the means of production during the Porfirian period. As early as 1905, one image attributed to Casasola renders the straight-on gaze of five male laborers at a glass factory, in such a collective pose as to suggest an art historical composition in the manner of the Spanish masters (Figure 14). An image, also from 1905, depicts two female workers in a tobacco factory, the probing look of both subjects in stark contrast to the listless environment in which they labor. In the darkness of this interior, and with faces that appear to be powdered for the photographic occasion—white face—the woman in the foreground peers suspiciously away from the lens at some undefined spot, her body and posture disarticulated from the spewing machine in front of her. A remarkable image of 1910 indicates a larger workshop for the assembly of carousel horses and other figurines

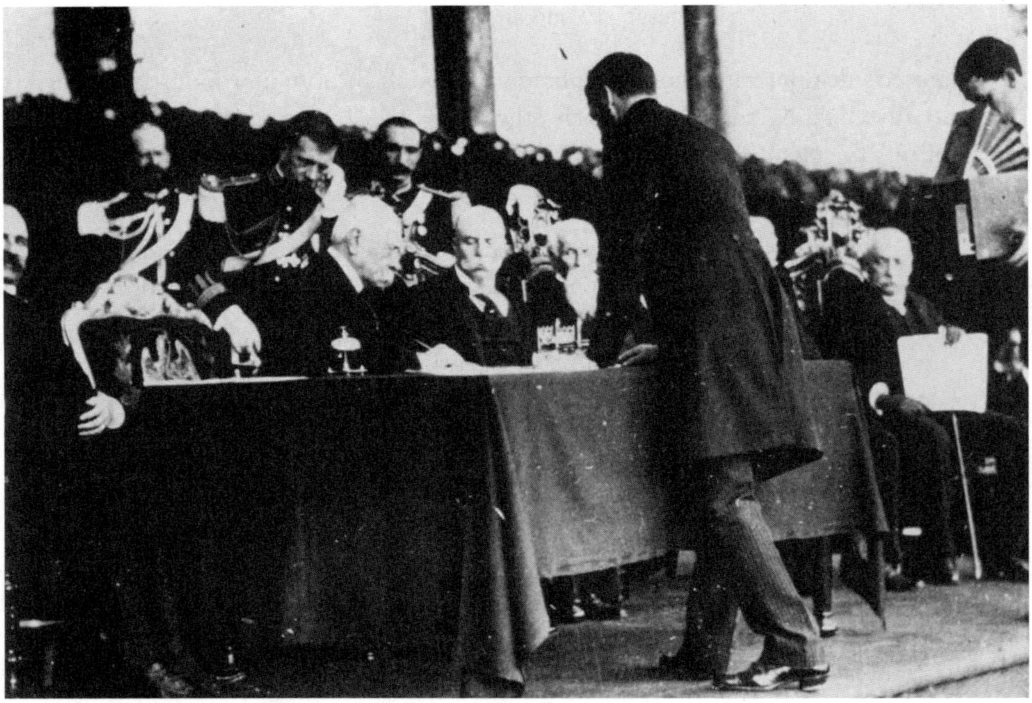

Figure 13. Agustín Víctor Casasola photographs Porfirio Díaz signing official declaration, 1910. Casasola Archive. Copyright SINAFO–Fototeca Nacional.

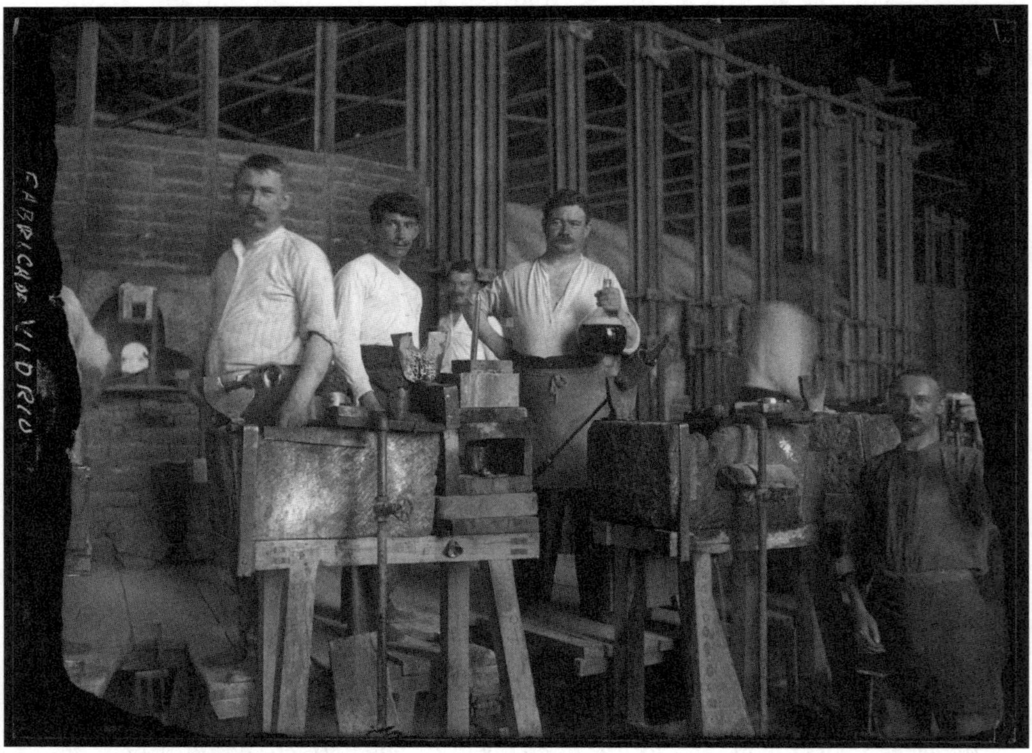

Figure 14. Laborers at a glass factory, 1905. Casasola Archive. Copyright SINAFO–Fototeca Nacional.

destined for public use, including the prominent Mexican eagle and serpent on a cactus. The men and women are arranged in ascending order—a hierarchical logic that is in no way ambiguous (Figure 15).

The ostensible immovability of power and material production, as well as the intricate links between them, are conflated in these photographs and cannot go unexamined. An image of Díaz at a ceremony commemorating former president Juárez in July 1910 (Figure 16) lies between two photographs of textile mills—one of 1908, another of 1912 (Figures 10 and 17). If, according to Allan Sekula, photography posed the "threat and promise of the machine" even as it was reflective of the leisurely or powerful classes, it nevertheless divulged an unhurried time of social "traffic."[24]

If we compare these images from the Díaz throne, and inside the Porfirian factory, with three others—two are anonymous, the other attributed to Miguel Casasola—we detect an overarching method of enunciation. All appear to be produced, both literally and allegorically, from a perspective in which composition is in keeping with the museum display. We need to recall the repugnant national-ethnographic show, the "Remarkable Exhibition," so as to corroborate that outdoor display with interior views, made during these same years, inside such visual institutions as the Museo del Chopo (Figures 18 and 19) or the Museo de Historia

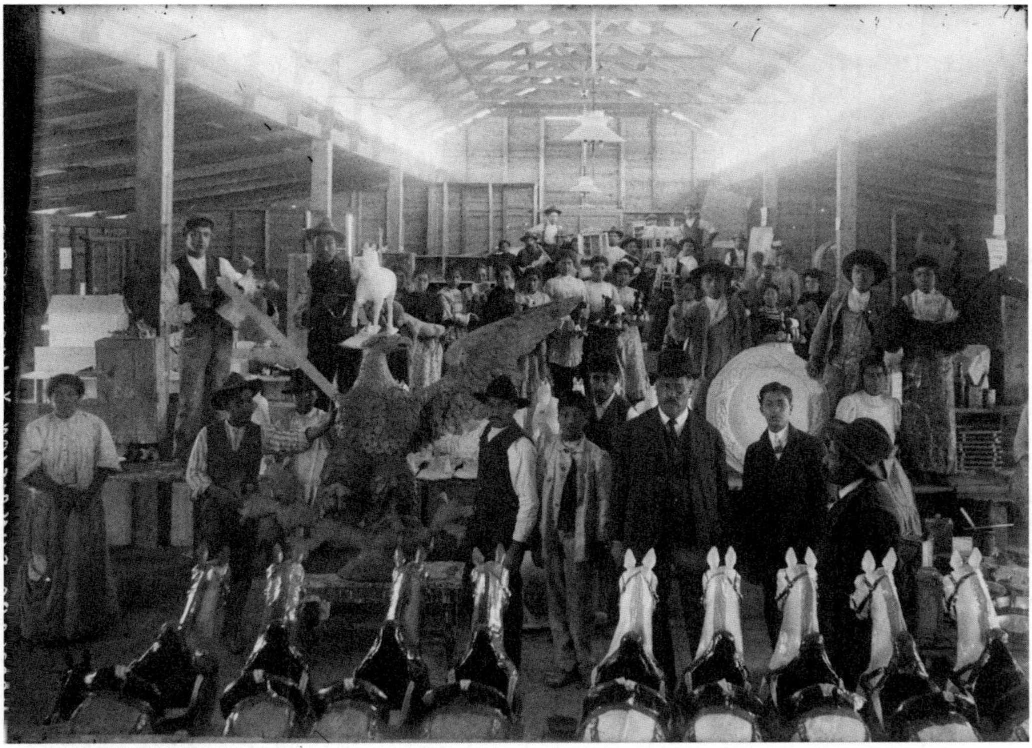

Figure 15. Figurine workshop, 1910. Casasola Archive. Copyright SINAFO–Fototeca Nacional.

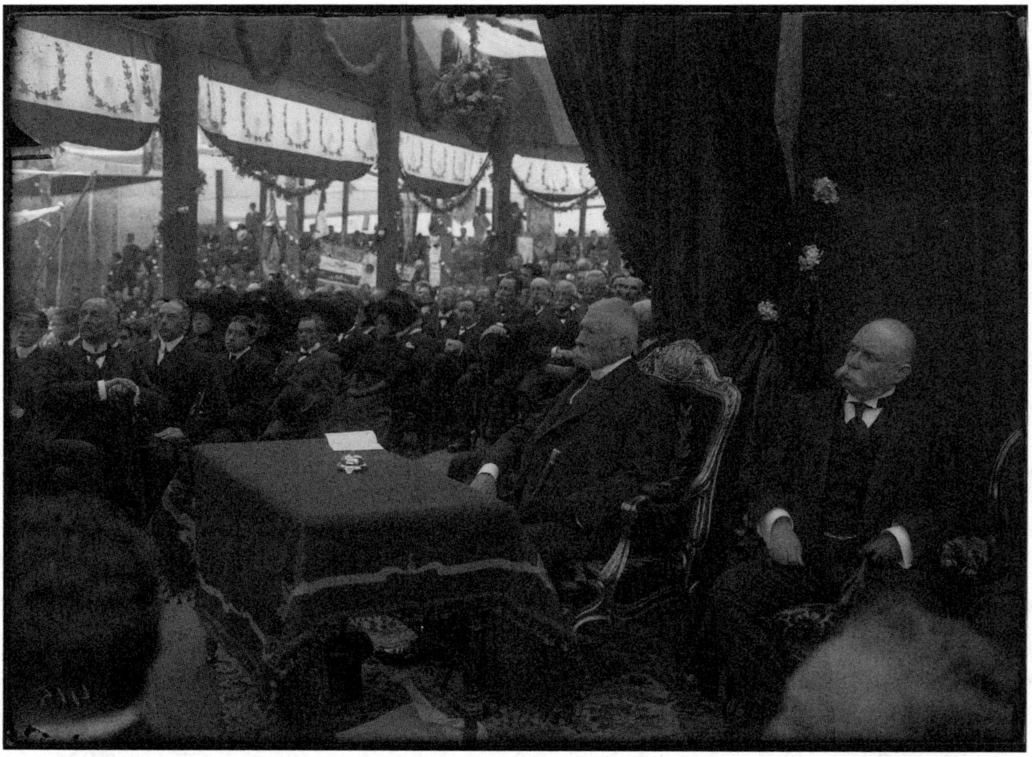

Figure 16. Porfirio Díaz at a ceremony in commemoration of former president Benito Juárez, 1910. Casasola Archive. Copyright SINAFO–Fototeca Nacional.

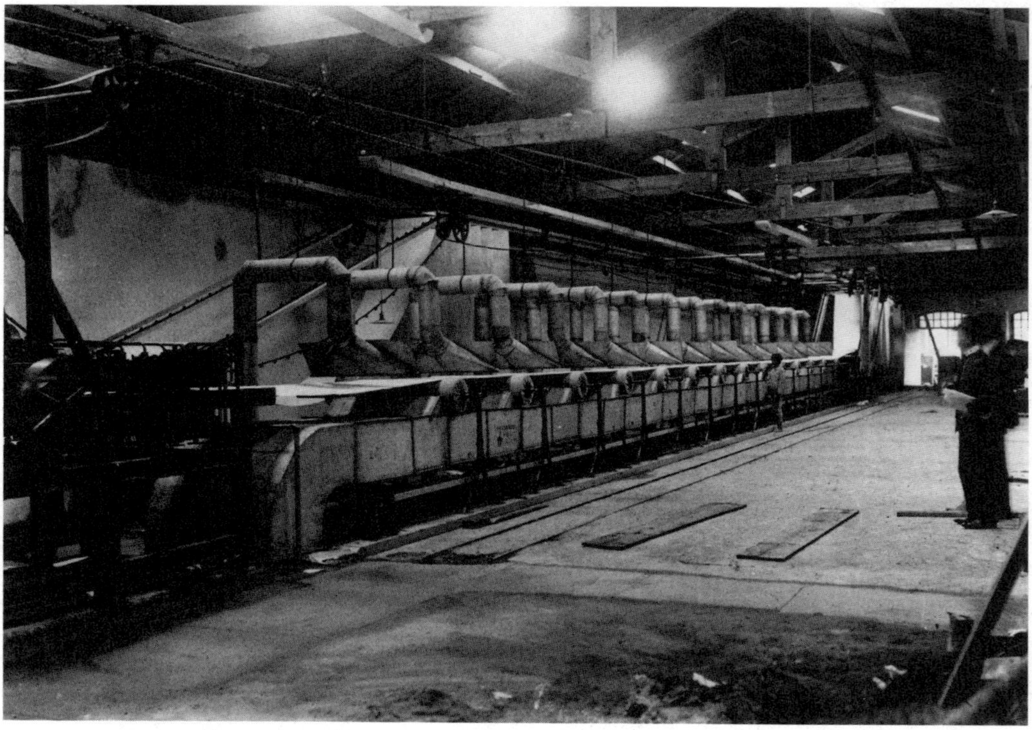

Figure 17. Textile mill and laborers, Mexico, 1912. Casasola Archive. Copyright SINAFO–Fototeca Nacional.

Natural (Figure 20). To varying degrees of visibility, a passive orderliness of distribution also permeates the political, social, and intellectual elites portrayed in the Casasola photographs. With the convenient perspective of time, we can trace how the archive houses and preserves a change in what Sekula identifies as the oscillation in the bourgeois image environment between objectivism and subjectivism. Oscillation gives way to movement. From the static to the mobile, from the monumental to the everyday, from the ceremonious and measured to the abrupt and overflowing, action takes over. On one important level, and viewed together in this way, the Casasola photographs pit one overarching visibility—and its practices of display—against a former facelessness now emerging in differential features and effects that were critical to mobilizing those agents formerly invisible within historical representation. Carlos Monsiváis has noted that in the absence of historians contemporaneous to the civil strife that followed the fall of Díaz, the Casasola photographs are an organizing principle rendering some of the cultural and social contradictions tangible.[25]

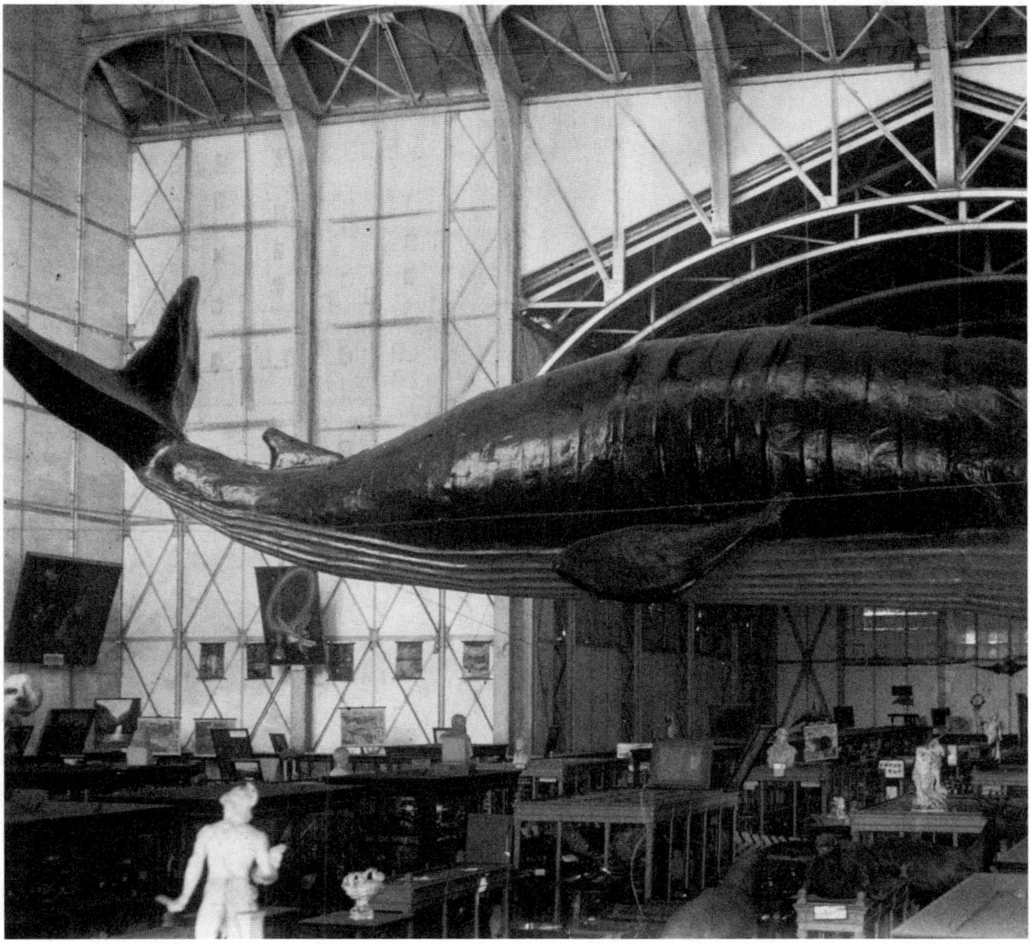

Figure 18. Museo del Chopo, ca. 1910. Casasola Archive. Copyright SINAFO–Fototeca Nacional.

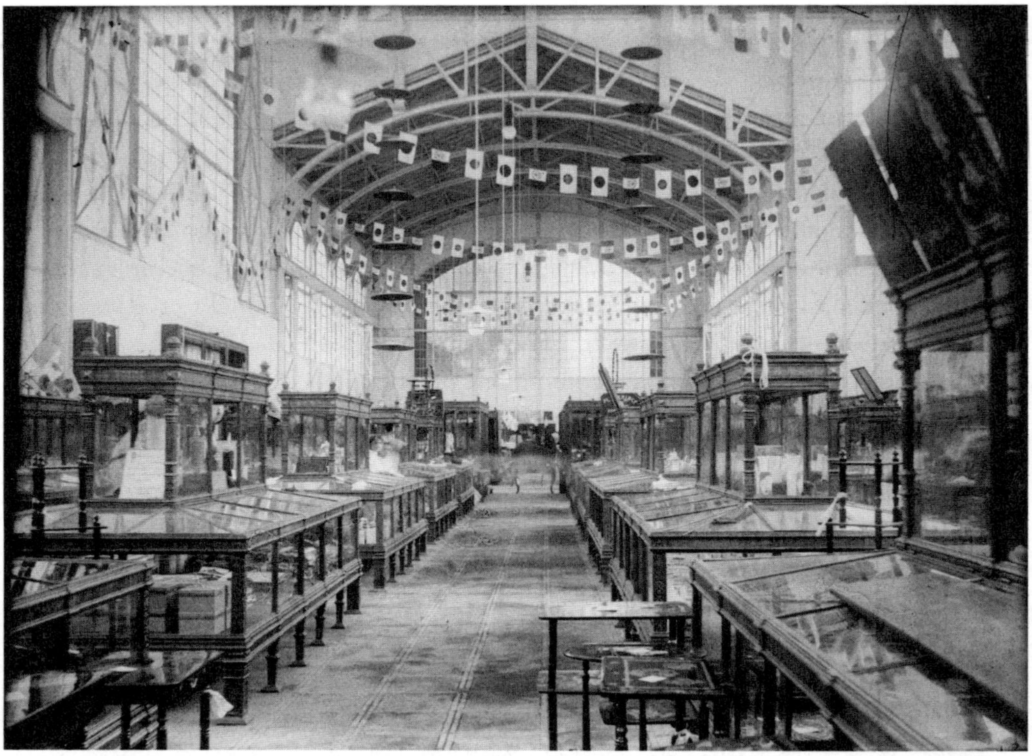

Figure 19. Museo del Chopo, ca. 1910. Casasola Archive. Copyright SINAFO–Fototeca Nacional.

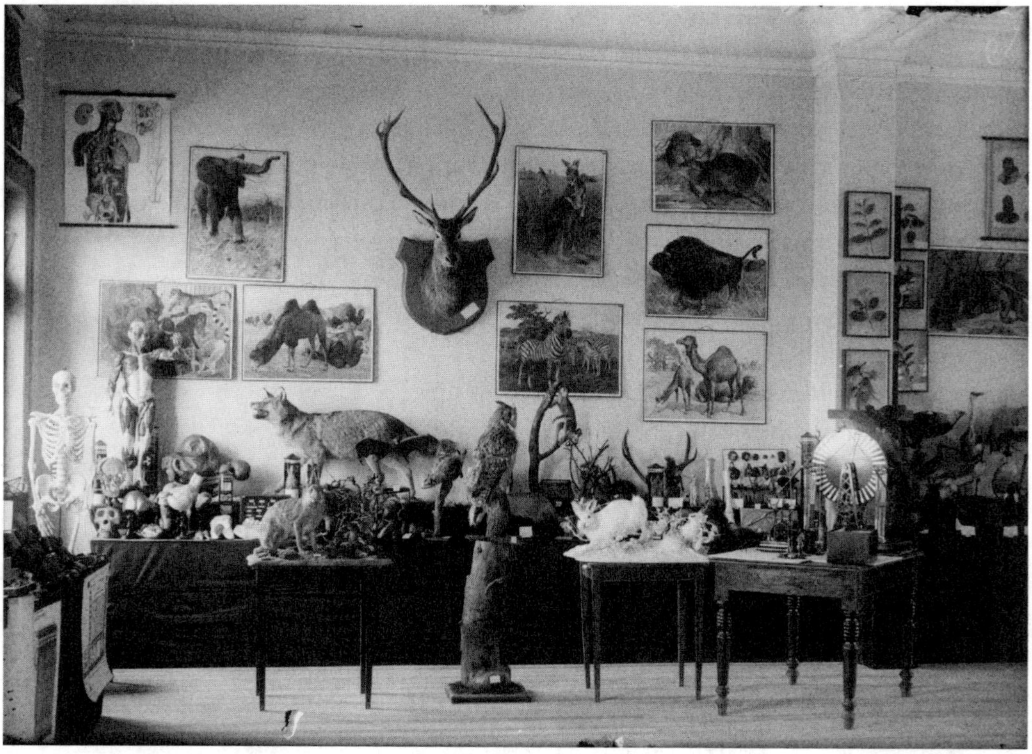

Figure 20. Museo de Historia Natural, ca. 1910. Casasola Archive. Copyright SINAFO–Fototeca Nacional.

Monsiváis refers to the multivolume *Historia gráfica de la Revolución mexicana* as a "sequential and purposeful progression,"[26] first assembled by Agustín Víctor Casasola in 1921 as the *Album histórico gráfico,* with subsequent updated editions published in 1940, and then in 1960, by Ismael and Gustavo. The material disposition of the *Historia gráfica* needs explanation. Among its pages, in chronological form, is the social demise referred to by Monsiváis. Part encyclopedia, part broadsheet, each volume begins with an initial print synopsis, followed by text and images relating, often in two-page spreads, the episodic accounts. To speak only of the first volume to the 1960 edition, these include the nonreelection movement commanded by the affluent landowner from Coahuila, Francisco Madero, as well as his various persecutions and exiles, and those endured by his supporters. A "purposeful progression" outlined in narrative form, the volume traces the parallel uprisings and armed rural mobilizations of Pascual Orozco, Francisco Villa, Emiliano Zapata, and Venustiano Carranza—in the tremendously complex, circuitous events of the Mexican Revolution—as well as the varied alliances and conflicting factions that finally gave way to the assault on the city of Juárez by a Maderista faction (against Madero's orders as led by Orozco) on May 10, 1911, and the resignation and flight of Díaz on May 25. The means by which the following ten years are organized in the *Historia gráfica*—and well beyond that period—is a chief example of how image technology could serve, a priori, to constitute the terminus of a teleology—the Revolution as an ongoing process. (The last edition, as already noted, spans the years 1900–60.)[27] Nevertheless, with its bestowal as an archive in the 1970s, a number of exhibition catalogs have appeared that have often included pictures deemed unworthy of the *Historia gráfica* but that have clear visual appeal—and political significance as well.[28]

For example, marching down a Mexico City street, demonstrators in a 1910 photograph can be seen carrying a banner with the insignia "Centro democrático antireelecionista" (Democratic center against reelection), a protest in support of Madero, as headed by the journalist R. de la Vega (Figure 21). In this exclusively male group of intellectuals and industrial workers and street hawkers, one of two youths in the foreground flaunts a newspaper's front page to the camera, as if to make patent an understanding that this very assembly, too, would be worthy of the print communication that circulated largely thanks to his own manual labor—or, in this particular case, the child labor exploited by the information industries. (We know that Casasola salvaged the press photographs from *El Imparcial* when it closed its doors in 1917, so that we can safely assume that images prior to that date circulated like this one, among the pages of that newspaper.)

A transition is further evidenced in the culminating 1910 photograph of Madero arriving by train to Mexico City, greeted by a throng of awaiting supporters (Figure 22). Here, a still relatively distant and static interface between the camera and its subject gives way to the commotion of the historical events, a perspective displayed in the picture of Madero's political tour in Cuernavaca on June 12,

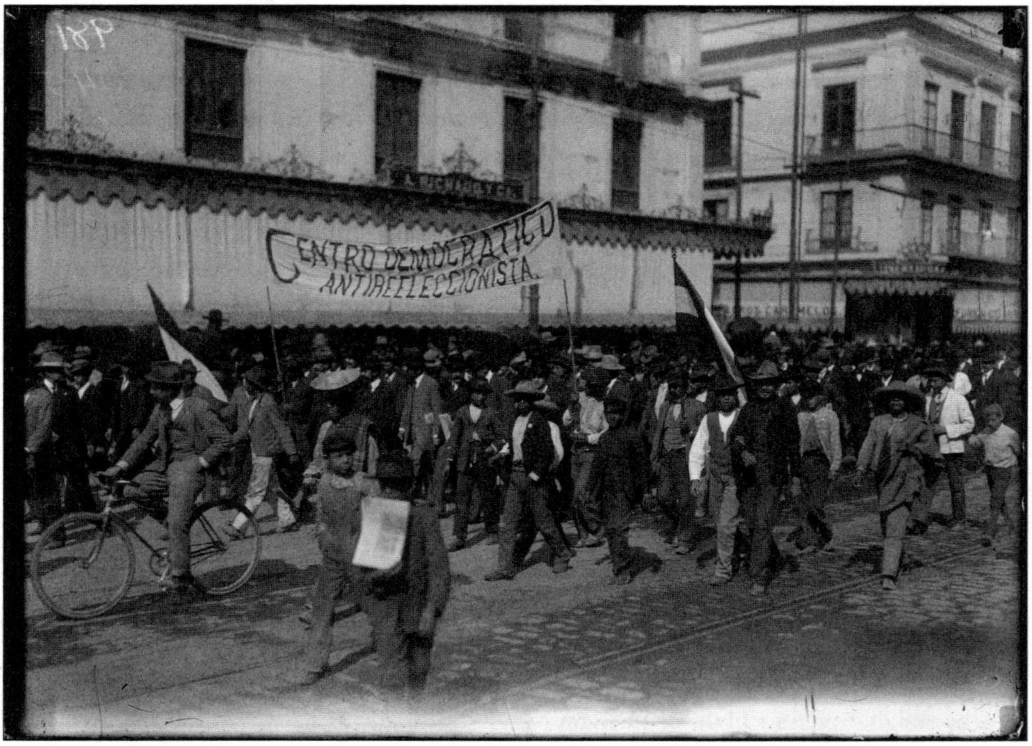

Figure 21. Rally in support of Centro Democrático Antireeleccionista (Democratic Center Against Reelection), 1910. Casasola Archive. Copyright SINAFO–Fototeca Nacional.

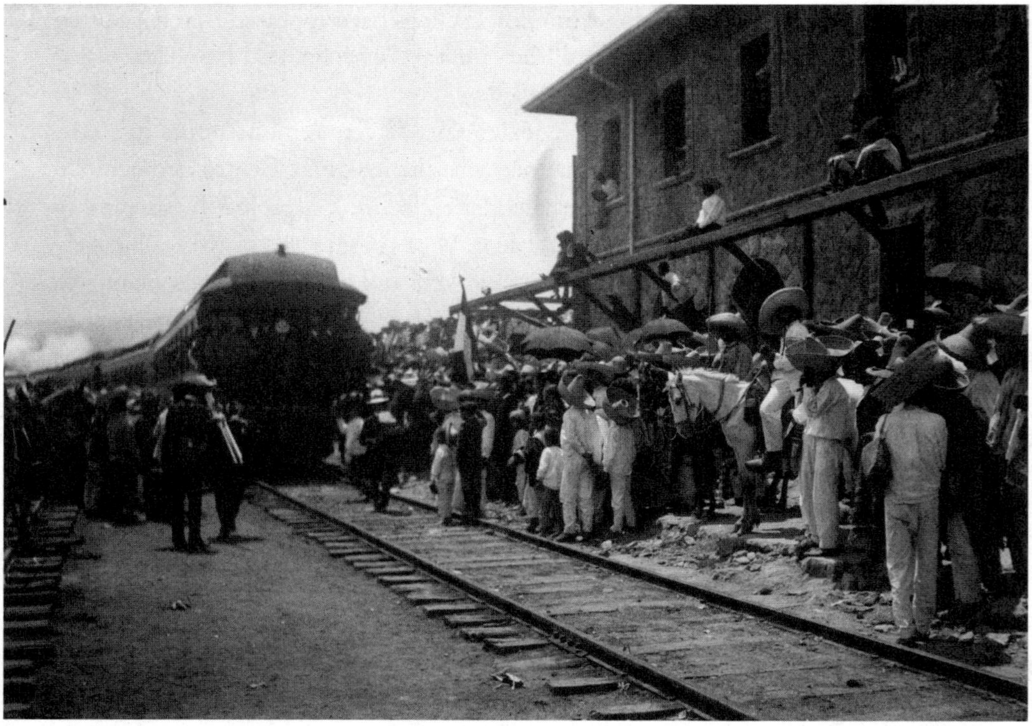

Figure 22. Francisco Madero supporters, train station, 1910. Casasola Archive. Copyright SINAFO–Fototeca Nacional.

1911 (Figure 23), and the more radical turmoil depicted in the image of bundled women and men passing the facade to a cantina ("El Club"), fleeing from the danger zone during the "decena trágica," or "ten tragic days" (Figure 24). In February 1913, Bernardo Reyes and Félix Díaz (nephew of Porfirio Díaz), escaped from their imprisonment to lead a bloody uprising against Madero in Mexico City, and "no one went abroad except under cover of a white flag."[29] First enlisted by Madero to retaliate, Victoriano Huerta ultimately joined with the opposing forces to topple Madero's newly instituted presidency. Further strife is dramatically portrayed in the 1913 rooftop view of the streets around Mexico City's railway station, where civilian men, women, and children are seen in frantic formation with the federal troops and volunteers under the command of Orozco (Figure 25). Selected in this way, many Casasola photographs trace the nature of the photographic image as it attended to the material and spatial predicaments occasioned by radical alterations in the everyday social environment. Parallel to this, they marked the change in societal and journalistic norms that regulated the photographer's movement in social space. What this past produces, writes Monsiváis, is a present desire "to understand how . . . faces . . . conceal and reveal, and the extent to which [Mexico has] given up or condemned the gestures and deeds that swept away a whole political, economic and social structure." Insofar as the Mexican Revolution altered the "facial landscape of Mexico," the Casasola Archive bears witness in the present tense as to the terms of an overturning: "Gone are [the manifestation of] generosity, provocative

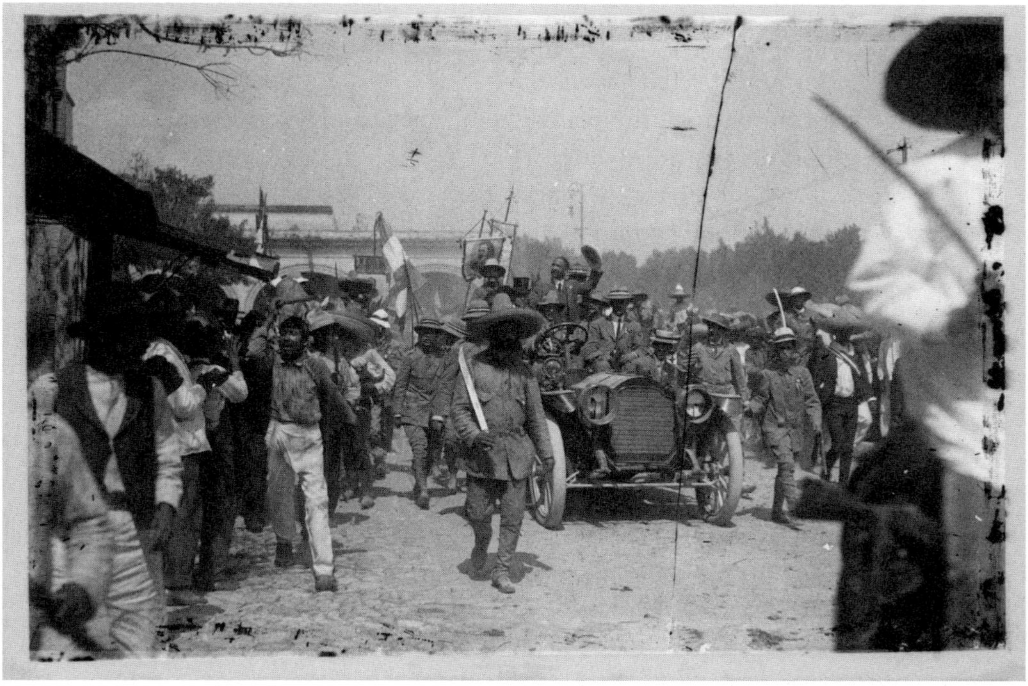

Figure 23. Francisco Madero's political tour, Cuernavaca, Morelos, June 12, 1911. Casasola Archive. Copyright SINAFO–Fototeca Nacional.

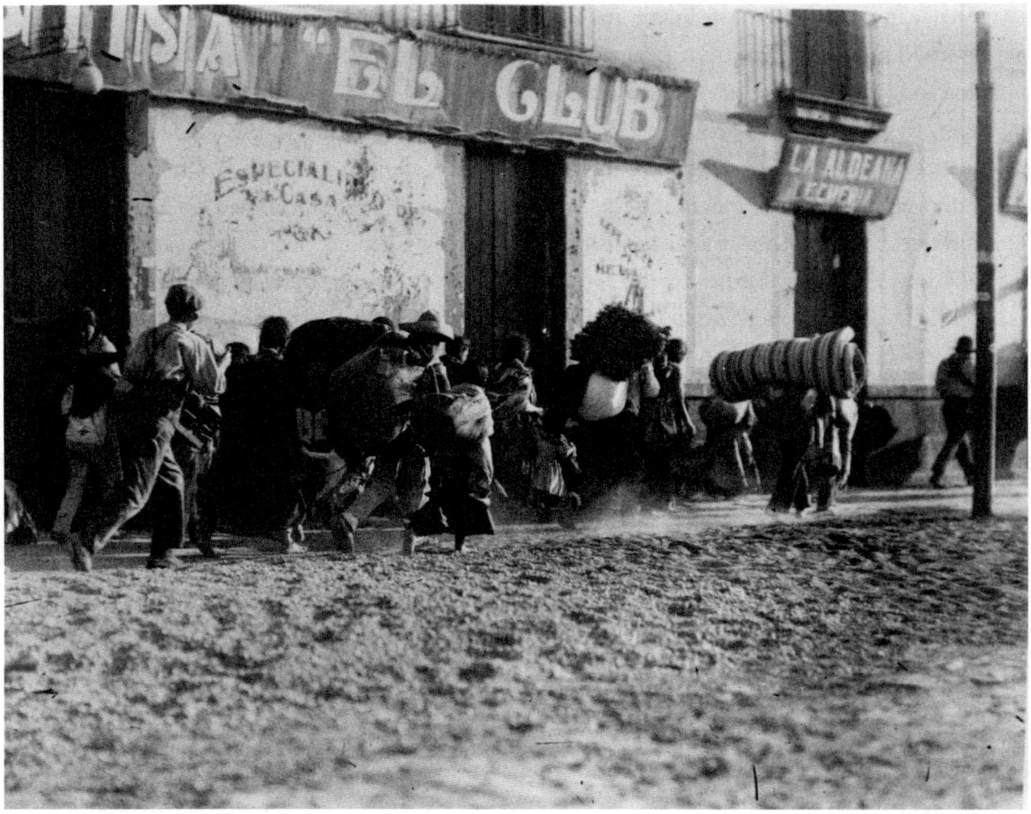

Figure 24. Fleeing from the danger zone during the "tragic ten days," February 9–12, 1913. Casasola Archive. Copyright SINAFO–Fototeca Nacional.

challenge, self-control, and command of bodily motion. A whole theory and practice of the uses of the face are no more."[30]

More than a physiognomy, the official locus of rigid power (expressed as bodily portrayal) gave way to public space—pressured between triumph and terror—and to what some historians have described as "rituals of rule" and "rituals of resistance."[31] To speak of Casasola is to name not a person (or set of persons) behind a camera but to localize an effect. In the matter of thirty thousand images, the name *Casasola* spans the international political pageantry, a civic spectacle that disguised the Díaz regime's more sinister consequences, even as it also managed to disclose the crisis of racialized national identity, the otherwise unrepresented means of production, and the mobilizations, violence, and individuation set into motion by the Mexican Revolution. These exist in a struggle between the spatial fixity of the museum and the open-endedness of the archive.

These archived images have been re-aestheticized because they embody how photography in the early 1910s in Mexico became a medium of a compromise—between object and subject but here also between what a social system could symbolically afford in a crisis of violent transformation and the demands for immedi-

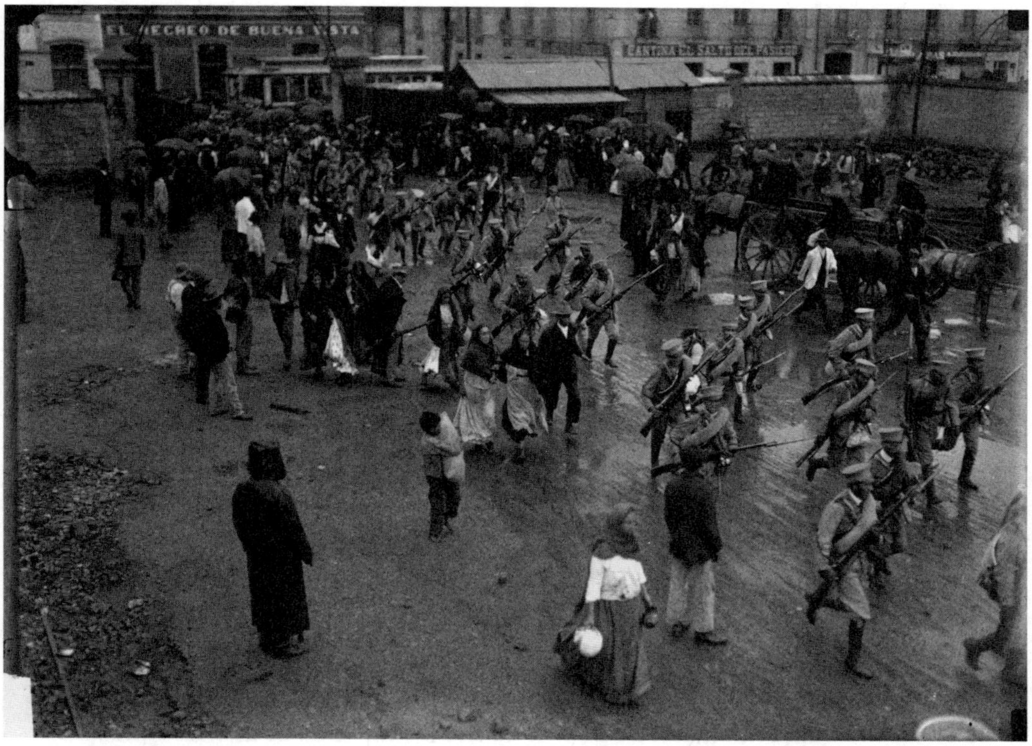

Figure 25. Federal troops and volunteers under command of Pascual Orozco, 1913. Casasola Archive. Copyright SINAFO–Fototeca Nacional.

ate meaning and consensus. Because the structures of the economic, the cultural, and the ethnosocial are incessantly negotiated in these pictures, they disclose a capacity as containers of the material and the ideal. This effect takes place whenever the regulatory space of the built environment provides a location for the spontaneous social aims of public protest; whenever the short-lived vehicle of the printed newspaper medium impresses the perception of a mass responsiveness and its mobilizations; and whenever an alleged cultural memory is contained as a perpetually emergent system.

The photographs go beyond the finite nature ascribed to them by Monsiváis (he speaks of "a limited number of images . . . a limited number of themes"). Political-aesthetic uses of the images have been inclined to legitimate a recent present as the effect of an originating cause (the institutionalized Revolution). Notwithstanding, the Casasola Archive provides access instead to what Nietzsche identified as an "access to the labyrinth of unfinished cultures,"[32] because it identified "representation" as a problem of capital consequence and as a question with a specific history of its own. The "Casasola effect" is a foresight and an intuition: to ignore such a history of representation is to be oblivious to the shaping of a population's corporeality; of personal, social, and political spaces; and of the internal and external differences that make them distinguishable. But it activates, too, the problem of photomechanical representation as it is linked to a philosophical category, which asks the question, is there a difference between the way a social order looks, and the way we act as if it looks? And does that difference alter over time, or is it settled and unchanging? Nietzsche had written, in 1886—with Díaz well into his second term and the year the muralist Diego Rivera was born—that the "historical sense" is hostile to what is self-sufficient and already developed in an art or culture, "the goldness *[sic]* and coldness displayed by all things which have become perfect." Nietzsche's centrality to the intellectual landscape of modern Mexico comes into focus at the cross-purposes of political stakes and historic measure. This is *Beyond Good and Evil,* where Nietzsche writes as well that what "we men of the historical sense find hardest to grasp . . . that which at bottom finds us prejudiced and almost hostile, is just what is complete and wholly mature in every art and culture. . . . *Measure* is alien to us, let us admit it to ourselves; what we itch for is the infinite, the unmeasured."[33]

To be sure, one unavoidable aspect of the Casasola photographs is that they render inoperative the conventional historiographical narratives, because the positivist value of a photograph as a mere visual document is so often betrayed by its inadequacy or failure to represent a categorical conclusion. While it is true that the foregoing may be said of many other mechanical images, it is especially conspicuous in a set of pictures that have so often been illustrative of, or used as source material for, the historical account—one accumulated during the reversal of positivism itself, as I show in what follows. Despite their intended function as evidence, or even more recently as aesthetic objects to be looked at, there is something indiscernible about these pictures that oblige us to account for not only the history of an archive but also "the history of a *concept in general.*"[34] To think of a Casasola *signature,* or effect, may prove useful in suspending the images between the various contexts they inaugurate: the authorial indistinctness of the proper name that is their source, their original function in the communication technologies of the time, their meaning as the material base for an ideal historical narrative about the development of modernity in Mexico, and their recent archival identity and advancement to the status of art. Insofar as the archive that divulges as it conceals the invention of a practice or concept, the Casasola signature provides access to a category—its shorthand is History—and to a "project of knowledge, of practice and of institution, community, family, domiciliation, consignation, in a word, the 'house' or 'museum' in the present state of its archivization."[35] This is made patent in the space covered by the Taft–Díaz images, telescoping out to the physical artifact of the *Historia gráfica,* and farther out again to the exhibition history of the images as art objects in the museum—to rejoin the 1910 pictures inside the Museo del Chopo and the Museo de Historia Natural.[36] In similar mode, *Casasola* is the proper name of a general perspective whose desired effect is to inaugurate an unrestricted origin. It stages metaphorically the "many as one" that time after time, as I have shown, serves to think the national community. It is a storehouse and, increasingly, a display of signs, structures, and historical subjects contained in an oscillating state of archival standing and aesthetization. Individual images, like those discussed above, can equally activate counternarratives to the totalities the archive also makes available. The Casasola Archive is situated at the point or pause before one function eclipses the other, before the lines of corroboration meet—that is, as the national dwelling place where time is meant to endure as so many unsettled tenures of land and light.

Immensity of a History

It is this Nietzschean yearning of the unmeasured or unfinished—the "historical sense"—that leads me from the Casasola Archive to the work of Henri Bergson, whose philosophy, widely read in the original and translated into Spanish, would prove to be of considerable importance to the intellectual elites of post-Revolutionary Mexico and relevant to my discussion of photography and its historical status. Throughout his writings—if perhaps with changing and apparently contradictory intentions—Bergson consistently invoked analogies of the camera, the snapshot, and the motion picture or cinema. In *Matter and Memory* (1896) Bergson identified a problem inhibiting discussions of consciousness, as long as "perception is imagined to be a kind of photographic view of things."[37] From the onset, Bergson makes the whole world photographic. This photographic analogy, however, goes farther. For Bergson, matter produces a multiplicity of images. Not only does every material object *emit* an image for us—matter *is* image. In this sense, the photograph (or image) "is already taken, already developed in the very heart of things and at all points of space."[38] Following this argument, Bergson goes on to claim that all image matter differs in degree rather than kind, as distinct from consciousness and memory.

In *Creative Evolution* and thereafter, Bergson builds from this assertion, almost entirely abandoning the still image in favor of the cinematographic and cinematic one to account for the workings of consciousness, perception, and memory—in the course of movement, time, and duration. This primacy of duration radically alters the category of matter. Here enters the question of body—an image itself that, in turn, produces major changes on other objects or bodies. As it directly undergoes and undertakes movement, the body constitutes a zone of indetermination at constant variance with itself. In this sense, we cannot speak of bodies or forms at all. For what is real as experienced by perception is "the continual *change of* form," and so, in this respect, *"form is only a snapshot view of a transition."*[39] The cinematic image would at first seem the perfect model for perception, except that between each cinematic frame (the unit of the filmstrip) there are "end points" that perception fails to register. Bergson here annexes the problem of movement, hence the question of time, and so brings to bear the cinematic sequence and its attempt to reconstitute movement. Though it presents itself to consciousness as image, matter cannot be external to itself—movement being a "translation into space" distinct from the space covered.[40] For Bergson, movement is the present-becoming-the-past, or the act of covering space—indivisible, heterogeneous, and irreducible. For displacement transpires in the interval between two points in space, or instants in time; in the unthinkable passage by which the present becomes the past; in the continuum whereby a difference is established between presence and absence; between what we frame and what gets left beyond the edges.[41]

Immediately striking is the degree to which Bergson understood the technology of the image during the time he was writing both *Matter and Memory* and *Creative Evolution.* More important, however, Bergson was subjecting to philosophical scrutiny the perceptual phenomenon of persistence of vision—first theorized by P. M. Roget and J. A. Plateau in 1825 and 1829, respectively.[42] Bergson's entire system of thought may be said to hinge on this long-identified experience: that an image appears to linger for a fraction of a second after the object has elapsed, the very effect that renders the cinematic illusion successful. Why is it, Bergson seems to ask by way of counterpoint, that we do not perceive the world in what today we would call strobe effect, or in the delayed traces of afterimage?

If, as Walter Benjamin noted, Bergson perhaps shut his eyes to "the inhospitable, blinding age of big-scale industrialism,"[43] it is not true, by contrast, that Bergson was unmindful of the power inherent in image technology, perhaps foreshadowing the ubiquitous presence it would command in this century and the philosophical implications to which it has since given rise. For the kind of modernity Benjamin foresaw was also a time in which the "transmissibility of the past" was being "replaced by its citability,"[44] posing additional problems with regard to mobility in general, concerned with the limits imposed by mechanical reproduction and its attendant questions of history and representation.

Bergson returns, time and again, to the phenomenon known as "persistence of vision," without which we would see indivisible passage as though resembling the choppy movement of the silent movie's sixteen frames per second. He addresses as well the notion of "division" or "halt" to describe the cutting-out process of perception. But, more to the point here, Bergson employs the halt to suggest the double transit of memory and the compensation performed by the creative mind in its viewing of a still image or photograph. In so doing, he entitles the mind or imagination, in its individual and social capacity, to compensate for that residual fraction of the afterimage. Hence the still photograph, in its arrest and hesitation of time, is afforded the fullness of the prior movements that led to the halt . . . and to the virtual future, which it contains and seemingly withholds.

In his "Theses on the Philosophy of History," and in other writings, Benjamin equates the processes of language to those of history—memory being the vehicle by which language is translated into history, and vice versa. If thinking involves not only a flow of language but its hesitation or grinding halt, so, too, memory must pause in an incalculable hover or stammer. If the instant is to perception what moments-of-passing are to duration—waiting for sugar to dissolve in water or lingering over the emergent forms of a photograph—the halt is that moment-of-passing by which we gain or lose awareness of our train of thoughts, by which we make the leap to that place where the erratic parcels of language and the shards of shattered images suddenly diffuse into a familiar environment—or into an abrupt, suspended state. Should the photograph be considered not a fixity but an insinuated flux in paradoxical pause? Not an instant, but a movement at a creative interval or remove from mind and memory? Do memory and the material calling-to-mind of a photograph differ at all?

If a photograph may be said, perhaps conventionally, to divide the continuous and to fix a becoming, and if the halt or hesitation allows us to see the whole as a sum of its parts, then we might conceive this arrest as consciousness itself in search of material form, as mind successfully finding itself in matter. It works by such release and contraction as to gather "into a single instant the incalculable number of small events which matter holds distinct, as when we sum up in a word the immensity of a history."[45]

In arguing for this magnitude of a history as summarized in the economy of a word or in the immediacy of a photograph, one must take Bergson at face value and maintain that the photograph does not merely constitute an aid to, or a category of, memory—it *translates* memory. Extending what Bergson has to say about memory to the still image proves useful in that both recollection and photography bring to mind all those past perceptions that are related to the present perception. They summon the anterior and suggest the ensuing multiplicities. In this sense, they bestow a perspective that compels a practicable or viable decision best suited. In that halt, multifarious moments of duration are made available that provisionally free us from the flow of matter or from the cadences of immediate need. A photograph hinges between what it contains and what it cannot, by its very nature, comprise. Hence the viewing of a photograph performs Bergson's twofold movement, for it is both immediate perception and pure memory.

For a photograph to be both perception and memory a translation must ceaselessly transpire—both in the sense of pure movement and of "carrying over." As Gilles Deleuze contends, the camera becomes an "exchanger" or generalized equivalent of the movement of translation, where "movement relates the object between which it is established to the changing whole which it expresses, and vice versa."[46] Doubtless, Benjamin addresses this point in his extraordinary framing of translation as a practice of difference and displacement: "Translation passes through continua of transformation, not abstract areas of identity and similarity."[47]

This double transit of memory as per the ways we visit a photograph is part recollection, part calling-to-mind. If memory complicates action, then photography makes memory ever the more intricate. What a photograph is to an "outside" resembles the process and effects of translation, whereby original and version are set into motion by a differential, historically meaningful relationship. (This conjunction, in turn, is not unlike cultural syncretism. Hardly irrelevant in a discussion of Mexico—where most cultural expression is defined by it—in syncretism contact leads to an often imbalanced but nevertheless joint transformation, never entirely one but neither altogether the other.) Like these phenomena, photography, too, is involved with "things in the making," with becoming. It is located at the interval, in the gap, is the liminal space of suspended momentum, of the present becoming the past. It is precisely this interval, however, that photography can never represent by unyielding fact. Because it is always external to itself, the photographic fraction, like consciousness, points to its other, the future tense.

Photography, like that of the Casasola Archive, had inaugurated an anxiety around the camera because of its increasingly everyday disposition, so ubiquitous as to potentially disable other forms of symbolic representation. It constituted a technology that circulated imperative images of power and was hence viewed as a science associated with the positivism being overturned by actors of the new social and cultural idealisms. The importance of Bergson's writings to the ethos of Revolutionary Mexico can now come into view as it was understood and amended by two of its decisive cultural producers: the philosopher Antonio Caso and the art critic Marius de Zayas.

Depicting an Action

Caso published his *Problemas filosóficos* in 1915, with acknowledgment to Bergson and Nietzsche, whose writings confuse the alleged dualism between intellect and intuition, as well as between the universal and particular:

> The philosophy of M. Bergson [proposes] the systematic correction of intellectualism with a constant appeal to intuition. This combination of purely rational and analytic procedures with direct and living intuition, that produces reality and clarifies it with science, penetrating the singularity of concrete irreducible beings, and not only the abstract definitions supplied by the intellect, is the exclusive and privative method of philosophy.[48]

That very year the United States officially recognized the Carranza regime—a relevant fact, given the antecedents. By 1914 Huerta, who had already toppled Madero's presidency, and now the chief executive, was embroiled in a diplomatic dispute with the Woodrow Wilson administration, which was supplying arms to Carranza and his Constitutionalist Army. Wilson had refused to recognize Huerta's legitimacy—the rising tensions were based on U.S. economic interest—and Wilson finally sent troops to occupy Veracruz. The port city became the provisional capital of Mexico—effecting Huerta's resignation—under the short-lived presidency of Eulalio Gutiérrez. Together with General Álvaro Obregón, Carranza and his forces entered Mexico City in August of 1914. Historians have viewed the middle years of this decade, especially 1915, as the bloodiest in the civil war, and this moment epitomized the rapid succession, the transitory impact of time, and the instability surrounding the brutal period of the Revolution.

Returning to Caso, the relevant intellectual biographies are unclear about the specific publication history of the individual essays that comprise that collection, but we do know that many were published in the years prior to 1915 in *El Tiempo,* and other newspapers in which the news reporting of Agustín Víctor Casasola, and others, found circulation. *Problemas filosóficos* refers to Bergson, Nietzsche, and other philosophers that Caso and his contemporaries deployed in a reversal of the positivism that permeated the social project of *los científicos* and the Porfirian regime. In a country ravaged by everyday strife, volatility, and radical violence, it is small wonder that Caso found appealing the Bergsonian category of intuition, as that which "produces reality and clarifies it with science, penetrating the singularity of concrete irreducible beings, and not only the abstract definitions supplied by the intellect."[49] As Rosa Krauze de Kolteniuk remarks: "In agreement with Bergson, [Caso] observed that philosophical systems artificially comprised the universe, leaving out considerations of an individual's hue, variety, and singularity. He doubted that one or two ideas were enough to encompass the truth."[50]

Caso was an active participant in the intellectual formations in Mexico committed to upsetting, as I have said, the positive philosophies that were complicit with the Díaz regime. He and others rose to recognition through a series of lectures, and the generation came to be identified by the place where they were first held, the Ateneo de la Juventud (Atheneum of Youth). The group refuted the positivist wave upheld by such ideologues and educators as Ignacio Ramírez and Gabino Barreda. Caso had studied under Barreda at the Escuela Nacional Preparatoria where positivism had become a "pedagogical routine" as imparted by those in such positions of power as to be the engineers of Mexico's national culture.[51] Caso and the Ateneo were apprehensive about the supposed incommensurability between "metaphysics and mathematics," and the relegation of ethics and aesthetics to mere emotive or evaluative meanings by Auguste Comte and his Mexican followers.

For Comte, the branches of knowledge were deemed to pass through different (and ascending) theoretical conditions: "The Theological, or fictitious; the Metaphysical, or abstract; and the Scientific, or positive." To the degree that Comtian scientism was central to the social architecture and image environment of Mexico's ancien régime, it's worth taking a closer look at "The Nature and Importance of Positive Philosophy," where Comte expounded claims that would be countered by Caso and other Ateneo intellectuals.

> In the final, the positive state, the mind has given over the vain search after Absolute notions, the origin and destination of the universe, and the causes of phenomena, and applies itself to the study of their laws,—that is, *their invariable*

> *relations of succession and resemblance.* Reasoning and observation, duly combined, are the means of this knowledge. What is now understood when we speak of an explanation of facts is simply the establishment of a connection between single phenomena and some general facts, the number of which continually diminishes with the progress of science.[52]

According to Comte, every phenomenon is subordinate to an unchanging physics—the material world as it is specified in forces, reactions, and internal structures—whose pattern it is the task of positive philosophy to discover in the smallest number of laws. Indeed, any kind of knowledge reaches the "positive," that is, the most preferable stage, in direct and most immediate proportion "to its generality, simplicity, and independence of other departments."[53]

As an optical innovation and communications advance, photography was broadly viewed as a mechanistic device of "science" with instrumental value. Yet because of the systems it prompted, and what it proffered in terms of human subject–object interface, the dilemma of photography was prepared to have upset those invariable relations of *succession* and *resemblance* so dear to Comte and his counterparts in Mexico. In opposition to the standardizing ends of positive philosophy were radical possibilities made available with image technology as it was employed not only in the industry of mass communication. (Indeed, Caso and Casasola came into eventual contact—linked by the sidelines of the camera—as a 1922 Casasola photograph of Caso testifies; there, the philosopher is represented in a moment of pause at a podium before an audience [Figure 26]). If, for the positive sciences, a "stability in fundamental maxims [was] the first condition of the social order,"[54] then the violent instability of the *political successions* that marked Mexican history from 1911 to 1920 ought also to have radically altered the idealized category of representation as an orderly, absolute reflection of social and spatial distributions. The function of photography, and ideas about it, should have developed in keeping with the physical and formal patterns of the unforeseen, the accidental, and the erratic—the elevated intangibles giving way to the realism of historic time as it was being played out in the hard matter of the Revolutionary wager.

For Caso philosophy was an inquiry by which existence and thought were made concordant, but he remained unable to see in the photograph a site for reconciling differences between a thing and its representation, between matter and memory, or between idealism and materialism. Like Bergson, he viewed the photograph with suspicion and deemed it a negative model of embodied positivist values. Caso believed, with Bergson, that science cannot account for the relation between images (in the broadest sense) as a material or mental difference, to the extent that the object of scientific inquiry is an image related to itself, an absolute value of identity. On this point of photographic representation Bergson and Caso err by incorporating Comte, and thus viewing photography as an explanation of particulars, as a "connection between single phenomena and some general facts,

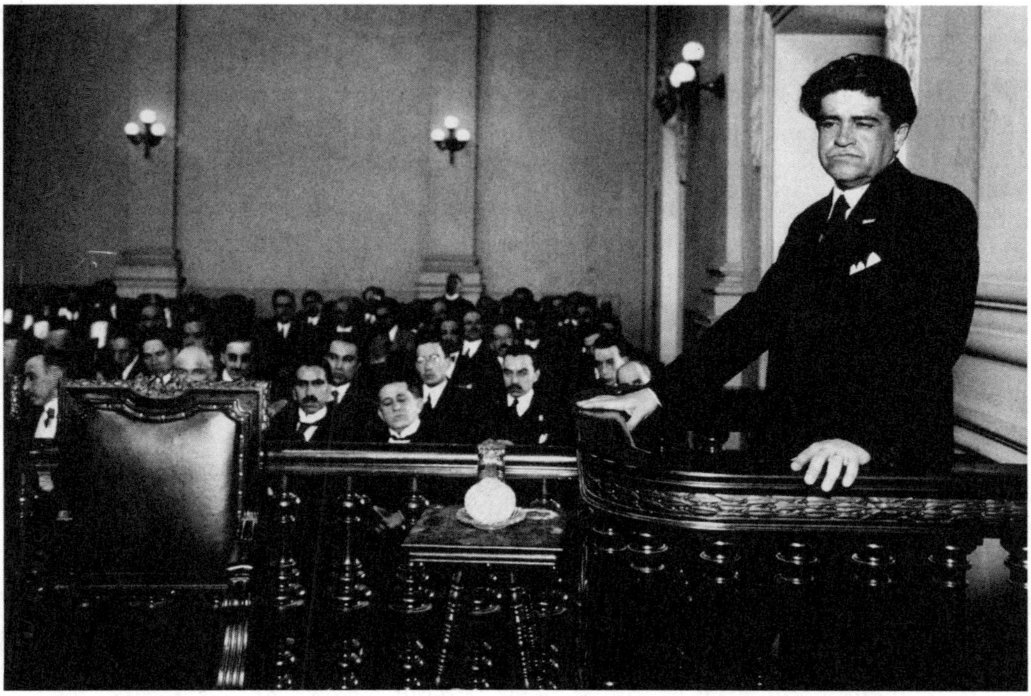

Figure 26. Antonio Caso at a podium before an audience, ca. 1915. Casasola Archive. Copyright SINAFO–Fototeca Nacional.

the number of which continually diminishes." If there is in matter something more than, but no different from, what is actually given, then there are two sets of systems, according to Caso and Bergson, and they are intermittent: the system of images called the universe and the body that contains "my perceptions" in relation to a system of images called the universe. As a writer for the print media, Caso was well aware that photography constituted a development in the discipline of knowledge as well as an advance in the sciences of light. What he has to say about Descartes and optics could have advanced his notions of resemblance in symbolic representation.[55]

That Caso allowed for the unknown variable is surprising, given the last section of *Problemas filosóficos,* "El nuevo humanismo" ("The New Humanism"). There, he points to the "mediated pragmatism" of Nietzsche and William James, and the philosophy of contingency advanced by Bergson and Emile Boutroux, as proof of the decidedly anti-intellectualist tenor of his times. In this view, man is not a simple surveyor of aesthetic forms, nor does he intone the harmonies of creation, nor is he a secondary phenomenon caused by the world he accompanies; instead, he is a collaborator and agent of existence. The world is no mise-en-scène but an arena: "There is something superior to the *spectacular sense* of the aesthetes, and it is the *life sense [sentido vital]* of the moralists who know the world is still in the making, that we are involved in the manufacture, and it is in perfecting it that we should spend our faith and breathing."[56] Caso goes on to cite Bergson's view of mind or reason, whose habits of economy represent effects in strict proportion to their causes, as opposed to nature or matter, viewed as investing more in the cause than is necessary for the effect—that is, prodigious and in excess of itself. This new humanism, this modern conception of man, regards reality as redundant, sees nature as superabundant. This new disconcerting universe is neither a copy nor a corruption of platonic archetypes but an endless overflowing and perennial flux. In such a world, philosophy becomes a complex social task in which "philosophic thought and the sciences are joined in a movement of constant intertwining, concomitant circulation, assiduous and mutual collaboration."[57]

In the last essay, "Aurora," it is at first unclear to what exactly Caso is responding when he critiques what he sees as an unhealthy entanglement between positivism and aesthetics. He remarks that positivism in philosophy and naturalism in the arts are identical movements of reaction, naturalism being an aesthetic positivism and positivism being a philosophic naturalism. He then develops the idea of aesthetic naturalism as "explaining movement in terms of number and space, chemical facts in terms of mechanics, biological reactions by virtue of chemical laws, and mind in terms of animal biology."[58] But the object of his unease soon comes into focus, and it is twofold. A photographic caveat should be expected at this point, but allow me to quote Caso in full:

> Aesthetic naturalism is identical to positivism in art; like its philosophical counterpart, it is a doctrine lacking in critical significance. When the naturalist reproduces ordinary life with its absurd representations, its countless irregularities, its nonaesthetic vacillations and the disconnected characteristic of phenomena; when he believes that the aforesaid is to produce an art that copies the profound nature of things, he does so forgetting that the reality of things does not subsist in disorderly practical manifestations: he forgets that reality is always ideal, that one finds it necessary to dismantle the conventionalism of daily experience to reach truthful aesthetic contemplation, and that, *finally, a being, a soul, or a thing are more real and more precise in the otherworldly limbo of idealist inspiration than in a photographic reproduction depicting an action.*[59]

The otherwordly, ideal, timeless, or static being is a matter of accuracy as compared with the irregularities, vacillations, and disconnected nature of movement in the reality depicted in a photograph. And it is the "disorderly practical" signs that betray Caso's second apprehension. The text goes on to isolate the gravest of the antiromantic reactions of the nineteenth century in the "practical positivism" of political economy, that is, the evolution of English utilitarianism and Marx's materialist conception of history. Though his language is equally scathing on the subject of capitalist excess—anthropomorphized in the figure of Rockefeller inverting the life chart so that property is valued over artistic production—Caso performs a deflection: he makes transcendent reference to World War I and completely overlooks the brutal civil strife in Mexico at the time. It is a deflection that verifies Caso's blind spot with regard to History and representation, one that haunts the whole of *Problemas filosóficos.* Caso had described History as an amalgam of "biography" and "biology"—a "creative copy" of material existence—but was ill equipped to see the photograph as "creative history," "an intuition of life that is no longer; this is to say, a simulacrum of life." Caso failed as well to grant the technique of photography the status of being in excess of itself—not a secondary phenomenon caused by the world it accompanies but a collaborator and agent of its ongoing history. Fearing the photograph to be a mere Comtean relation of succession and resemblance—the repetition of the same—he doomed the photograph to the category of aesthetic positivism, to a descriptive function, and not to the productive amalgam of mathematic and metaphysics (active intuition) that he found himself elsewhere prescribing. While Caso admitted that a photograph could *depict* an encounter, he was blind to its potential for prompting action.

Not Even an Art

So as to further unsettle the identity of Mexico in the mirror of "photography itself," I turn now to New York City of the 1910s and to the largely unremarked writings of a deracinated Mexican national: Marius de Zayas.[60] Born into a prosperous family, de Zayas had come into his own as a political caricaturist for the newspapers his father published in his native Veracruz, as well as for one of Mexico City's leading newspapers, *El Diario.* In the introduction to her collection of his writings and correspondence, Francis M. Naumann underscores how the calls for democracy and the antidictatorial positions against Díaz endorsed in the newspapers published by the de Zayas family "obliged them all in 1907 to abandon their homeland and to take exile in the United States."[61]

In New York City, de Zayas gained employment on the staff of the *New York Evening World* where his caricatures of the city's beau monde celebrities and intelligentsia gained the particular attention of one in particular he portrayed. Alfred Stieglitz went on to exhibit the work of de Zayas in his Little Galleries of the Photo-Succession, or "291." But more important to my purposes here, de Zayas began to write in English—with the first significant article on Picasso to appear in the American press—and to contribute essays to the milestone journal *Camera Work,* where they were intertwined with writings by others that included Sadakichi Hartmann, Alvin Langdon Coburn, George Bernard Shaw, Maurice Maeterlinck, Benjamin De Casseres, and excerpts from the philosophy—not surprisingly—of Bergson. In the January 1913 issue, number 41, and then again in a subsequent issue were published two articles that nominate de Zayas as a link between the photographic practices of the United States and Mexico, and of the shared histories of symptomatic ambivalence and blindness that are betrayed in the discursive positioning of photography as an identity in relation to the other visual arts.

Published in 1913, "Photography" and its companion piece of that year titled "Photography and Artistic Photography" both participate in a series of rhetorical attitudes that, since the inception of mechanical reproduction, have sought to theorize the media-specific discrepancies inherent to the photograph.[62] (A later chapter rehearses a subsequent but related text, "Photographs: Graphic and Anti-Graphic," written by another associate of Stieglitz, the art dealer and photography advocate Julien Levy.) De Zayas's two essays trace a transition evident already in the repetition and variance of their opening statements that range from an initial act of disowning to a subsequent admission—that is, between "Photography is not Art. It is not even an art" to "Photography is not Art, but photographs can be made to be Art." The two essays mark a resonant avowal; it is one rife with ambiguities, in writing that is alternately ingenious and excessive, and I want to bring it into view adjacent to the foregoing analysis of the Casasola Archive, Caso's writings, and Bergson's philosophy. For the emergent or troubled nature of these tracts betrays itself throughout the text in a number of inconsistencies and uncertain recurrences—contradictions I make productive.

"Photography is not Art. It is not even an art." In *Camera Work*—along with images by Julia Margaret Cameron (of Carlyle and Herschel, among others)—and by Stieglitz himself, de Zayas continues his aphoristic commentary as follows:

> Art is the expression of the conception of an idea. Photography is the plastic verification of a fact.
>
> The difference between Art and Photography is the essential difference which exists between Idea and Nature.
>
> Nature inspires in us the idea. Art, through the imagination, represents that idea in order to produce emotions.

De Zayas's opposition of art and photography is developed by means of a rhetorical recourse to a set of contrary terms: presentation versus evidence, idea versus nature, the similar versus the identical, feeling versus fact, imagination versus matter. This is finally to make incompatible a visual distribution reflective of the given with the creative faculty that is productive of the new. But before going any farther it is necessary to address the thorny ethics of racial evolutionism that informs his aesthetic: for it is within the context of the preceding that de Zayas also distinguishes between the "refined" and the "savage" as symbolized and actualized between Europe and Africa:

> A peculiar evolution of Form corresponds to each one of the states of anthropological development. From the primitive races, to the white ones, which are the latest in evolution and consequently the most advanced, Form, starting from the fantastic, has evolved to a *conventional naturalism*. . . . In the savage, analysis and discrimination do not exist. He is unable to concentrate his attention upon

> a particular thing for any length of time. He does not understand the differences between similar and identical, between that which is seen in dreams and that which happens in real life, between imagination and facts; and that is why he takes as facts the ideas inspired by impressions.

There is a great deal to unpack here. To begin, de Zayas equates his abhorrent evolutionary model of white supremacy with cultural or creative progression of the forms and shapes produced by humankind in History. In this, it is reflective also of the Comtean positivism whereby, as I showed earlier in this chapter, reasoning and observation, duly combined, are the means of a knowledge understood as "the establishment of a connection between single phenomena and some general facts" whose number diminishes with the advances of science. Therefore, de Zayas regarded eclecticism, and the appropriation of the non-Western, in the contemporary arts of early modernism as a *deformation.* De Zayas, preoccupied with art as the actualization of some preordained idea or form, posits the ideal over any realization of it—and thereby commits a deflection. The Casasola photograph of the "Remarkable Exhibition" comes to mind when de Zayas deploys the cannibalistic metaphor of art seen as greedily consuming itself: "Art is devouring Art." In reference most notably to Picasso, de Zayas needed the evolutionary model to posit that, while the human brain has been developing, "perfected under the influence of progress and civilization," the elements for the creative faculties whose function is to produce new images and ideas have been exhausted. Imagination leads man away from the truth of Form, for Memory retains not the substantial representation of form but its "synthetic expression." Therefore,

> in order fully and correctly to appreciate the reality of Form, it is necessary to get into a state of perfect consciousness. The reality of Form can only be transcribed through a mechanical process, in which the craftsmanship of man does not enter as a principle factor. There is no other process to accomplish this than photography. The photographer—the true photographer—is he who has become able, through a state of perfect consciousness, to possess such a clear view of things as to enable him to understand and feel the beauty of the reality of Form.

De Zayas goes on to claim that photography has removed "the veil of mystery" that was the function of Art when it enveloped the represented Form. Photography is conceived as the developmental terminus that allows man to understand the "cause of facts." Hence a photograph is identified by de Zayas with truth of form.

> Photography represents Form as it is required by the actual state of the progress of human intelligence. In this epoch of fact, photography is the concrete representation of consummated facts. In this epoch of the indication of truth through materialism, photography comes to supply the material truth of Form.
>
> This is its true mission in the evolution of human progress. It is not to be the means of expression for the intellect of man.

De Zayas returns to the topic as if to correct his initial claim, now stating that although photography is not an Art, "photographs can be made to be Art." It is this twin function and outcome of the camera that de Zayas examines in "Photography and Artistic Photography." In this corrective text, de Zayas differentiates the category of "pure" photography, which he sees not as a new system to represent Form but as a "negation of all representative systems." In the discourse of objectivism and subjectivism, materialism and idealism, de Zayas deems that the artist photographer veils the object with subjectivity; hence, his aim is expression and pleasure. The pure photographer, on the other hand, simply performs a "process of indigitation" (mindlessly releasing the camera shutter) and therefore expresses objectivity, his aim being knowledge. One (as represented by Edward Steichen) is the "perfect fusion of the subject and object"; the other (as characterized by Stieglitz) is the "elimination of the subject in represented Form to search for the pure expression of the object."

> It would be difficult to say which of these two sides of Photography is the more important. For one is the means by which man fuses his idea with the natural expression of Form, while the other is the means by which man tries to bring the natural expression of Form to the cognition of the mind.

In this rhetoric of "fusion" and "elimination," de Zayas perceived the fraught standing of a photograph in its *synthetic* and *exclusionary* functions. Given his exile status in the United States and his second-order relationship to the English language in these writings—and as a Mexican national with ambivalent notions of human variation, of "purity" and "mixing" that surround *mestizaje* as the colonial difference—de Zayas performs a series of contradictions whose perplexity is marked with the desire for hierarchical categorizations inherent to both racism and formalism, with its valuations of "superior" to "inferior," of "civilized" to "primitive," and of art to photography, of the "lack of analysis" vis-à-vis "the indication of truth through materialism, [wherein] photography comes to supply the material truth of Form."[63]

I want to conclude by evoking the images of the Casasola Archive, together with the writings of Caso, de Zayas, and Bergson, to make some larger claims. With Bergson, a photograph is the juncture linking a once and future passage, the always already and the as yet to be. In the Casasola Archive, every photograph is an addition to the open set of images, but it is also a subtraction from the becoming whole, because it operates only by way of its metonymic office. Added to this double movement of inclusion and abstraction is the variability of a framework, by which a photograph's actual maker may be said to radically foreground the primary center of indetermination—that is, for Bergson, the body. Caso situated representation in the "otherworldly limbo of idealist inspiration" but failed to see that an image achieved though mechanical reproduction, like the ideal reality that he hypothesized, necessarily dismantles the "conventionalism of daily experience" and therefore resembles aesthetic distance—a reflection severed in part from its source. In a photograph, movement is no longer a translation, a link in space and time between photographer (or viewer) and subject, but the expression between perception and action.

In Bergson's poetics of the residual, and the politics of the archive inaugurated by Casasola—the quantity that is left out, the potentiality that remains latent—a photograph effectively marks historical calendar time in its desire and specious capacity to detain transition. But a photograph is also the negative endorsement of a duration, whose viewing enacts a twofold halt, a double memory whose outcome is a future relationship between artifice and life. This, in the words of Deleuze, is "a double system, . . . a double régime of references of images": on the one hand, the "duration *wherein we see ourselves acting*" and, on the other, "the duration *wherein we act,* a duration wherein our states melt into each other."[64]

In the cut-out enacted by a photograph something is added and something else gets cast aside through an interplay of presence and absence. An arrest in time is laid open and filled in by a photograph's viewing. Indeed, a narrative leading to the suspended moment is imagined and followed by a series of ellipses latent with sequential potentiality. A photograph situates us at the interval between matter itself and our conscious perception of matter. It inhabits the liminal spaces between the becoming of life, the encroachment of matter, and the progress of history; between consciousness and matter; and between phosphorescence and translation. Bergson came very close but fell short of theorizing how photographs function in life *as life*—both *depicting* and *promoting* action. But we can transpose his claims about memory to say that a photograph

> no longer *represents* our past to us, it *acts* it; and if it still deserves the name of memory, it is not because it conserves bygone images, but because it prolongs their useful effects into the present moment.[65]

By arresting the present and preterit as stages passing from one to the next, a photograph places us in the environment of duration as a "becoming that endures, a change that is substance itself."[66] Because they radiate with a historical phosphorescence imbued by previous and eventual viewings, a photograph constitutes a wager on the future: it is both an agent of memory and, located between the plane of action and the plane of desire—and groping toward a palpable "anticipation" of the future—it is a reminder of movement as ever-penultimate passage.

In light of collective memory, photographs stand as the index of personal and collective change, of individual duration and of universal becoming in opposition to the predictability of calendar time. According to Benjamin, calendars do not "measure time as clocks do; they are monuments of a historical consciousness."[67] Photographs, however, refuse to be solely monuments of historical consciousness. They capture things invisible to the human eye, which alone is unable to overcome or detain persistence of vision. If the arrested image stands for a privileged instant, it is only in the sense that Benjamin attributes to the photograph, in that the "camera introduces us to unconscious optics as does psychoanalysis to unconscious impulses"—symptoms recognized in the presumable future of a viewing.[68]

Still images are duration's performative surrogates. Not unlike Bergson's assessment of "the comical" (perhaps even its pressing double), "the photographic" also delights in the mechanical order—or lifelessness—of life. As such, photographs do more than what Charles Baudelaire famously attributed to them, as the Casasola Archive reveals, "to rescue from oblivion those tumbling ruins, those books, those prints and manuscripts which time is devouring . . . and which demand a place in the archive of our memory." Because a still image can measure both the relative predictability of matter and the relative unpredictability of life, a photograph can be the measure of our action in the world—of those already depicted and those emergent. Together, all existing and possible photographs allude to the "fluid continuity of the real." But the "photographic" is that which cannot be represented in fact; it is the sum total of discontinuous images that serve as reminders of the passages between them. I submit that in Mexico these considerations of measure and scale as per the photograph have made the image environment a privileged locus from which to view a culture. The image environment awakened between the Casasola Archive, Caso, and de Zayas is equally inclusive of political geographies and their representation, as well as visual and discursive distributions; at cross-purposes they allow us to point to the possible in a given past, but with a present view to passages that conceal in measures rivaling what they promise to make public.

2. Experiment in Related Form: Weston, Modotti, and the Aims of Desire

Photography begins to be Photography, for until now it has only been art.

—Marius de Zayas

Marius de Zayas reappears at this juncture with watchwords that would have gladly animated either one of the previous two chapters. A decade after he published the extravagant speculations on photography in Alfred Stieglitz's *Camera Work,* the sentence in question traveled back to Mexico City in October 1923 to serve as the epigram on printed invitations to Edward Weston's milestone exhibition in the mezzanine gallery of Aztec Land, "a Madero Avenue tourist shop and tea salon."[1] (The aphorism, incidentally, is to be found in neither of the *Camera Work* essays, so for the provisional purpose of what follows we can assume it consisted of an overheard remark or a paraphrase coined for the Aztec Land exhibition.)[2]

Tina Modotti (1892–1942) and Weston (1886–1958) had departed earlier that year from Los Angeles to make Mexico City their expatriate residence, and at the Aztec Land launch Modotti "presided over the guest register, whose first entry was her own: 'Long life to your work—The only thing which never fails you—Tina Modotti-R, Mexico, 1923."[3] Suspended as such by long dashes, the communication is symbolic of various concerns, even as it half obscures the reference in question, namely, the object that "never fails" in the avowal. Does it point to Weston's work or to Modotti's own signature and its adjoining markers of time and geography? Encapsulated in the foregoing scene, then, is an appeal to "photography proper," the borderline between "work" and "life," between the "foreign" and "familiar" and other relations of identity and difference, as well as the shifting nascent values of (modernist) achievement and failure. Image environments opened up as a result of Modotti and Weston's relocation to Mexico, and their practice in that migratory encounter enabled the decisive foregoing elements to come together—along with others I explore.

A 1997 George Eastman House exhibition, *Modotti and Weston: Mexicanidad,* was the first to discuss sexual difference at work in environments of deep-seated cultural and social alterity—a subject I also pursue—and its curatorial intent helped upset the evaluative hierarchy often upheld between Weston's and Modotti's work in earlier photographic accounts.[4] Even as it disavowed the romanticizing legend of Weston and his "protégée-lover" turned artist-as-revolutionary, and despite foregrounding the work of Modotti who, until quite recently, had been relegated to a lesser status or to mere biographical foil, the exhibition could not help but reify romance in the process. I'd like to further examine whether that collaboration, as read within the broader context of its cultural production, necessitates a reading invested in "romance"—that is, on the one hand, perhaps as a political allegory about modernist representation and its investments in "pure form" and, on the other, "social reform."[5]

Commentators agree that the extraordinary biographical facts of Modotti's life have too often eclipsed actual consideration of the photographs. In relation to Mexico's modernizing project during the 1920s, I locate Modotti's work as an impressive corpus of photographic images she made in association with, and independent of, Weston. I look also at frameworks that submit the photographs to discerning inquiry that renders sexual difference productive: a meaningful socio-aesthetic distinction that can be discursively effected. But is it possible to think sexual difference in an optical regime unmediated by language—or are those differences necessarily rhetorical ones? The answer to this question necessitates a series of detours. I begin by discussing migratory structures and the notion of hybridity, and trouble the overarching notion of the heterosexual "male" gaze by finding points of vulnerability in Weston's *Daybooks* and photographic work. I turn to psychoanalysis for insight into vision and sexual difference in terms of drive and sublimation, and I apply this to the modernist "object" of photography. I then interrogate the sole artist statement Modotti wrote for her 1929 exhibition at Mexico City's National Library, as well as her familiarity with the writings of Friedrich Nietzsche, in light of a 1929 series of photographs at odds with the claims of her manifesto. With the photographic articulations of Modotti and Weston, sexual and cultural difference constitute a migratory practice whose "experiments in related form" are performances of cultural translation. That process uncovers threshold regimes that, suspended discursively, account for sexual difference.

The Adjacent Space

There have been a significant number of commitments in the last two decades—but particularly in the last ten years—to Modotti's life and photographic works, in the form of exhibitions, biographies, and critical research.[6] Among these, Andrea

Noble's *Tina Modotti: Image, Texture, Photography* troubles the facile associations often made between biography and photographic meaning, even as Noble sets out to identify certain strategies in earlier feminist accounts of Modotti's achievement, as well as recent uses and abuses of Modotti's market value. To this end, Noble seeks to uncover the "correlation between visual culture and the social and psychic construction of sexual difference."[7] Her project can claim to be feminist in the twin sense of reinstating woman in her role as cultural producer, that is, it interrogates how visual representations of women circulate and how sexed perception and social relations bestow an image with meaning.

The "positive aesthetics" of former feminist critiques relied on overly optimistic claims about Modotti's marginalized position—as a woman, a "Mexican," and a photographer left out of the patriarchal histories of the medium. This inclination not only deprives Modotti of social and aesthetic agency but also transforms her into a "feminist commodity."[8] If there is no one-to-one relation between a theoretically "marginalized" position and an "exemplary" practice, in what ways—if any—does Modotti's status affect the many images she made of native Mexican or mestizo women, children, and men? Noble refuses to accept that Modotti was immune to the objectification of others on the sole ground that she herself had been the object of the male gaze, most notably Weston's. Rather, Noble reads the social and sexual marker of the sombrero in so many of Modotti's photographs as the synecdoche of a racialized body politic, and the abject body as viewed by a maternal or "matrixial" gaze.

To distinguish a "female gaze" is to compel first a theory of the relationship between bodies and space. In her reading of *Open Doors* (1925) (Figure 27), Noble convincingly describes Modotti's photograph—the frame of an interior doorsill, the door partly open, and the glimpse it affords into the tentative visual passage of the adjacent space—as a composition distinct from any that might have been produced within the muralist project that was contemporaneous with Modotti's work, but as Noble points out, remarkably masculine in its structure. (The male-centered formation of the Mexican avant-garde is taken up at later junctures.) Two facts are essential to the reading of Modotti's photographs: first, that Modotti herself was a model in at least two of Diego Rivera's frescoes, and second, that Rivera and José Clemente Orozco both commissioned Modotti, between 1926 and 1930, to photograph sections of the murals they painted during that time.[9]

Rivera's *In the Arsenal*, a panel of the *Corrido de la Revolución* mural at the Secretaría de Educación Pública (SEP), features Modotti, along with other artists and intellectuals—Frida Kahlo and David Alfaro Siqueiros, among them—distributing arms to the restless masses in a scene of revolutionary uplift and insurrection. In this work, the viewer's overly determined place, Noble contends, is one that relies on the "ultimate in authoritative frames," that is, the "nation's official spaces [wherein] urban viewers were to pursue the largely rural Indian bodies [en masse] in a visual experience whereby the embodied gaze conferred upon the viewers a combination of scopic and physical mastery."[10] Whereas I find less

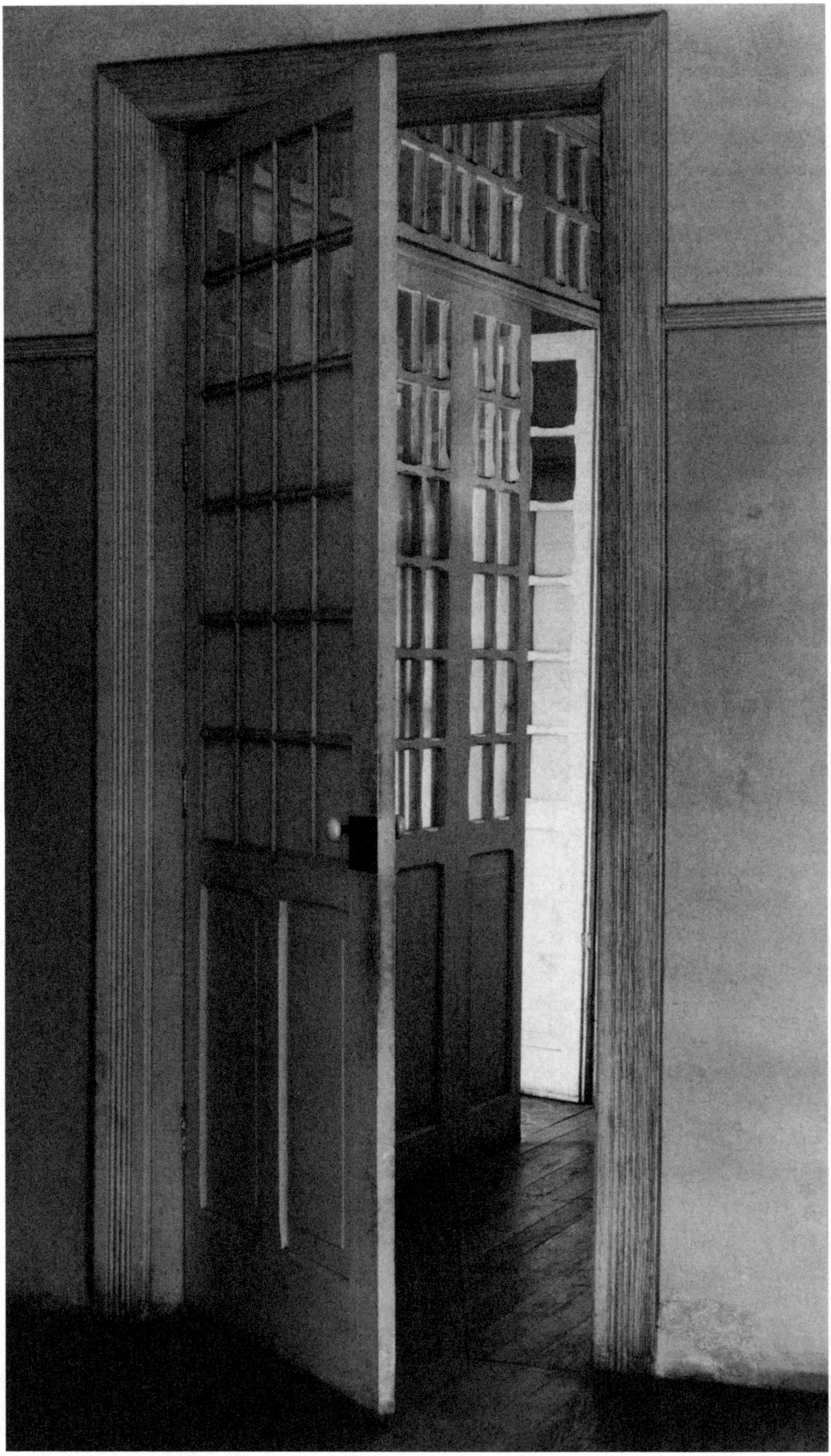

Figure 27. Tina Modotti, *Open Doors,* 1925. Copyright J. Paul Getty Museum.

convincing the notion of "mastery" with regard to the look—it implies a finishing point and totality, something unfamiliar to the gaze, insofar as photography has a structurally inbuilt partition—I find appealing Noble's comparative view of *Open Doors* and its "secret-space" beyond the limits of the frame: "To enter the space of the image, the viewer must relinquish her position of visual mastery *outside* the frame, in a conceptual leap that problematizes the stability and fixity of the subject-object relationship."[11] Insofar as this photograph makes use of the lattice-pattern windows to stage a sidelong distortion or swerve of the compositional grid while pointing also to a location neither identical to itself nor internal to the image, *Open Doors* depicts a "splitting of consciousness" that is the psychic pressure of the threshold state,[12] and therefore that which is added to the economy of vision by this feminine gaze; in short, it points to feminism's outside or "beyond." Variations on the theme briefly outlined here can be summarized with a line of inquiry: Are manifold subject positions, and their disseminating movements in the built environment, contained within the temporal arrest of the photographic frame? Does *Open Doors* inaugurate a "feminine gaze" by inviting stress on areas external to the image? Does it awaken sexual difference as "tentative visual passage of . . . adjacent space"?

Moving to Define

Modotti published a text titled "On Photography" on the occasion of her 1929 exhibition in the vestibule of the National Library in Mexico City.

> But, those of us who use the camera as a tool, just as a painter uses a brush, are not bothered by *opposing ideas.* We have the approval of persons who recognize the merit of *photography in its many functions,* and accept it as the most eloquent, direct medium for capturing and registering the present time.[13]

I look more closely at this manifesto below, but for the moment I want to highlight the theoretical currency of Modotti's self-professed openness to ambiguity and incommensurability, that is, to the "opposing ideas" afforded by the camera.[14] It is in this sense I examine how the "expressionist formalism of the equivalent" or the "referential literalism" of the New Vision photograph was itself being troubled by the cultural difference of Mexico,[15] its hybridity or syncretism, and the epistemological reframing—the double take, or second visibility—it imposed on the outsider.

In the contact zone, feminist difference connects with debates about racial, cultural, and class differences in global studies, cultural and postcolonial studies, anthropology, and geography. The prevailing concept of the "border" in cultural theory is relevant, therefore, to feminism insofar as it marks a separation even as it recognizes a contiguity and connection. From a first- and second-wave feminism, concerned with silence and invisibility—giving voice and shape, the enterprise of restoration and recovery—a third-wave feminism emerged whose emphasis on location and interrelatedness looks to positionality, situatedness, and "the geopolitics of identity within differing communal spaces of being and becoming."[16] This entails, as Modotti prefigured in her 1929 statement on photography, an embrace of oppositions and a welcoming of symbiotic, interactive formations (both social and formal), so as to inhabit modalities of dislocation and change. Another contested account is that of the global binaries of first world versus third world, or of the West versus the Rest, accounts that obscure how "conquest and colonialism are worldwide phenomena."[17] To the masculine–feminine divide there is a need to broaden the multidirectional flows of power and desire in the dialogue about race and class, as well beyond the calcified pure binaries, and to make relevant the interlocking character of "home" and "elsewhere."

Insofar as there is no such thing as an encounter between pure differences—no dividing line to relate one component to its adjacent term—feminism compels us to read at the border it shares with other progressive discourses that examine the effects of postcolonialism, globalism, multiculturalism, and, in what follows, alongside early twentieth-century discourses on photography. In this mode it is instructive to read *Open Doors* alongside a letter Modotti wrote to Weston the year she took the photograph. There, Modotti relates the aesthetic function of creation (i.e., photography) to the question of sexual difference. Because so much of its rhetorical efficiency relies on layering and repetition, I quote the letter at length:

> July 7th Eve [1925]: . . . I am convinced *now* that as far as creation is concerned (outside the creation of species) women are negative—They are too petty and lack power of concentration and the faculty to be wholly absorbed by *one thing*. . . .
>
> I cannot—as you once proposed to me "solve the problem of life by losing myself in the problem of art"—Not only I cannot do that but I even feel that the problem of life hinders my problem of art.
>
> Now what is this "my problem of life"? It is chiefly: an effort to detach myself from life so as to be able to devote myself completely to art—.
>
> And here I know exactly that you will answer: "*Art* cannot exist without *life*"—Yes—I admit but there should be an even balance of both elements while in my case life is always struggling to predominate and art naturally suffers—.
>
> By art I mean creation of any sort—You might say to me then that since the element of life is stronger in me than the element of art I should just resign to it and make the best of it—But I cannot accept life as it is—it is too chaotic—too unconscious—therefore my resistance to it—my combat with it—I am forever struggling to mould life according to my temperament and needs—in other words I put too much art in my life—too much energy—and consequently I have not much left to give to art—.
>
> This problem of "life" and "art" is my tragi-comedy—the effort I do to dominate life is wasted energy which might be better used if I devoted it to art—I might have more to show for—As it is my efforts are wasted so often—they are futile—.

> That is why I say: Women are negative—(again I am generalizing) well, at least, I am negative as far as creation is concerned.[18]

If to be woman is to have a negative relation to art, this is not because Modotti confesses to "generalize" but because she cannot be absorbed by any one thing or single ideal. The recurrences and ambiguities of the text perform a distribution—a perspective open to heterogeneity and to energy in excess of itself, that quantity of "too much art in my life." Image technology and photographic practice were agents that restructured the too-clean divisions between "life" and "art"—or, as I rehearse below, between "truth" and "untruth." Hence Modotti struggled with the fact that the camera produced hybrid effects that rendered a split between the subjective and the objective, between the visually given and the optically made. As a hybrid medium, photography participates in what constitutes the "beyond" as a concept in discourse. In the period Modotti made *Open Doors,* she referred to photography as a representational technique severing the heretofore known conceptual categories of relation and knowledge. The "beyond" suggests a more comprehensive range of categories that include forms of synthesis, coincidence, and creative confusions, habitual or experimental meanings, spatial or temporal partiality, and political modes that foreclose or grant access to instances and agencies that are site specific. Modotti was pointing to a migratory difference whose predicate function sets the visual field in motion.[19]

The Gray Zone

The phallocentric regime that views woman as complement or counterpart is a symptom that has historically vexed Modotti's photography in relation to Weston's. By looking at Modotti's work "in relation to the norm established by Weston's—the norm as both she and Weston construed it," Carol Armstrong has made productive the sexual variance at work between two visual centerings.[20] The difference is one between a fixed look at an object and a variable participation in an action, between a gaze that offers a "direct experience" (a transparency and "purity of vision") and a scopic regime that is a field of displacement, an itinerant phenomenon in the production of symbolic meanings.

In repeated disavowals at various points throughout the *Daybooks,* Weston refutes the sexual or erotic content of his work *Nautilus Shell* (Figure 28), and others like it. Instead, he foregrounds otherworldly significance with the terms "physical" and "spiritual." Armstrong relates this disclaimer to the structure of sublimation, which she defines as an "uplifting of base sensuality to the authority of the sensuous abstraction, the distilling and purifying of the bodily" while keeping the erotic component as close to the surface as possible, albeit hidden underneath.[21] That is, displaced to the "outer shell" of perception, sublimity constitutes the quintessential effect of the successful modernist photograph, its "truth of form"—but more on this in a moment.[22]

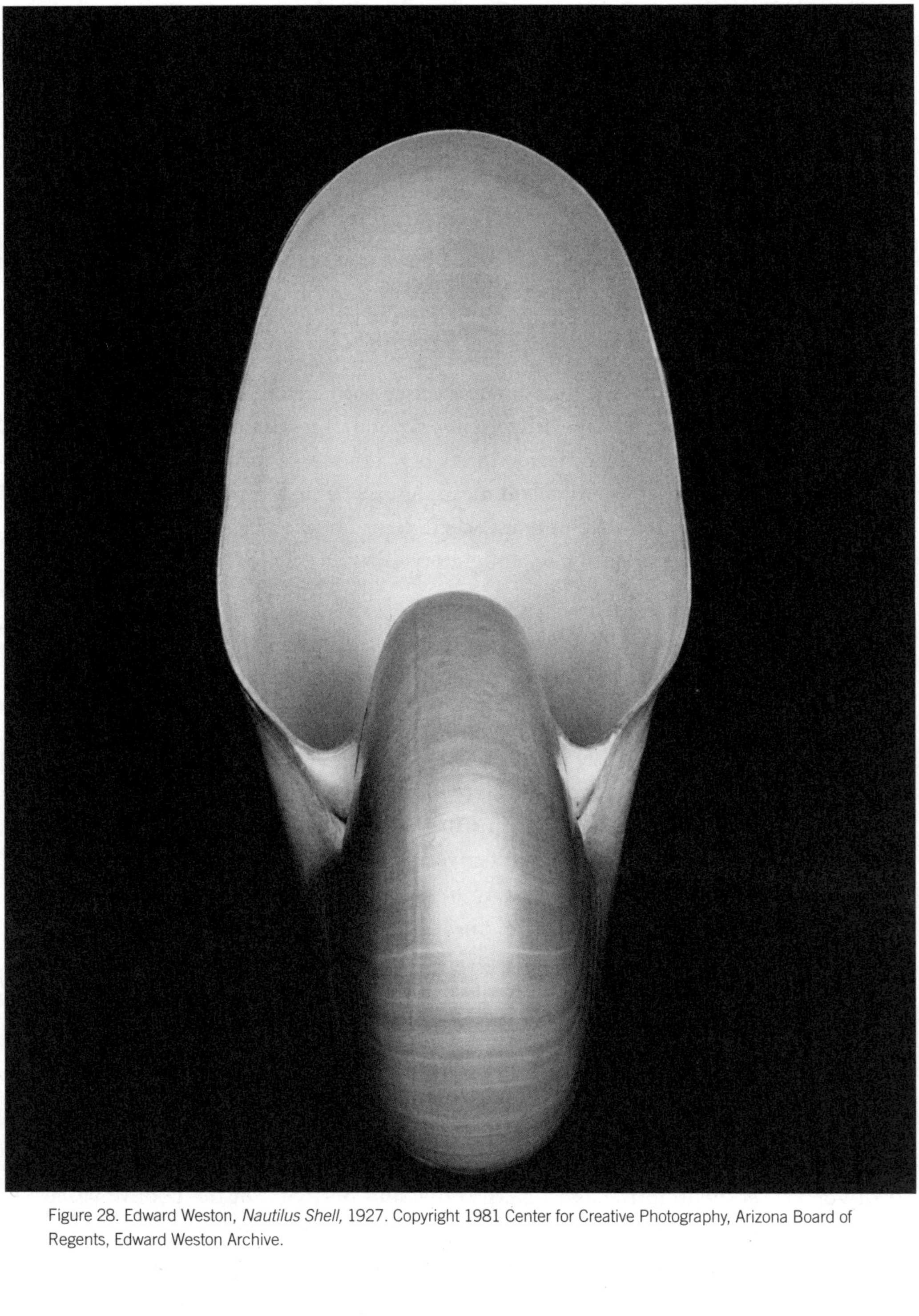

Figure 28. Edward Weston, *Nautilus Shell,* 1927. Copyright 1981 Center for Creative Photography, Arizona Board of Regents, Edward Weston Archive.

Here is the contradiction Armstrong detects: Weston's repeated claims to, and assertions about, the thing-itself, remained chiefly futile, *and in excess of his intended aim.* No matter how much he willed otherwise, the alleged one-to-one relationship between the object under the scrutiny of his lens and the represented object in the frame of the photograph, Weston's thing-itself suggested, rather, *other things* not only to other viewers (Modotti's "lilies and embryos") but to Weston as well. Are images such as *Roses* (1924) or *Calla Lilies* (1925) (Figures 29 and 30), Modotti's chronologically earlier efforts to render the "one single beautiful thing," any different from Weston's subsequent endeavors in this direction—and if so, how? (Modotti: "They [women] are too petty and lack power of concentration and the faculty to be wholly absorbed by *one thing.*")

Insofar as it is representative of the "difference between Modotti's and Weston's photographic taste," Modotti's now iconic *Roses* performs a commitment to the surface indeterminacies that proliferate in this extreme close-up of four roses whose

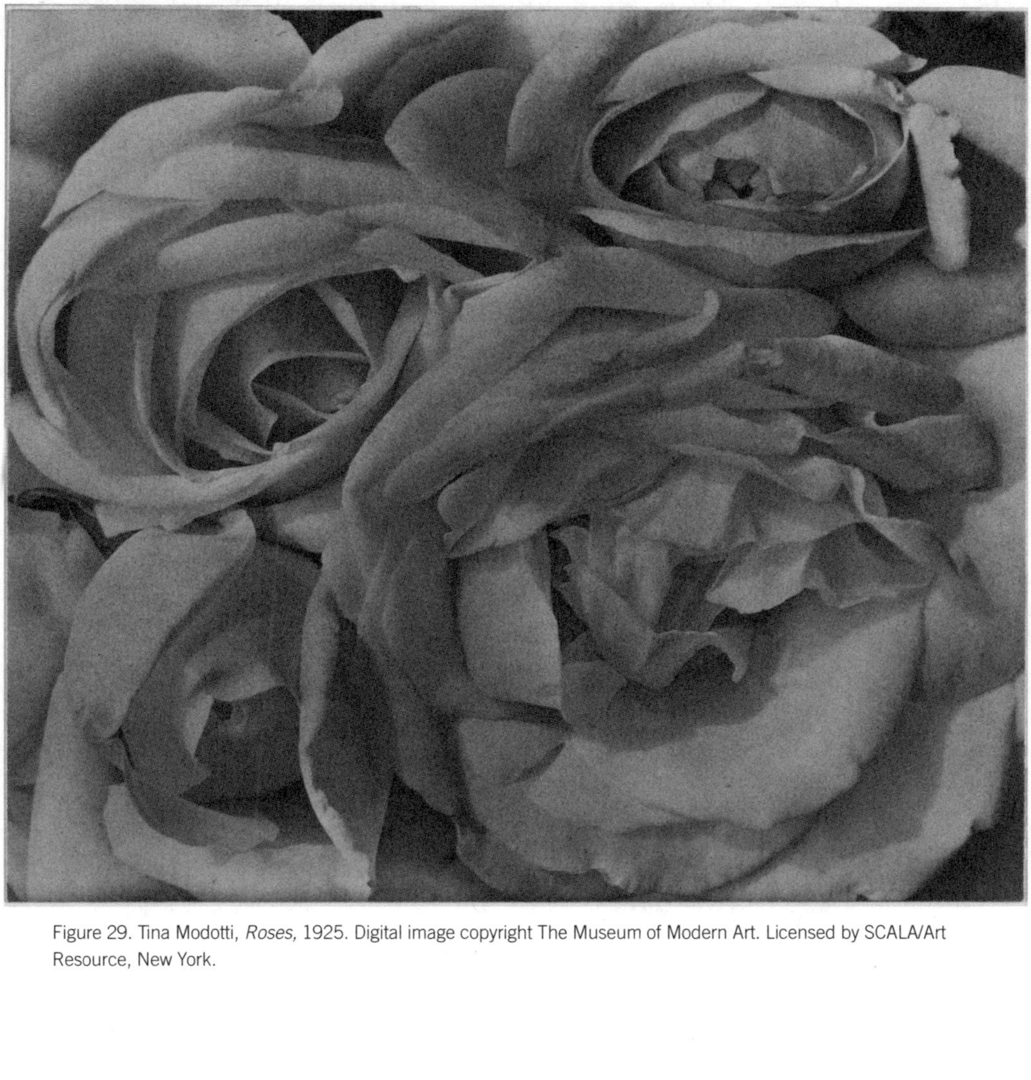

Figure 29. Tina Modotti, *Roses,* 1925. Digital image copyright The Museum of Modern Art. Licensed by SCALA/Art Resource, New York.

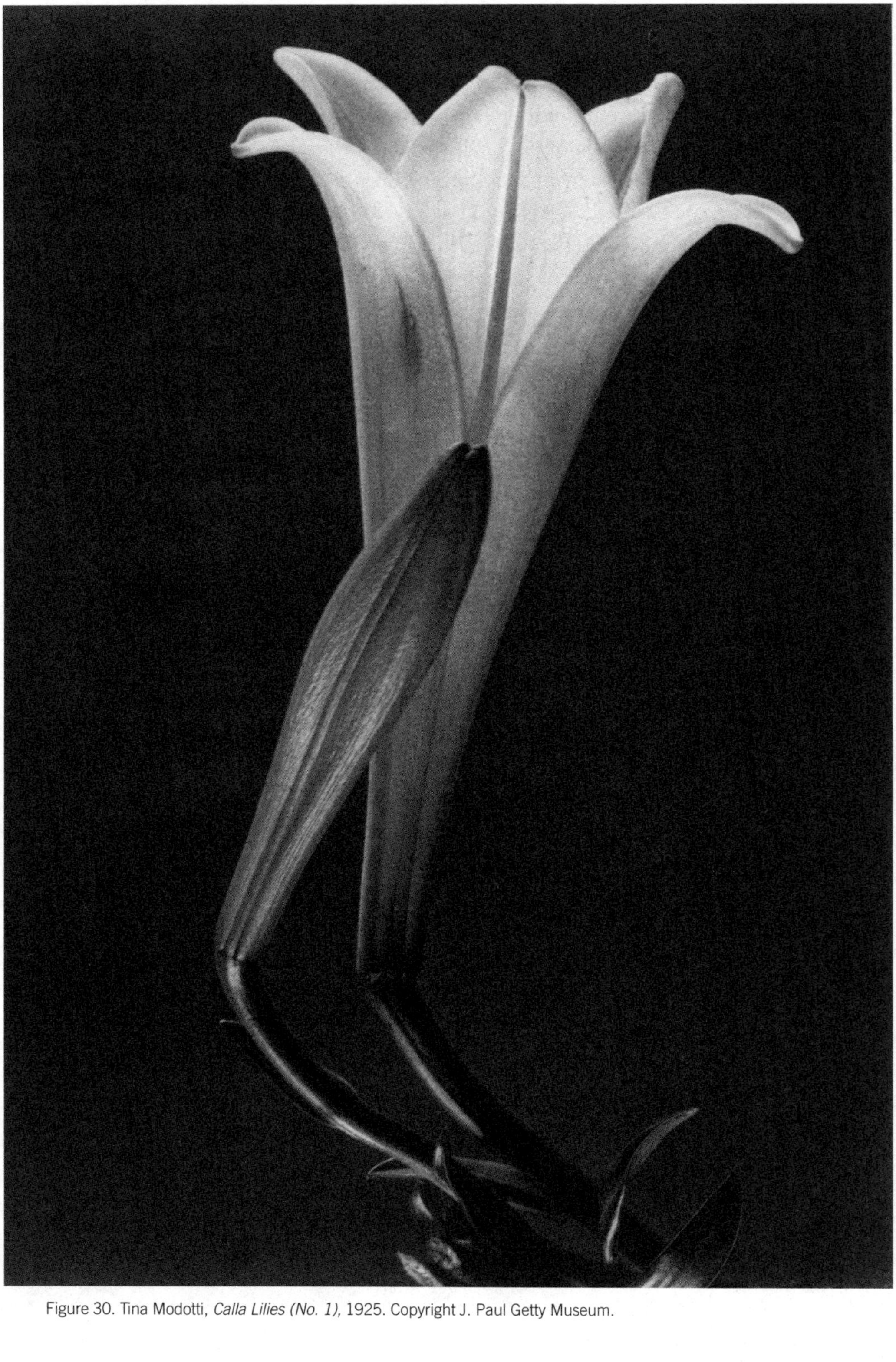

Figure 30. Tina Modotti, *Calla Lilies (No. 1),* 1925. Copyright J. Paul Getty Museum.

half-visible interiors insinuate a rhombus of focal points otherwise made unstable by the surrounding proliferation of fleshy petals in a palpitating curvature of fold on fold—so much roundness and quivering, so much restraint and abundance, that the visual rhythms suggest both the immediacy of the material occasion and the frail prospect of the flowers' physical demise. Because the photograph is "not transcendent in its opticality"—actively inhering, as the photograph does, to its touchable attributes—Modotti's image is, unlike Weston's architectonic or "self-spawned inner structure," committed instead to the "call of the haptic" and so "to the eye's desire to touch what it sees," that is, to render "touch at odds with sight rather than sight extending and sublimating touch."[23]

Weston's *Hands, Mexico* (also known as *Hands and Kimono,* 1924) (Figure 31) and Modotti's *Hands Resting on Tool* (1927) (Figure 32) make a provocative claim in terms of sexual difference as a visual identification:

> It is tempting to read the hands in *Hands Resting on Tool* as male hands. . . . But closer inspection of the blurred background of cloth [worn by the subject] suggests a Mexican woman's belt-seamed and pleated shift, and leads to another possible understanding of the hands themselves, which against that ground and under their caked and creased dirt begin to read as the slender, relatively hairless *hands of a woman,* while their restful pose, despite the apparent masculinity of the tool they hold, begins to be coded as "feminine." Or perhaps one might understand the resting upper hand as "feminine" and the fisted, thickened lower hand as "masculine"? All of which still suggests an analysis of labor as at once classed and gendered.[24]

The claim that in fact these are a woman's hands remains unconvincing—for it applies too much pressure on the "truth effect" of a photograph, and one wonders if the verifiable difference would make a remarkable difference at all. Instead, it is appealing to think that the image invites a partial viewing that must *activate the various visual functions associated with sexual identification,* and sexed spectatorship.[25] The comparison of this image with the Weston photograph is an evocative one. Whereas Weston was transforming Modotti's body—in this image and in all manner of nudes he made of Modotti and other women—to elevate his own pictures into icons of modernity that mediate "between the expressionist formalism of the equivalent and the referential literalism of the sharply focused 'straight' photograph," Modotti's image manages to "bring the visual field of aestheticisms back down to the ground of manual labor . . . [to] a realm of physical relations between body and world that goes beyond the body and itself functioning as the sign of the formalist photograph's internal relation to itself."[26] This is to say, then, that Modotti's photograph successfully accomplishes a transforming effect—the "classed and gendered" hands *become* the racially specific labor base on which the post-Revolutionary society was reliant. Weston's *Hands, Mexico* is seen, however,

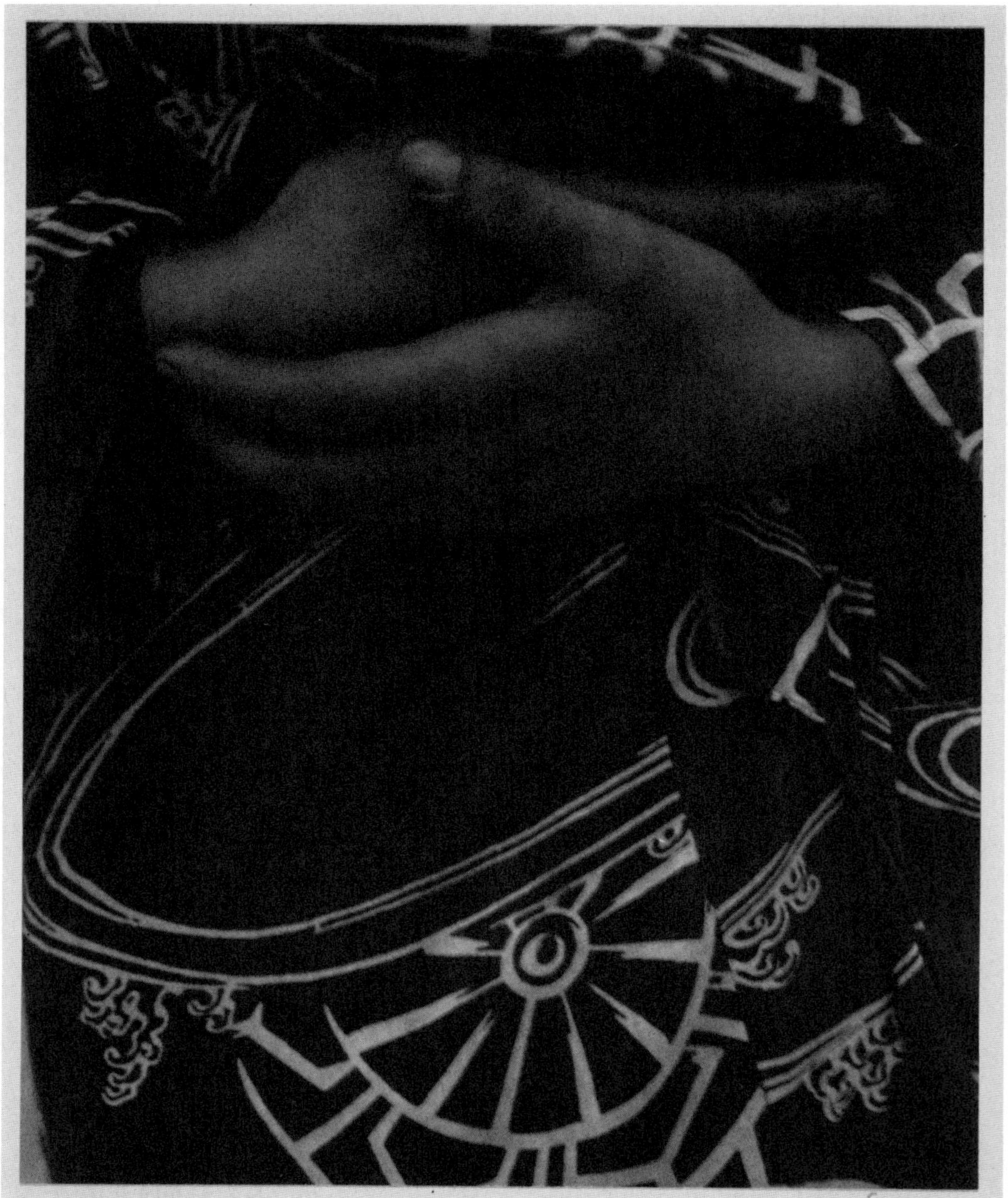

Figure 31. Edward Weston, *Hands, Mexico,* 1924. Copyright 1981 Center for Creative Photography, Arizona Board of Regents, Edward Weston Archive.

to fall short of metaphor because it isolates the body part from the larger social context to which they refer; hence it is a "simile-driven equivalent" for Weston's "art-sublimated ardor."[27] While I recognize the "haptic" quality of Modotti's images, I have trouble accepting that Modotti's photographs, no matter how different from Weston's, are not also products of sublimation.

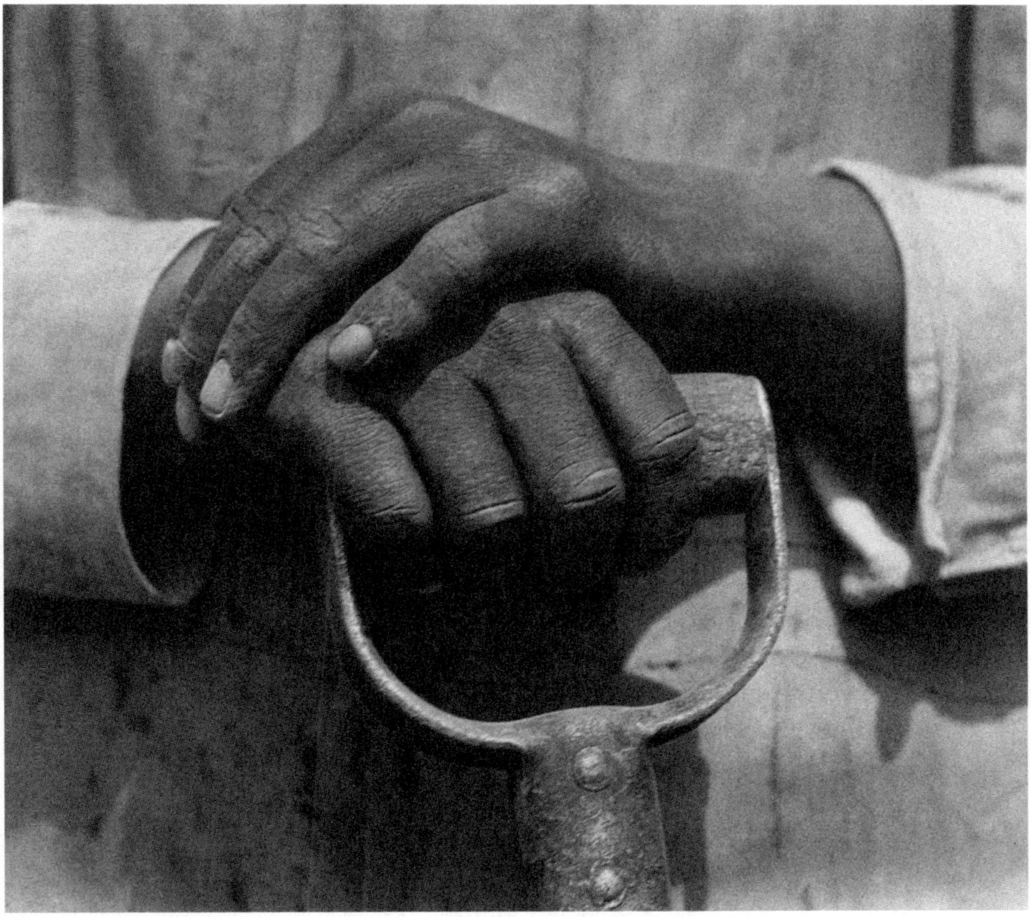

Figure 32. Tina Modotti, *Hands Resting on Tool,* 1927. Copyright J. Paul Getty Museum.

The material and political facts on view in Mexico were so unfamiliar as to unsettle outsiders such as Modotti and Weston. But in this context Modotti served as *translator*—in both the restricted and general sense of the term—securing Weston and herself admission into the country's cultural elites.[28] Correspondingly, even when Modotti struggled, as she claimed, to detach herself "from life so as to devote [herself] completely to art,"[29] her photography, in keeping with a progressive involvement in Mexico's intellectual milieu, its art and its political life, repeatedly addressed, albeit in abstract terms of unspecified space, the aims of agrarian and artistic production, while trying to think their distinctiveness.

To be sure, Modotti was aware of a crisis that took place in the radical art nexus of Mexico during the 1920s. After reviewing *Hands Resting on Tool* in relation to the cultural nationalism of the Mexican Revolution, whose aesthetic and extra-aesthetic overtones were unapologetically masculine—and heterosexist, as I discuss below—I want to examine the assumed normativity of Weston himself, as well as the sexual and social estrangements that trouble his work. Having completed that task, I can turn my attention at length to a significant theoretical text—the manifesto Modotti wrote for her 1929 National Library exhibition—and to a largely underdiscussed series of photographs of that same year.

Modotti's commissioned photographs of mural works by Rivera and Orozco provide evidence of a conversation that Modotti established between painterly and photographic idioms, and the relevance of hands to her habits of framing.[30] *Hands Resting on Tool* asks whether photographic authority can withstand the vicissitudes of connoisseurship that are applied, for example, to painting and the graphic arts. That is, can a photograph, as a textured surface, disguise or suppress the unique signature or authorial markings traceable on the surface of the image? *Hands Resting on Tool* speaks also, perhaps inadvertently, to a debate that surfaced between two literary avant-garde movements with which Modotti associated—and to a mural by Rivera that mediated them. Directly or indirectly, *Hands Resting on Tool* has something to say to certain writers of the literary and graphic arts movement known as *estridentismo* and to the group of poets known as the Contemporáneos. In Mexico, Modotti quickly became involved with revolutionary art and politics, including the aesthetics of *estridentismo.* Fronted by poets and printmakers who were familiar with Italian futurism, the Estridentistas advanced a theory of images and typography based on spatial volumetrics. In manifestos, these artists embraced radical social practice, the electrically powered industrial world of the machine, and the visual and phonographic communication technologies. A poem ("Revolución") by one of the group's founding members reflects this new socio-aesthetic attitude in its references to Mexico's "aircraft landscapes," a "political economy" of factory smoke, and the "eclectic hum of uprising."[31] In poems and manifestos, the Estridentistas viewed images as driven by "infinitesimal calculus controlled by means of a geometry in space" and as "centripetal claims upheld by gravity."[32] Such claims were not inconsistent with a libidinal anxiety regarding masculinity that marks the second Estridentista manifesto of January 1, 1923, signed, among many others, by its two most visible practitioners: Manuel Maples Arce and Germán List Arzubide (who authored the poem above). One sentence boasted: "To be Estridentista is to be a man. All eunuchs will be barred."[33] The pronouncement inaugurated a tradition in which political and aesthetic *efficacy* was seen as incommensurate with *effeminacy,* and it led to a kind of swagger that found frequent opportunities—such as the one detailed in a 1927 chronicle of the movement—to bait their literary rivals, the Contemporáneos, composed mainly of poets, many of them openly homosexual, in different degrees of social and writerly candidness. As functionaries of the state's cultural apparatus, the Contemporáneos were viewed with suspicion as having betrayed revolutionary practice by favoring the cozier shelters of bureaucracy. Importantly, the chronicle—List Arzubide's *El movimiento estridentista* (1926)—featured a photograph by Modotti: *Telephone Wires* (1925), known also as *Partial View of Telegraph System.* In a scarcely veiled allusion to the Contemporáneos, List Arzubide wrote:

> *Estridentismo* was anchored in triumph: [as opposed to] the confirmed poetasters [who] were spotted at the Alameda Park, accompanied by those of feminine probabilities and they were forced by the Police Examiner to *declare their sex* and prove it, charged with extortion of the kind relative to decreasing virility.[34]

Revolutionary nationalism and aesthetic radicalism, in Mexico as elsewhere, were constructed on one level by making a spectacle of sexual variance. Elizabeth Grosz describes this process as an expulsion, insofar as "the threat that homosexuality poses to heterosexuality is its own contingency, and openendedness, its own tenuous hold over the multiplicity of sexual impulses and possibilities . . . its own unnaturalness, its compromised and reactive status."[35] Modotti was familiar with the codified homoeroticism in the poetry of her Contemporáneos colleagues inasmuch as her assignments for the art magazine *Mexican Folkways,* edited by Frances Toor, "kept her in touch with non-Communist intellectuals like Xavier Villaurrutia [and] Salvador Novo who . . . had their portraits done by her."[36] The erotic veiling and unveiling, enacted especially in Villaurrutia's series of lyric "Nocturnes," cannot have escaped Modotti's notice. If *Hands Resting on Tool* activates the *instrument* by which we visually determine sexual identification, and if it brings the field of aestheticism to the ground of labor, perhaps Modotti's photograph demonstrates that to ask these hands to "declare their sex" is to render class a category capable of obfuscating or blurring the boundaries between sexually differentiated workers. Alongside these debates among the Mexican intelligentsia arising out of a specific masculine anxiety, *Hands Resting on Tool* belies the relation to the campesino class celebrated by the Revolutionary cultural elites. The photograph is also about the false resemblance of manual labor to aesthetic production, and about the incommensurable gaps separating physical expenditure and (its) representation. The image obliges us to rethink our visual assumptions about sexual differentiation—but it is a difference that, at certain crossroads, may not make *all* the difference, or so Modotti's photograph seems to say.

Should this point appear belabored, I submit additional evidence. The year Modotti made *Hands Resting on Tool* falls within the period (1923–27) that Rivera was completing his ambitious series of murals at the Secretaría de Educación Pública. As previously mentioned, Rivera had commissioned Modotti to document the frescoes. (There are seventy-one photographs of just these walls in particular.) One panel is titled *El que quiere comer, que trabaje* (*Work If You Intend to Eat,* Figure 33). Below an upper strip of background depicting an industrial landscape of oil rigs and factory smokestacks is a cluster of four figures—three men and a woman wearing bandoliers and carrying rifles or muskets; there are, among them, differences of skin color and distinguishing markers of rank. One

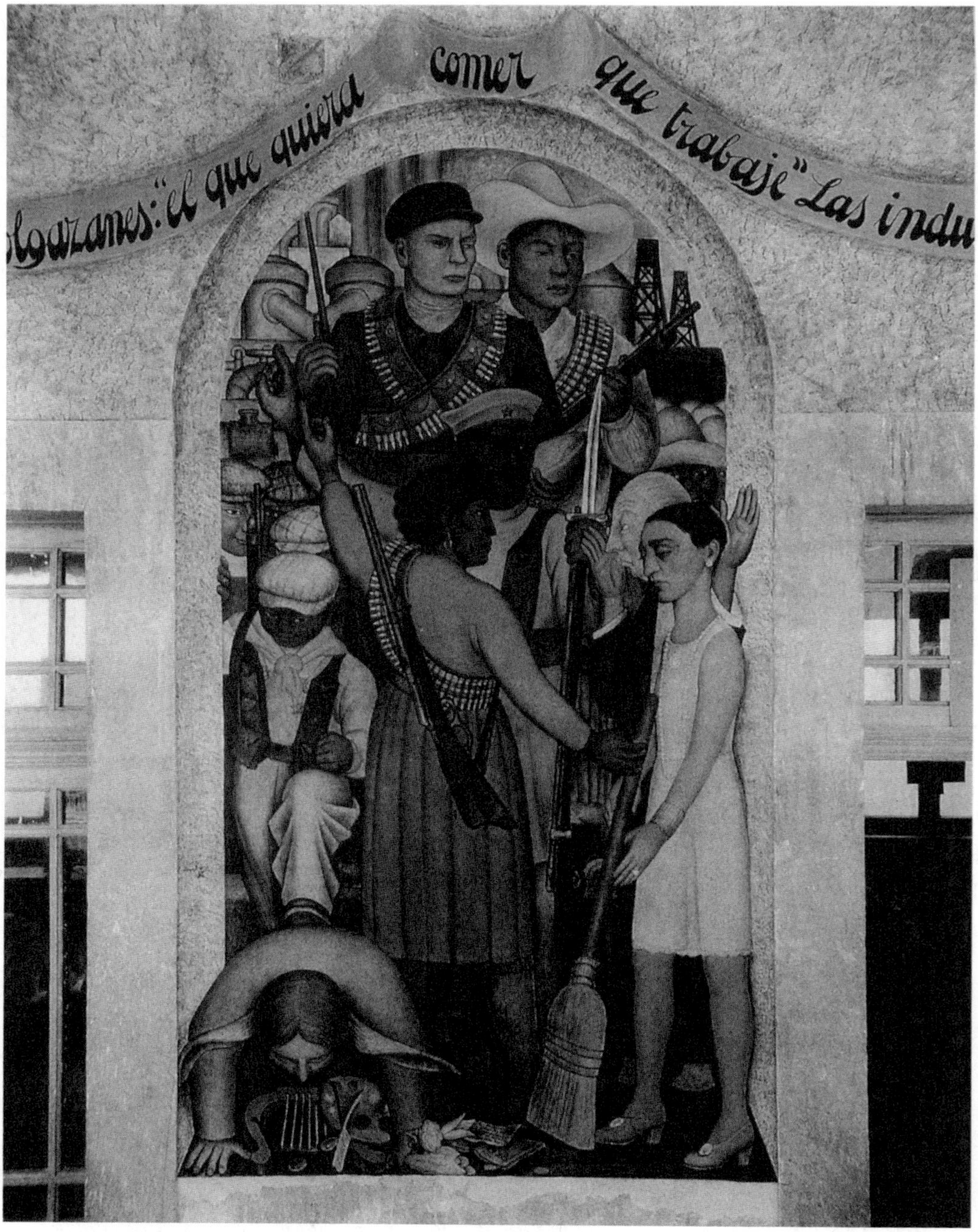

Figure 33. Diego Rivera, *El que quiere comer, que trabaje (Work if you intend to eat)*, 1923–27. Mural at Secretaría de Educación Pública. Photograph by Tina Modotti. Archivo Fotográfico del Instituto de Investigaciones Estéticas de la Universidad Nacional Autónoma de México.

insurgent, the woman, hands a broom—as per the imperative of the title—to the fairer figure of Antonieta Rivas Mercado (a writer and arts patron associated with the Contemporáneos). The figures are surrounded by armed youths; one, in the lower left-hand corner, has placed a foot triumphantly on the back of another (male) figure associated with the Contemporáneos. This figure is depicted with the elongated ears of a barnyard animal, and he is huddled over a lyre, a quill, a palette, and a pair of spectacles. In his left hand he clutches a torn bag of coins and a flower. These are found next to a 1928 issue of the literary group's eponymous journal Contemporáneos. Resting on the journal's spine is a sheet of paper inscribed with the following text: "The *Contemporáneos* / Ulysses King of Ithaca / and of Sodom / are formed also by the Trojan horse (James Joyce)."[37]

In 1927, the year she made *Hands Resting on Tool,* Modotti photographed the mural segment in question, and three details. One detail frames the crouched-over Contemporáneos figure. Another is a close-up of three hands that meet in their disparate gestures (Figure 34): one (male), clutching a rifle, and the other two (male, female) pointing, it would seem, to the Revolution's future prosperity as proffered by the landscape of production on the horizon. What interests me is the idea that these parallel representations inform *Hands Resting on Tool*—whether by anterior or posterior relation. Read together with these photographic details, Modotti's depiction of *Hands Resting on Tool* emerges as an exploration of the social relations ordinarily excluded when focus is affixed exclusively to what the philosopher José Ortega y Gasset called the "outskirts of attention."[38]

Against this background, the hands in *Hands Resting on Tool* are freed of fixity. They remind us that the encounter with the wholly other is fraught with ethical questions: is it possible to represent cultural difference without resorting to essentialist notions of identity or reducing different subject positions to the status of exchangeable terms in a system of more or less arbitrary equivalences? Faced with, but reticent with respect to, the demand to declare their sex, the hands in *Hands Resting on Tool* challenge viewers to push beyond satisfaction by way of formal pleasure: "work if you intend to eat." Insofar as it is possible to represent sexual and cultural difference, these hands stand for the figured periphery that Gayatri Spivak claims is "as much a concealment as a disclosure of the margin [so that] where s/he discloses, s/he is singular."[39] As is so often the case in Modotti's work, where it is difficult to determine in what language a photograph was originally named, the Spanish title of *Hands* is *Manos sosteniendo un palo,* that is, hands *holding* a shovel. The object at once held and withheld in this photograph—where hands and tool are rendered both one and discrete—is "the margin as such, the placeholder . . . of the wholly other, the figure that makes impossibility visible."[40]

If *Hands Resting on Tool* obliges us to suspend our predetermined visual assumptions about sexual identification, Weston's alleged and overarching "male gaze" is unavoidably troubled by so many of the parallel images he made alongside

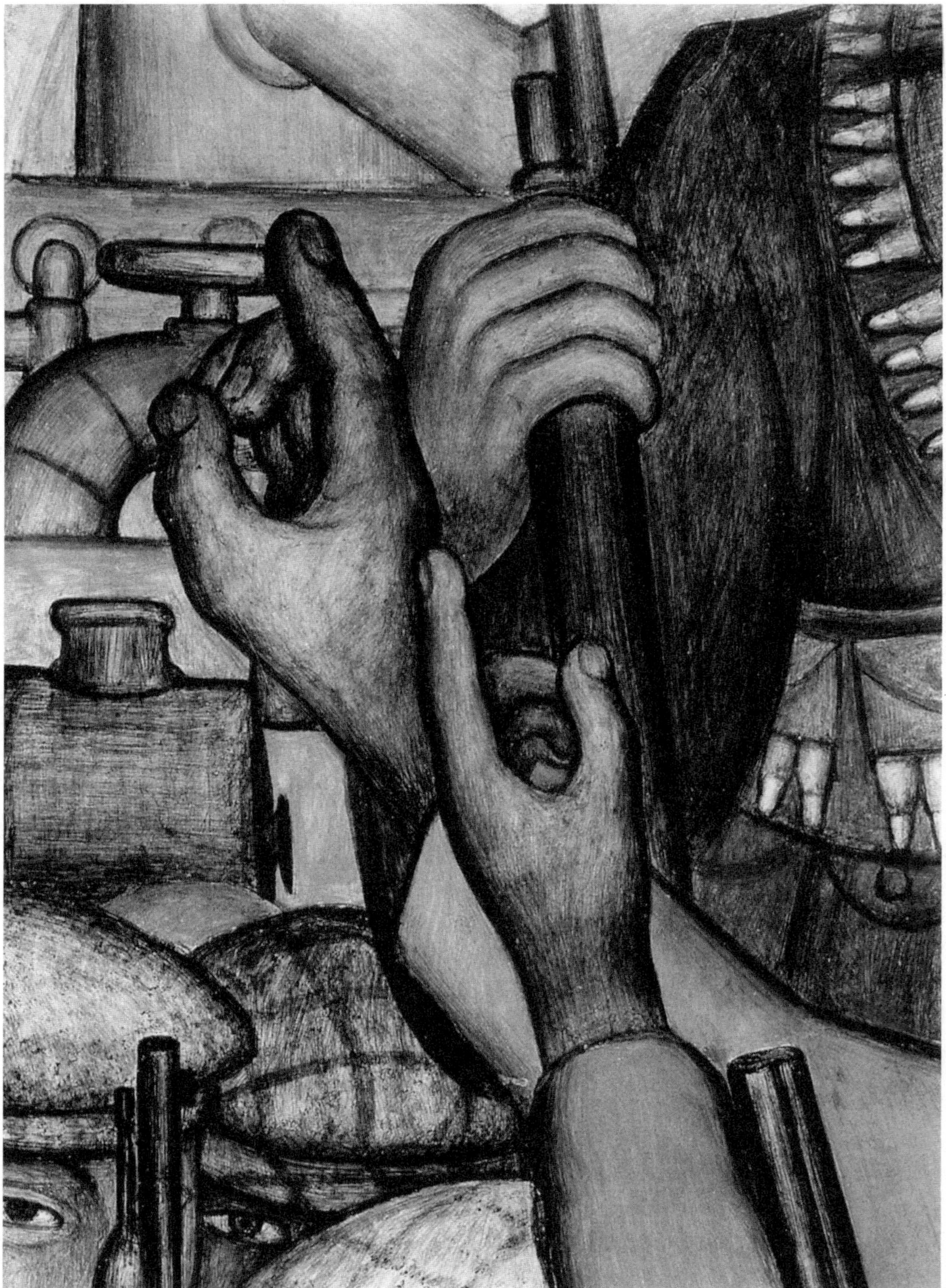

Figure 34. Detail of *El que quiere comer, que trabaje.*

his nudes, *Nautilus Shell*, or *Hands, Mexico*. What are we to make of a contemporaneous image, the vaguely autoerotic, possibly homoerotic, polymorphous pairings of his 1929 *Peppers*? (Figures 35 and 36). One need only refer to Weston's *Daybooks* where on July 13, 1929, he wrote, "I have been working so enthusiastically with the two peppers—stimulated as I have not been for months," to find evidence of his sexual investment in these photographs. But I want to venture further and unsettle the *Daybooks* with the following claim. There are far too many willful and unsuspecting admissions in the *Daybook* entries to ignore the fact that this artist, so often figured as the Elder of Modernism, the "Grand Master of the Photographic Beautiful," the unquestionably virile exemplar of a heterosexual "male gaze" that supposedly structures his photographs of female nudes—his models included Modotti, Anita Brenner, and Margarethe Mather, with whom he was erotically obsessed in spite, or because, of the fact she was "mostly, though not wholly, a lesbian"[41]—too many traces, finally, to ignore the fact that Weston clearly derived writerly satisfaction from that which today we call "queer pleasures," including what Grosz has defined as the "quirkily heterosexual." With that in mind and in what follows, I follow Grosz's lead to expose how "homosexual relations and lifestyles, expelled from and often ignored by the norms of heterosexuality, seep into, infiltrate the very self-conceptions of what it is to be heterosexual."[42] There are numerous indications to suggest this is operative in the persona Weston fashions for himself in the *Daybooks*. One passage I take as especially indicative—given the fact that Weston destroyed most of the contents in the *Daybooks* prior to 1923—for he virtually inaugurates the published version with the following memory at a downtown Los Angeles bar:

> A room full of sailors with here and there a collarless nondescript—but mostly those not in uniform were that type of effeminate male who seek the husky sailor to complement their lacking vigor—One such fastidiously dressed—unmistakable person—presented to us a most lascivious picture of impatient desire—his foot twitched continually—his whole body quivered—his lips fairly drooled—until finally with several others of his kind—a bunch of sailors were "dated up" and off they went in a limousine—Sailors danced together with biting of ears and open caresses—some sprawled over their tables down and out—everyone had a bottle on the hip—while an officer of the law amiably overlooked his opportunity to enforce the 18th amendment— . . . Margarethe [Mather] was the only girl in the place besides the waitresses—But we were too differently dressed—too conspicuous and I wonder we did not land in the street—I should like to go again under different circumstances.[43]

Readers today may rightly feel anxious about the caricatured depiction of "lascivious desire" and effeminacy as "complement" to what is lacking in vigor—although this is telling in itself, as I show below—but I am more interested now in what appears to be Weston's descriptive partiality to, and unabashed rhetorical

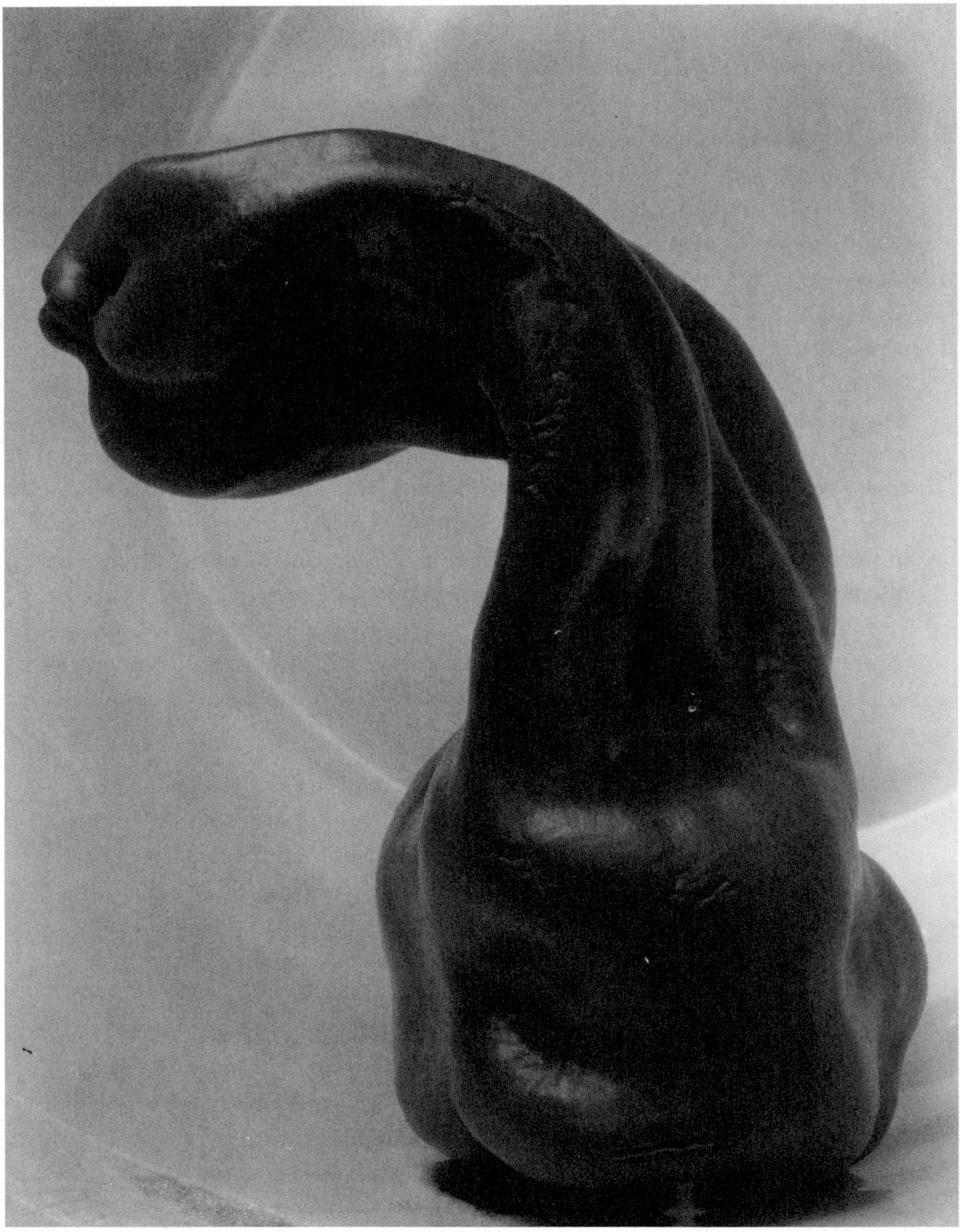

Figure 35. Edward Weston, *Pepper,* 1929. Copyright 1981 Center for Creative Photography, Arizona Board of Regents, Edward Weston Archive.

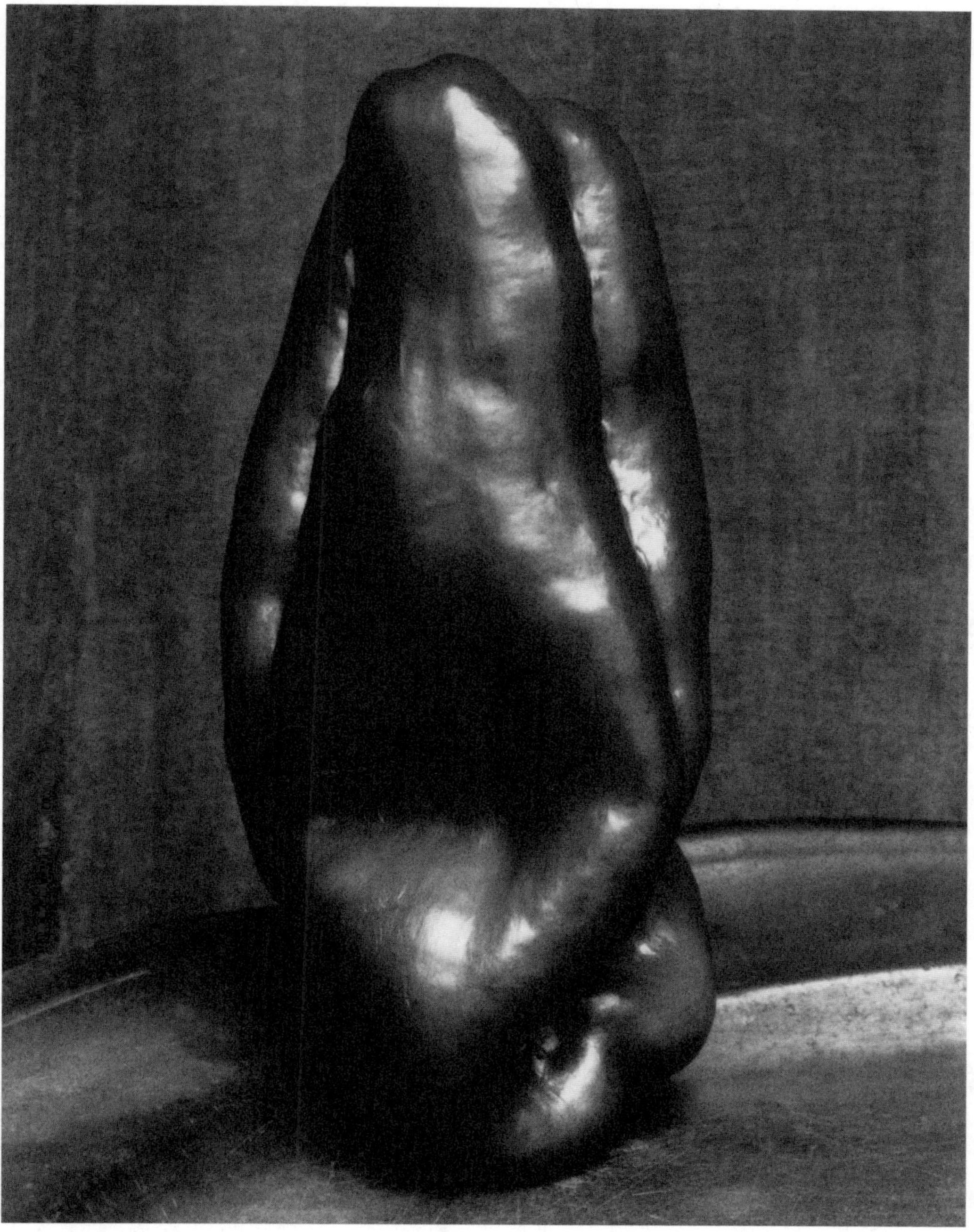

Figure 36. Edward Weston, *Pepper,* 1929. Copyright 1981 Center for Creative Photography, Arizona Board of Regents, Edward Weston Archive.

relish in, this homosexual social scene. Although it is not within the scope of my remarks here, there is also a need to address more thoroughly the ambivalent relationship between Weston and his friend Ramiel McGehee, described by one of Modotti's biographers as "a homosexual writer and former dancer of the Ruth St. Denis Group, who had spent five years in the Far East and had developed a keen interest in Buddhism."[44] Elsewhere in the same account, a footnote admits:

> McGehee was believed to be much in love with Weston and utterly devoted to him. Their relationship was described as "delicate and complex." Maddow, *Edward Weston,* pp. 44 and 60–61. According to Mildred Constantine [one of Modotti's first biographers] Weston too "was most certainly bisexual, and in the final analysis loved no one but himself," Letter to Maddow, June 6, 1975. The J. Paul Getty Research Institute, Los Angeles.[45]

This is hardly incidental, given McGehee's repeated appearance in the *Daybooks.* Images of him in Weston's reverie, usually prompted by the arrival of a letter, educe the most doting and tender of terms. An example nearly chosen at random divulges such ensuing raptures:

> From Ramiel the most beautiful letters of my life. He alone from out of the potpourri of friends and acquaintances has emerged a definite clear-cut figure from whom I cannot part—Ramiel! Keenest of my critics, tenderest and most understanding of my confidants![46]

The *Daybooks* are complicated by a significant number of passages that include an amusing description of some dinner party banter between Lupe Marín, then Rivera's wife, and the writer–painter Nahui Ollín, on things homosexual in Mexico,[47] as if in prelude to Weston's euphoric description of an evening on which he and Modotti cross-dressed for a Mardi Gras soiree:

> The Mardi Gras party went off with a bang! Many funny and some quite beautiful costumes. Masking, costuming, and drink loosen up the most sedate. Tina and I exchanged clothes, to the veriest detail. I even squeezed into a pair of mannish shoes which she had just bought. She smoked my pipe and bound down her breasts, while I wore a pair of cotton ones with pink pointed buttons for nipples. We waited for the crowd to gather and then appeared from the street, she carrying my Graflex and I hanging on her arm. . . . We imitated each other's gestures. She led me in dancing, and for the first few moments everyone was baffled. After a while I indulged in exaggerations, flaunted my breasts and exposed my pink gartered legs most indecently. Lupe was enraged by my breasts, punched at them, tried to tear them loose, told me I was a sin vergüenza—without shame. I treated Tina shamefully in my "take-off"—even beauty can be made ridiculous. I hope I have not "cramped her style!"[48]

The description of the scene anticipates, by a matter of paragraphs, Weston's oft-cited meditation on "the thing itself"—a subject still to come. First, however, let me be very clear that I'm concerned not with claims to a dormant homosexual identity for Weston but with what is rhetorically sexed and unsettled in relation to these passages. I mean to suggest that such discursiveness cannot be insignificant to the practice of his photography—and the so-called purity of its (libidinal) vision. Although we cannot ignore the all-too-familiar rehearsals of heterosexual seduction and conquest in Weston's manuscript,[49] if we bring these other accounts provisionally to the foreground, I submit that they disturb the supposedly unmovable masculinity depicted in his writings and the "male gaze" of his photographic representations. But I want to locate a notion of sublimation as related to the drive, inasmuch as sublimation is something that happens to the drive.

Joan Copjec has formulated the following question: "How does drive determine human embodiment as both a freedom from nature and a part of it?"[50] Insofar as drive traverses the human body, and bodies are the vehicles by which drive becomes the end itself instead of attaining satisfaction in an object, drive can be said to have no goal; it is only an aim. "It is not a means to something other than itself," writes Copjec, "but it is itself other than itself." Inasmuch as drive is a "changing of the object itself" and is "never identical to itself,"[51] that bipartition for photography—especially at this historic and culturally specific juncture—takes place in, and is thereafter internal to, the photograph itself. And to the degree that this bipartition takes place within the photograph, what a (sexed) viewer rediscovers there will always be doubled in addition to what the image contains.

This allows us to read sublimation itself as an effect, which is not one. Insofar as photography poses specific problems relevant to the ways representation structures history, and the ways history structures representation—and similarly between subjectivity and collectivity, cause and effect, matter and the nonmaterial—it is reflective of drive: of the split between the eye and the gaze that structures the scopic regime.[52] I submit that it is hardly immaterial to notice that when Weston wrote the "thing in itself" entry cited below, it was consecutive to that evening he and Modotti dabbled in a little bohemian transvestism. An added quantity is at stake in such seemingly innocent role-playing insofar as it rehearses earlier identifications of "spatial reciprocity."[53]

To this effect Weston claims: "I indulged in exaggerations, flaunted my breasts and exposed my pink gartered legs most indecently. . . . I treated Tina shamefully in my take-off." It is in the aftermath of such excitement—deemed worthy of inclusion in the *Daybooks,* or not so undeserving as to be deleted—that Weston turns to his more "momentous" reflection on the thing-itself:

> The answer comes always more clearly after seeing great work . . . based on conventionalized nature, superb forms, decorative motives. That the approach to photography must be through another avenue, that the camera should be used

> for a recording of *life,* for rendering the very substance and quintessence of the *thing itself,* whether it be polished steel or palpitating flesh. . . . I shall let no chance pass to record interesting abstractions, but I feel definite in my belief that the approach to photography is through realism—and its most difficult approach.[54]

Weston had written only paragraphs earlier about the exorbitant pleasure he derived from his female impersonation of Tina and the reactive response it solicited among the invited: "Lupe was enraged by my breasts, punched at them, tried to tear them loose, told me I was a *sin vergüenza*—without shame. I treated Tina shamefully in my 'take-off'—even beauty can be made ridiculous." In the scopic drive, exorbitant pleasures are compelled for a subject so as to mirror self-seen sexual characteristics as viewed by others.[55]

The photographic thing-itself was thus engendered by Weston to the degree in which it was no one pure thing, no one pure sexual identity, transgendered as such in the scene prior to its "investiture," and therefore conferred from its inception with such impurity and sexual indeterminacy that, thus partially borne, the beautiful thing could "be made ridiculous"—that is, so outlandish as to be reflective of the shame by which the thing-itself was conceived. (About Weston's *Nautilus Shell,* Modotti had remarked that it was "something so pure and at the same time so perverse.")

In keeping with drive, the sexed sideline of photographic viewing likewise *displaces* its object only to reinvest or reinaugurate the form it sought. If drive is that force relating a subject to the system in which that subject circulates, I move to associate psychoanalytic drive with the drive of photography in the system of modernism—not possessing a goal but being an end in itself. By "object" I refer to its broadest philosophical sense as that which "a change, a verb, or mental attitude is 'directed at,'"[56] and to its art historical proposition (as in the "status of the object"), but I do not want to altogether abandon its psychoanalytic meaning whereby "reality is never completely severed from the pleasure with which hallucination is associated"[57]—simulacra, fantasies, false appearance, or the "untrue."

On Truth and Lies in a Photographic Sense

If the modernist thing-itself was sexually othered from the outset, what to make of the art historical assumption that modernism was primarily the development of a self-referential or self-critical abstraction? Ortega y Gasset in 1925 had called "infrarealism" an organizing principle meant "to upset the value pattern and [to] produce an art in which the small events of life appear in the foreground with monumental dimension."[58] Having earlier looked at movements of adjacency, hybridity, displacement, and the thing-itself, I now address photography as a valuative technique that confused modernism's "status of the object." In this, I want to relate the psychoanalytic drive to the aesthetic drive—or at least with a strand of modernism produced by Modotti in "On Photography." In all manner of signifying overtones, the *given-to-be-seen* in Mexico offered image technology the hard matter and dormant opportunity to initiate a writerly process of cultural judgment and interpretation alongside the emergence of photographic modernity and its attendant value systems—of which the *Daybooks,* for example, are evidence. Modotti and Weston produced groundbreaking photographic works during their time in Mexico to the varying degrees they were prompted by the visual force of their new environs and the social limits ensuing from that practice of displacement—such a sight of relations as to invert the hitherto privileged terms of representation and aesthetic value. Not only did Modotti make *photographs* that took part in the visual deliberations about modernity in Mexico and its resulting modernisms, she also produced *writing* and was very much an agent in the discourse that inflects the legacy of visual culture thereafter. On this matter of relation between visual and textual practices, Johanna Drucker has structured the debate as a "lineage of precedents and responses, dialogues, and disputes, internal to the history of modern art."[59]

Camera culture was variously conceived as a set of primary technologies that enabled a transformation of human experience and knowledge. In the burgeoning nation-state of Mexico, immersed in industrialization and urban growth, the practices around mechanical imaging mobilized evaluative judgments about photographic representation in light of the medium itself—in a logic that sought to define those differentials internal to mechanical image making when set against a wider field of visual convention, habit, or recurrence. This is to speak of the medium's drive, namely, to address a discursiveness in pursuit of photography's so-called structural *truth.*

It is surprising, therefore, that Modotti's best commentators have overlooked or paid scant attention to the brief but obligatory text on photography the artist wrote in view of her culminating exhibition at the National Library of the National Autonomous University (December 3–14, 1929). Earlier that year, Modotti had been witness to the public murder of her then companion and comrade Julio Antonio Mella (1904–29), whose death had severe social and political implications for Modotti in the form of dubious and lengthy court actions in which she found herself accused—falsely, and in the end acquitted—as an accessory to the crime. Moreover, a series of student conflicts at the university led the administration of provisional president Emilio Portes Gil (1928–30) to implement legislation granting the university autonomy—an important status of political relevance in Mexico to this day.[60] To address properly this manifesto requires quoting from it at length. For the exhibition, it appeared with the following epigraph by Leon Trotsky: "Technique will be converted into a much more powerful inspiration of artistic production; later it will find its solution in a higher synthesis, the contrast that exists between technique and nature."[61] Modotti's text begins:

> Whenever the words "art" or "artistic" are used with respect to my photographic work, I have an unpleasant reaction, most surely because of the improper, abusive use of those words. I consider myself a photographer and nothing more. If my photographs are different from those generally produced, it is precisely because I try to produce not art, but rather, honorable photographs—without any tricks or manipulations. Most photographers, however, are still looking for "artistic effects" or an imitation of other types of graphic expression. These tendencies lead to a *hybrid* product and do not achieve the most valuable feature that a work should have: PHOTOGRAPHIC QUALITY. There has been a great deal of discussion in recent years regarding whether photography can be considered a work of art comparable to other plastic art creations. Naturally, opinions vary between those who accept photography as a medium of expression just as any other, and others—those who are shortsighted—who continue to look at the twentieth century with eyes from the tenth or even the eighth century. They are, therefore, incapable of accepting the manifestations of our mechanical civilization. But, those of us who use the camera as a tool, just as a painter uses a brush, are not bothered by opposing ideas. We have the approval of persons who recognize the merit of photography in its many functions, and accept it as the most eloquent, direct medium for capturing and registering the present time.[62]

In preceding pages, I looked at how de Zayas upheld a discursive opposition between art and photography by resorting to the contrary terms of presentation versus evidence, idea versus nature, the similar versus the identical, feeling versus fact, and imagination versus matter. Similar to de Zayas—but siding more strongly with an identical status ("I consider myself a photographer and nothing more")—Modotti too perceived a crucial conflict between art and photography. The difference of her practice—as opposed to art—is constitutive of truth as opposed to trickery, and of "objective reality" as opposed to dissimulation. Artistic effects in photography engender a hybrid appearance that stages an attempt to deceive; it is a lie to be shunned. (That Modotti had been standing trial as an accomplice to Mella's political assassination during the foregoing months cannot be overestimated in this context.) But her disavowal of false appearance in "On Photography" now contradicts her letter to Weston two years earlier. There she described her reaction to the shell photographs as a "purity of vision" to be "conveyed"—not an immediate presence but a mediated rediscovery cut off from its source, that is, veiled appearance or misapprehension. I am concerned as much with the urgent nature of this axiology as with the terms of its criteria—that is, as much with the all caps of "PHOTOGRAPHIC QUALITY" as with "photographic quality." One cannot overlook the manifesto's divisions of painting and photography: its distribution of those who accept photography as a medium of expression and those who do not, with an appeal to the past in order to privilege the present. One cannot help but notice, consequently, how the collective refusal to accept photography as a means of expression, in this assessment, is a disavowal of mechanical civilization, modernity, and the contemporary, with whose opposing ideas the author claims to be "at home." In this discursive performance of valuations and revaluations, manifold borderlines are further bolstered and dissolved. The text continues:

> It is not important to know whether or not photography is an art. What is important is to distinguish between good and bad photography. What should be understood by good photography is that which accepts the limitations inherent in photographic technique, and which takes advantage of all the possibilities and characteristics offered by the medium. Bad photography should be understood as that which is produced, one could say, with a kind of *inferiority complex,* without valuing what photography has to offer as its very own. In this latter case, all kinds of imitations are used, giving the idea that the one producing the work is almost *embarrassed* by making photographs and tries to *hide* everything that has to with photography from the work, using *tricks and falsifications* that can only be pleasing to someone with a *perversive* taste.[63]

Photography constitutes a problem. It is "artless" because it establishes a "truth effect," but it nevertheless compels a critique of judgment. Those practitioners who "add" to the truth do so because they are ashamed of the fact the medium has been "exposed" for what it is—mere mechanical reproduction, pure positive science, a sole record of the perfectly observable—hence they disguise the aesthetic inadequacy, thereby neglecting the specificity of the medium. The will to turn photography into a means of illusion is thus seen as perverse. Disavowing any equivalence between photography and art, Modotti reiterates her concern for value, but psychologized with a rhetoric of limitation and technique. It is for that reason one is further struck by this "perversive" taste to which Modotti alludes—following the metaphorics of deceit, lowliness, and shame that are the cause of "false" photography.[64] It is in this sense that Copjec has linked the disavowal of sexual difference to perversion, what Modotti nominates the "perversive":

> In perversion . . . the law of sexual difference is instead treated as an arbitrary law of culture. . . . Perversion seeks to ensure that gaze and vision, desire and law, conscious and unconscious no longer contradict each other but inhabit the same plane, and attempt to force them to coalesce.[65]

Even as it argues for a form of self-sufficiency, "On Photography" struggles with two terms productively confused and amalgamated: the "one thing" and the "many functions of photography," that is, the "purity" of modernist form (the status of the object, and the presumed self-identity of the photograph) and the diversified field in which society and history are structured through the medium. Modotti was struggling against the hybrid effect or perversity of photography itself. Modotti had been publicly assaulted in the press that year, linking her to Mella's murder, with photographs and newspaper copy depicting her as someone to be morally reviled.[66] As a public spectacle of ignominy, it is especially relevant to her discussion of purity, or of the inferiority and shame she attributes to "perversive" taste. But in her refusal to merge the categories of media, in the writing of "On Photography" Modotti inadvertently unveiled the hybrid or perverse structure of photographic practice and image making. In reference to Stieglitz's pictorialism and to the photo-club amateurism predominant in Mexico, Modotti's disavowal of a *stylistic* constituted, perhaps even despite Modotti herself, an *unmasking of representation as such.* Modotti was not historically positioned to see the potential of hybridity as a differential that upsets the notion of the first and second order, of dominant and subordinate terms. In this text Modotti at once betrays a belief and performs a reversal: the supposed "transparency" of the lens makes it a guarantor of the "true" and the "pure" ("These tendencies lead to a hybrid product"). Earlier, I outlined how a specific structure can compel a less-powerful internal term to its cultural forms or, inversely, how a supposed lesser force can undermine the authoritative field to displace and redirect the convenience of oppositions. In both models, hybridity constitutes a drive that unsettles, ironizes, and transgresses within a historical location. Modotti had insight into these competing pressures constructive of photographic imaging, at the very least within her own production, as the sum of its parts makes patent. How else but as a hybrid effect could she have accounted for the "pure form" of *Roses,* for example, in relation to the "social reform" of *Hands Resting on Tool,* to say nothing of the intentional differences between the "commissioned" portraits, the magazine work for *Mexican Folkways,* the muralist fresco reproductions, and the final gestures in the 1929 series made in Juchitán, Oaxaca? In Mexico, Modotti and Weston participated in the kinds of modernist photography whose legacy insinuates a formalist romance about the moment "photography became photography." In those accounts, whereby the small events of life were made to appear monumental in the foreground as "the microstructure of sentiments, social relations, [and] characters,"[67] "photography" became "Photography" (until then it had only been art), for, like the movement of drive in sublimation, photography so willed to show "what photography has to offer as its very own" that the axiologies it found and founded were indistinguishable from the object of its (self) inspection.[68] (A few years prior to "On Photography" Ortega y Gasset had written: "An object is more and other than what is implied in the idea of it.")[69]

There is yet another movement rehearsed in "On Photography." Insofar as the photograph became the site of a crisis, negotiation, or productive interruption between two things—the camera and its object—photography was incorporated into the propositions that structure material fact into that which *is* true and that which *makes* true. One of Modotti's biographers further confirms Nietzsche's currency in Mexico's 1920s bohemia. As I showed earlier in terms of Antonio Caso and the Ateneo, Modotti's investments in the philosopher's writings are said to have derived from "notions that one must, at all costs, avoid a herd mentality."[70] "On Photography" comes very close to prefiguring—and then disrupting—"belief that a work of art is equivalent to its status as an object" or that "formal values are self-evident," that is, art historicism's investment in constructing "the ontology of the object."[71] Insofar as her manifesto belongs to a line of rhetorical practices or rehearsals of a negative aesthetics that point back to *Beyond Good and Evil*—recall the negative ascription to woman in her 1925 letter to Weston—Modotti may also have been prompted by Nietzsche's assertion that "ocular evidence" is an effect that does not follow cause, so that the true and the false, the good and the bad, are therefore surface beliefs: "It is no more than moral prejudice that the truth is worth more than appearance."[72]

For Modotti, the importance of differentiating good and bad photography was thus in direct proportion to the limitations of technique—"what photography has of its very own"—whose internal laws were judged to be productive of its identity. The truth of untruth in the visual distribution of life—the secret law of aesthetic truth—is reflective of the will to differentiate, insofar as, on the axiological scale, photography's inferior status to art need not be therefore cloaked or hidden with the false. In the vicissitudes of such photographic faith, the camera's framing produces a window onto, while remaining independent of, its source in any "intractable reality." In the manuscript "On Truth and Lies in a Nonmoral Sense," Nietzsche wrote:

> Surfaces. Forms.
> Art includes the delight of awakening belief by means of surfaces. But one is not really deceived! [If one were] then art would cease to be. . . . Thus art treats *illusion as illusion*; therefore it does not wish to deceive; it *is true*.[73]

In her 1929 text, to the degree that she was immersed in a redistribution whose object was truth in a photographic sense, Modotti gained access to the insight that photography's identity is transvalued insofar as it is also something rhetorically produced, hence contingent on the place photography should hold in social production and history—an aspect yet to be rehearsed in the final section of "On Photography."

Truth or Consequences

There is visual evidence to support Modotti's understanding of the wedge photography introduces between writing and optical representation. Modotti's photograph titled *Mella's Typewriter* (1928) is a celebrated image the photographer made by framing, at high angle and in extreme close-up, the geometries offered by the writing machine's keyboard, ribbon reel, type tray, and carriage (Figure 37). The particular typewriter in question belonged to Modotti's lover Mella—the anti-Machado revolutionary, exiled from Cuba in Mexico. With this writing machine the ideologue and author had produced his political tracts. Noble has brought this image to bear not only on the conflation of portraiture and communist philosophy—the subject "Mella" is encapsulated in the device that turns his practice into principles—but similarly on a "photograph of politics" becoming a "politics of photography." In the upper right-hand corner taken up by the sheet of paper, viewers can see a series of typed words. The complete legible phrases are "inspiración," "artística," "en una síntesis," as well as "existe entre la."[74]

Noble remarks that the writing on the page ends at the interstitial or threshold space between the words "entre la," the interval or gap *between* terms, so that the text is "patently unfinished," purposefully failing to tell the whole story. The text, furthermore, is the very passage from Trotsky's writings that Modotti would use as the epigraph to her 1929 manifesto—linking that text and this image in crucial ways. In English, again, Trotsky's statement reads: "Technique will be converted into a much more powerful inspiration of artistic production; later it will find its solution in a higher synthesis, the contrast that exists between technique and nature."[75] I read the image as a profound meditation on a series of gaps, most notably the radical dislocation that exists between the discursive and scopic regimes.

The final section of Modotti's 1929 statement was written, it is important to recall, within a year of Mella's death. In her conclusion, as she addresses the relation between a photograph and its place in social production, Modotti makes a set of claims that refer back to the photograph in question. Until now, the text had primarily focused on questions of photographic value and "truth." In yet another repositioning, Modotti suggests how, as a critical practice of social representation and as an ethical imperative, image technology has the power to structure a positive knowledge of the past:

> Photography, because of the single fact that it can only be produced in the present and based on what objectively exists in front of the camera, is clearly the most satisfactory medium for registering objective life in all its manifestations. For that reason, it has documentary value. If we add to all of this some sensitivity and understanding of the matter, and above all, a clear orientation of *the place photography should hold in history,* I believe the result is something [that] deserves *a place in social production,* something to which all of us should contribute.[76]

The distance between technique and agency, between human resource and raw matter, or between the instrumental and the given, had been the subject in part of *Hands Resting on Tool.* In *Mella's Typewriter,* however, there appears to be such added tension in the diagonals that separate the keys in the lower left corner with the writing in the upper right, as to compel technique to coalesce with its material and conceptual effects. Insofar as all representation is determined by technological meanings (the social consequences that occurred with the appearance of the typewriter and the camera, for example), and layered with the symbolic effects produced in the use of that technology (in radical doctrine or in a photo-

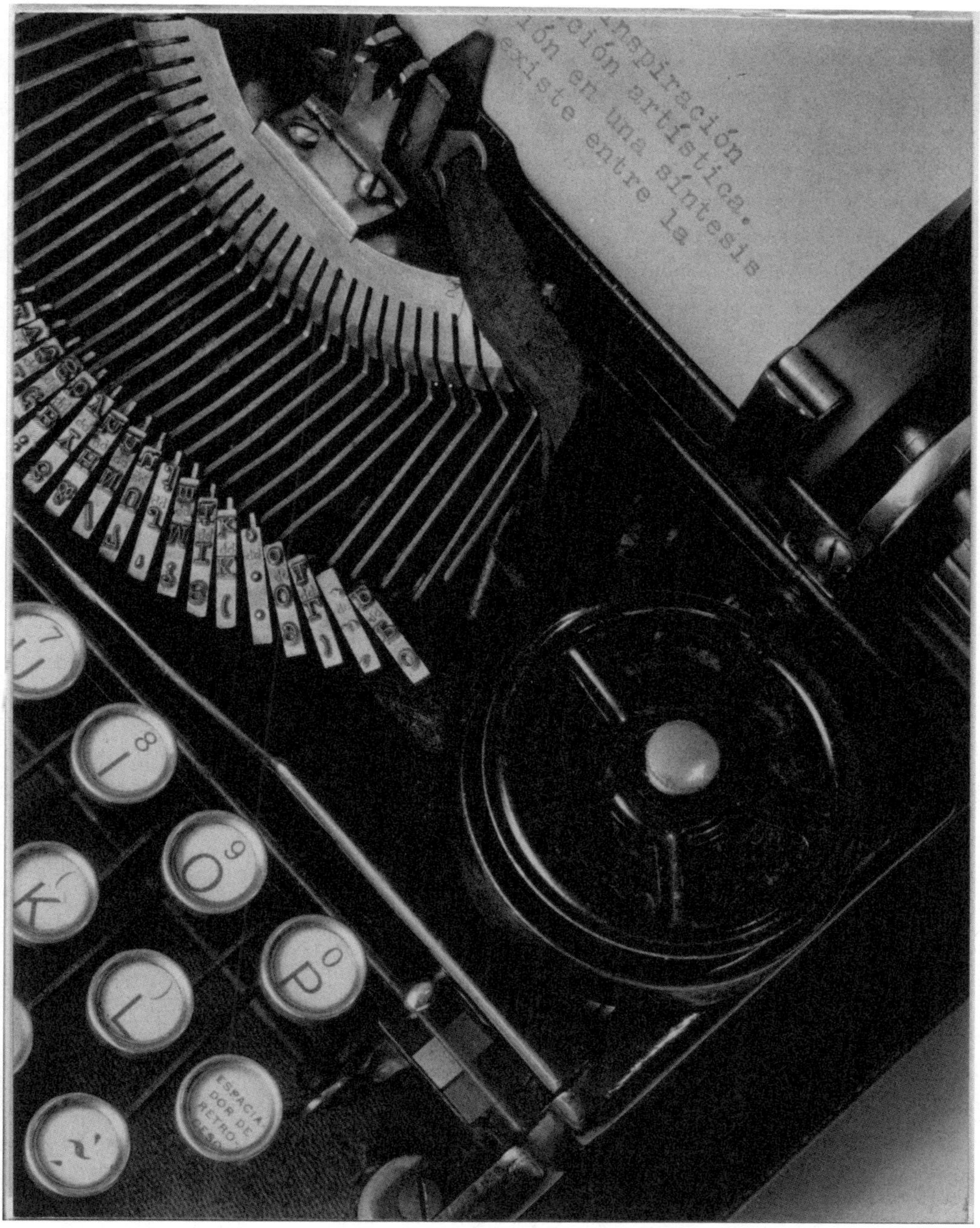

Figure 37. Tina Modotti, *Mella's Typewriter (La técnica),* 1928. Digital image copyright The Museum of Modern Art. Licensed by SCALA/Art Resource, New York.

graph), the solution the camera seeks in this photograph, certainly Modotti's most self-critical, is the higher synthesis that is supposed to uncover a contrast between technique and nature. As the camera and writing machine square eye to eye, as the space narrows between the lens and its object, and as the visual centering oscillates between text and image, the impossibility of that synthetic enterprise is laid bare, allowing us to see the disjunction there is between the *photographed* (a typewriter: the technology of which by 1928 had been largely naturalized) and the *photograph* (the effect of another technique: the camera). The fragmented Spanish text on the sheet of paper in the typewriter, a translation of Trotsky's original Russian, suggests that the disjunction between the photograph and the photographed constitutes a kinship corresponding "to the caesura between a translation and the original."[77] Walter Benjamin suggests that, like translation, photography is based not on a system of equivalences. Instead, it refuses to structure the world based on similarity or resemblance, insofar as a picture, like translation, is able to confuse the division between essence and appearance, and between original and representation. Photography constitutes a limitlessness where "more and less are always going a point further."[78]

What *Mella's Typewriter* encapsulates is that partition, made more intimate and imposing with the camera, between optics and language, but also the links between social formation, visual purpose, and language difference—the secret kinship of variety and vision. If the printed word in translation had been at one time the most effective and enduring process for tracing cultural description and difference over time and geography, this translation effect soon surrendered aspects of its sway and creative force to the representative "truth" claims of photography. That is, Modotti viewed photography and translation as internal to one another, that the technology of the image and the afterlife of written meanings labored jointly to expand the imaginative and political reaches of what there is in the world and how we come to know it.

In *Mella's Typewriter,* the angle of the composition was consciously chosen to privilege the key bearing the Spanish diacritical marks in the lower left-hand corner, as well as another barely legible key. The limited area on its round surface and the length of the Spanish word inscribed on it produce a visual poetics out of what amounts to the word for "backspace":

ESPACIA-
DOR DE
RETRO-
CESO

In a distribution worthy of Estridentista aesthetics, the backspace key in *Mella's Typewriter* (literally, the "backward movement spacebar") puts further stress on the insurmountable hyphenation between pictures and words. Moreover, it is uncanny to observe that among the multiple reproductions of this image in catalogs and books—the most highly circulating forms of the mechanical copy—the text to the backspace key is often printed so diffuse or with such variable contrast as to render "espaciador de retroceso" illegible. I accept this technical variability as relevant to its meaning, for it reinforces the vexed copy–original status of photography that is the photograph's theme, insofar as the backspace allows one to add to or amend a typescript when the accidental or "unconscious" aspect of writing interrupts. The backspace, standing in for that which cannot be properly represented, is thus the blind spot that structures sight and renders vision possible. Psychoanalysis uncovers the split between the eye and the gaze as a force activating "the dialectic of truth and appearance." Constitutive of perception, this rift makes subject and object accountable to matters of aesthetics, insofar as it functions in large measure as a "visual centering."[79]

Because the synthesis is deferred into a future (Trotsky's statement promised that "later, [technique] will find its solution in a higher synthesis"), another backspace explored in this photograph is the relation of the photograph to its present (Modotti: "what objectively exists in front of the camera") and how the present–past of a photograph structures history in the viewing present. Eduardo Cadava speaks to the caesura, halt, or arrest that is mutually compelled by photography and translation:

> If a space must separate the present from what it is not in order for the present to be itself, this space must at the same time divide the present. In constituting itself, in dividing itself, this interval is what Benjamin calls "space-crossed time"—time-becoming-space and space-becoming-time.[80]

Similar again to *Hands Resting on Tool, Mella's Typewriter* points to the fault line between social and aesthetic production, the extreme contiguity that nonetheless separates the means of production in labor from that in art. Modotti's contemporary and the author of *Mexico, An Interpretation* (1923), the journalist Carlton Beals, remarked, in a 1929 issue of *Camera Art,* that the photograph was "taken at an angle that conveys a kind of mystery—almost frightening—to this compact instrument, probably never observed by those who strike its keys to earn a living."[81] Friedrich A. Kittler in *Phonogram, Film, Typewriter* has demonstrated that with the appearance of the typewriter—advance in the discourse networks of information storage and retrieval—"Woman" was released from her fixed position as idealized form, to the degree that women began to enter the work force as typists.[82] Given its conflation of the contrary technologies of the written and the visual, and of the historical identities the tools imply, *Mella's Typewriter* could equally have been titled *Modotti's Camera.* With the photograph at its discursive and visual upper limit—where the copy overwrites, reverses, or cross-spaces the original as though it could successfully go back in time, correct its failures, and so provide itself with an alibi—fissures and ruptures are brought into conceptual possibility.[83]

With the cultural form photographed in *Mella's Typewriter*, and at the levels of form and content, we are both in proximity to, and a long way from, the natural form photographed in *Roses*. But it is precisely culture that is at stake here, and especially that photographic culture that had begun to retreat on itself. If I apply too much allegorical pressure to what was the given-to-be-seen of any typewriter at the time, it is to make vibrant the radical difference that opens up between *Mella's Typewriter* and a sequence of photographs Modotti made in its wake on a trip to Juchitán in 1929.[84] To account for that difference in these photographs is already to speak of a kind of reversal, backspace, or overwriting. The series may be viewed in any number of sequences—there is no record of their chronology—but they span a matter of weeks and were made only months prior to Modotti's writing of "On Photography." One possible succession begins with *Woman Carrying Yecapixtle Gourd* (or, *Woman of Tehuantepec*, Figure 38), and *Mexican Mother and Baby* (or, *Woman Carrying Child*, Figure 39) and concludes with *Market Scene* (Figure 40) and *Women and Children by Riverbank* (Figure 41). In light of *Mella's Typewriter*—indeed, in relation to almost any other Modotti photograph—they appear so remarkably unstudied, so unbridled by the laws that structure her prior work, the progressively more casual quality of their compositional framing so devoid of self-conscious spectacle, as to be understood as a disavowal or overturning of modernist truth—which is to say now the "untruth"—of form. As the everyday practices they depict inform the otherwise unremarkable formal support, these photographs stage a relaxing or dilation with a view to deployment. For example, the clipped iconic structure of the portrait *Woman Carrying Yecapixtle Gourd* gives way to *Mexican Mother and Baby* in which the pregnant woman in corporeal profile (her head remains outside the frame) holds the fleshy folds of her infant child clutched to the side. The tension of the statuesque and the fragile in this photograph is even further surrendered in *Woman and Children by Riverbank* and *Market Scene* where several photographic subjects recognize the presence of the photographer and camera—though it is not the recognition of the camera that matters here but the uneventful means by which it is encapsulated. Together, these images Modotti made in the Isthmus of Tehuantepec perform a doubling: to speak of the everyday practices that is their *content* is to speak of their *method*.[85] These images double back to describe the tactic Modotti locates as a refusal to capitalize in terms of controlling time. These photographs do not colonize to the extent that, with the everyday practice outlined by Michel de Certeau, they transform "another person's property into a space borrowed for a moment by a transient."[86]

We can begin to situate a difference in Modotti's work, not in any one particular image but at the junctures modernism opened up between a thing made visible and another emptied or ghosted of itself. In this sense, the Juchitán series prefigured a response to what T. J. Clark has termed the "bad dream of modernism." Clark looks to those spaces historically ignored or veiled to examine how capitalist energy has used them as the profitable representation now of what it had formerly made invisible. Modernism proposed to explore the other of Western bourgeois experience—the outside, the primitive, the childish, the deviant, the underside of reason—"insofar as these margins have been posited and organized as new territories on which representations could take place." Predictably, the result was benefit for the bourgeoisie. That is, even the "outskirts of attention" were not out of reach of capitalism for long before they, too, were transformed in visual commodities. For Clark, the bad dream of modernism implies that no matter how "urgent the

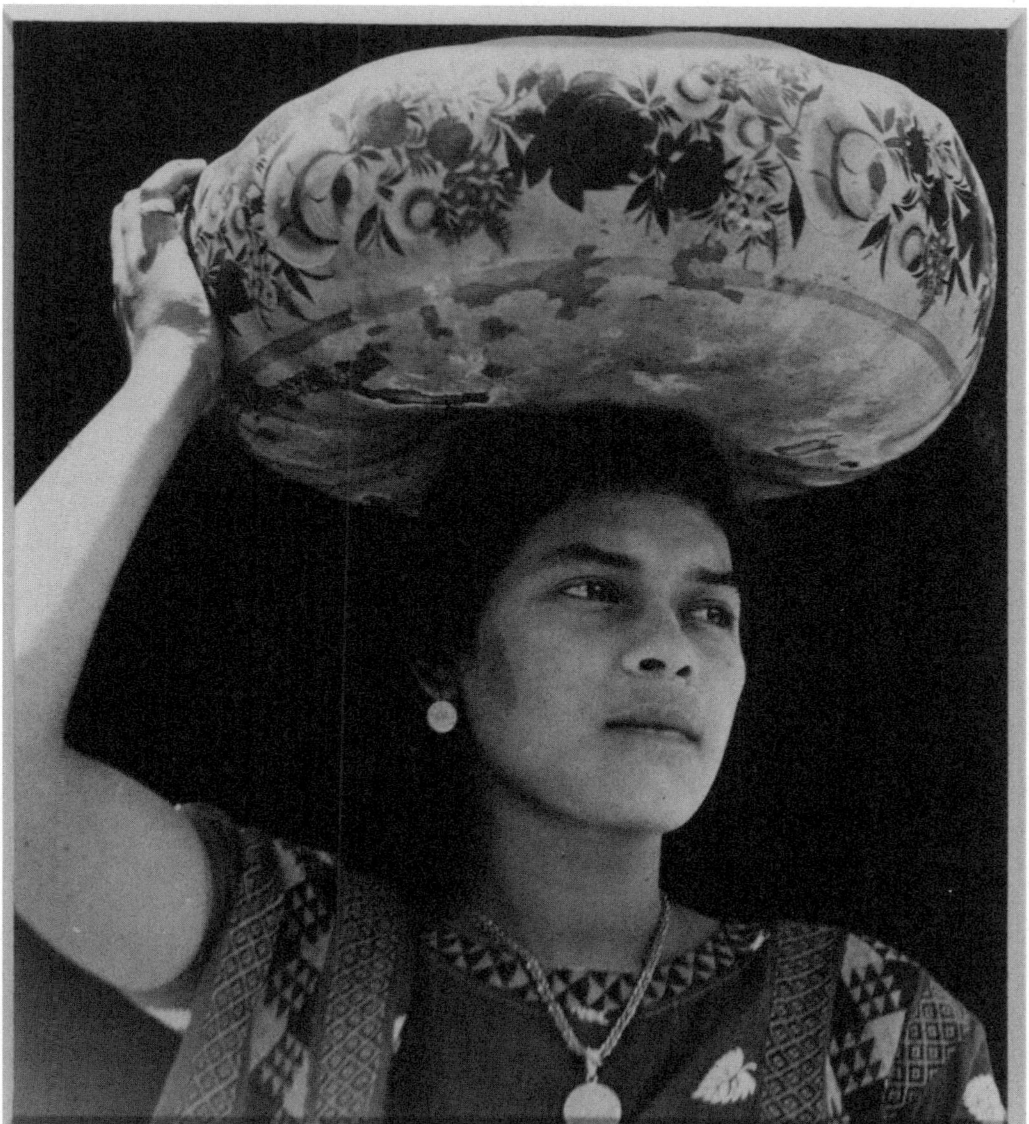

Figure 38. Tina Modotti, *Woman of Tehuantepec,* 1929. George Eastman House, Museum Collection.

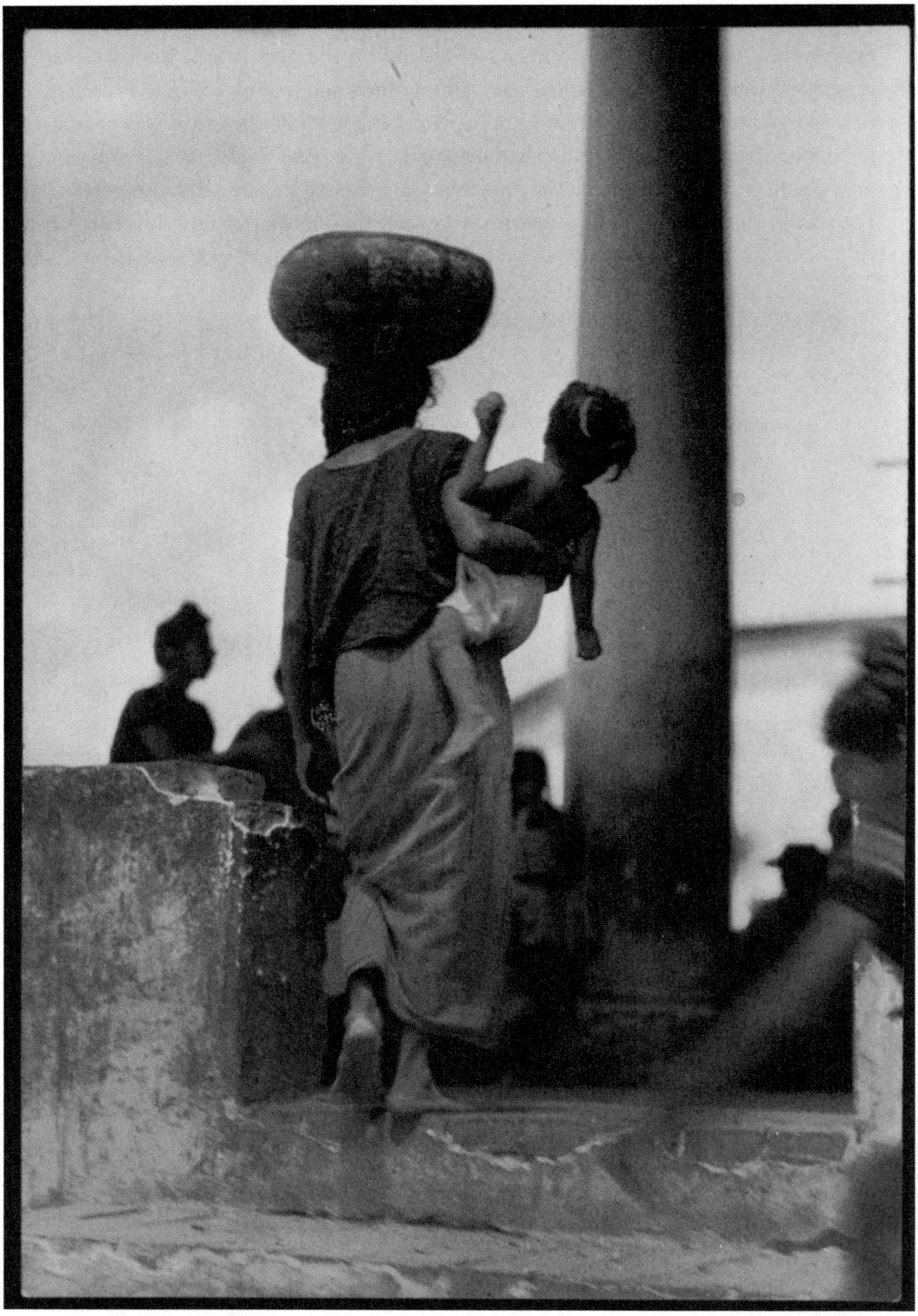

Figure 39. Tina Modotti, *Woman Carrying Child,* 1929. George Eastman House, Museum Collection.

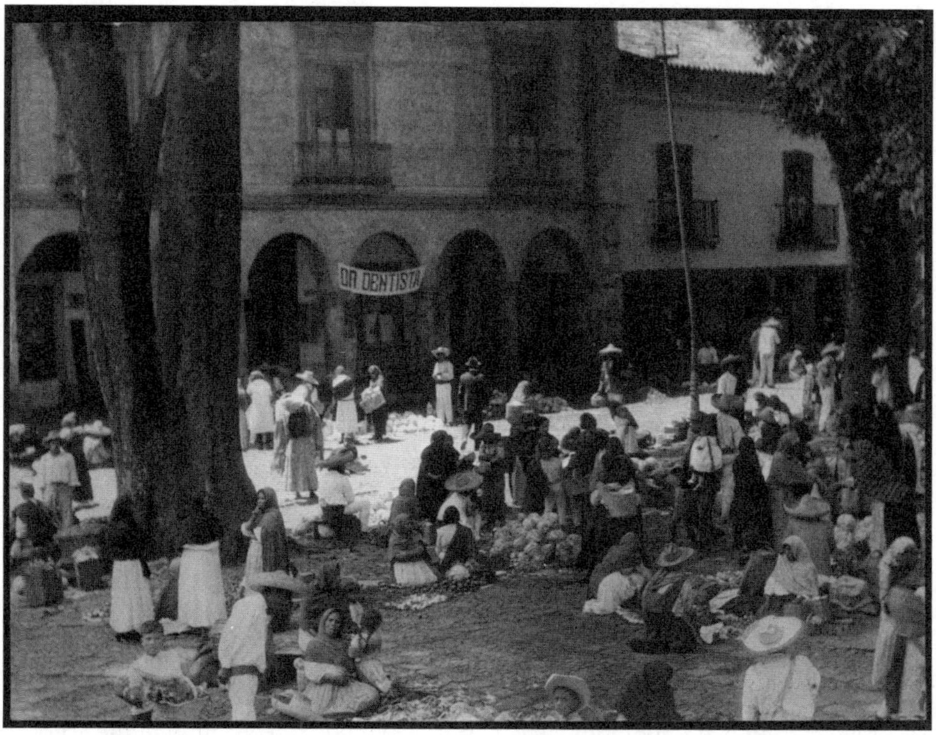

Figure 40. Tina Modotti, *Market Scene,* 1929. George Eastman House, Museum Collection.

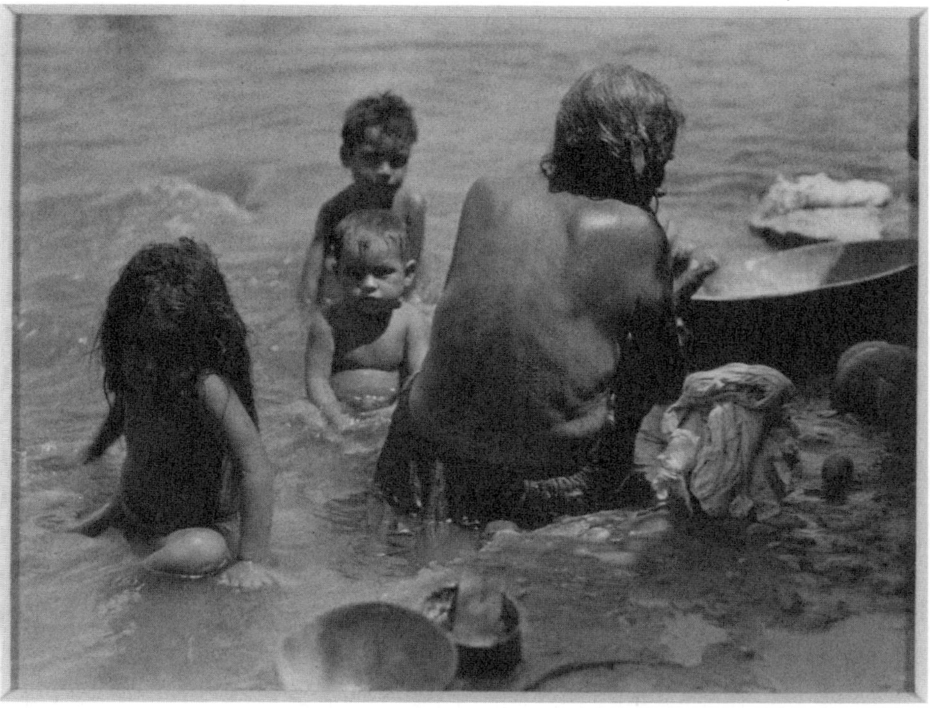

Figure 41. Tina Modotti, *Women and Children by Riverbank,* 1929. George Eastman House, Museum Collection.

impulse had been to alter the aesthetic and move out into uncolonized areas of experience, all that resulted was a thickening—a clotting—of the same aesthetic mix."[87] From the technique of photographic curtailment—to make less as if by cutting off or away some part—to the local tactic of the habitat—a deployment in the sense of spreading out, utilizing, or arranging strategically—Modotti's images are reflective of what Gayatri Spivak has termed "withheld specularity,"[88] whereby the radical other has the right to refuse the onlooker's gaze, hence beating foreclosure to the punch. In another double movement, in the primary gesture afforded by this series, Modotti goes a point further by beating the visual culture of which she was a participant—that is, modernism's formal foreclosure—to the punch as well.

If "the modernist past [is] a ruin, the logic of whose architecture we do not remotely grasp,"[89] it is because such a vision suspends photographic efficacy as a series of cultural causes and effects severed from the present in events remote now in time and place—a romance with form that never reformed, the partial function that failed to bring together the representative whole. With Modotti's Juchitán photographs, and with the Certeau of *The Practice of Everyday Life,* we might also discover the discontinuous narrative, as Modotti did in this sequence of photographs, of "escaping" modernity without leaving it altogether. Constructed from these late Modotti photographs, that narrative would closely simulate the account of syncretism of which Certeau speaks, and of which Modotti's photographs are more than simply reflective:

> The ambiguity that subverted from within the Spanish colonizers' "success" in imposing their own culture on the indigenous Indians is well known. Submissive, and even consenting to their subjection, the Indians nevertheless often made of the rituals, representations, and laws imposed on them something quite different from what their conquerors had in mind; they subverted them not by rejecting or altering them, but by using them with respect to ends and references foreign to the system they had no choice but to accept. They were other within the very colonization that outwardly assimilated them; their use of the dominant social order deflected its power, which they lacked the means to challenge; they escaped it without leaving it.[90]

A substantial body of images within Modotti's brief but comprehensive career, the Juchitán series both *documents* and *encapsulates* syncretism itself, thus troubling those accounts invested in rendering modernism "pure," readable "under some dismissive fantasy rubric . . . of 'opticality,' 'formalism,' 'elitism,' etc." Produced by a nonnational who was able to deftly translate into photographic images the debates of a nation caught between the divisive effects of modernization and modern art, the pictures are reminders of those forces that continue to resist any notion of modernity's ultimate triumph over all structures of life and representation.

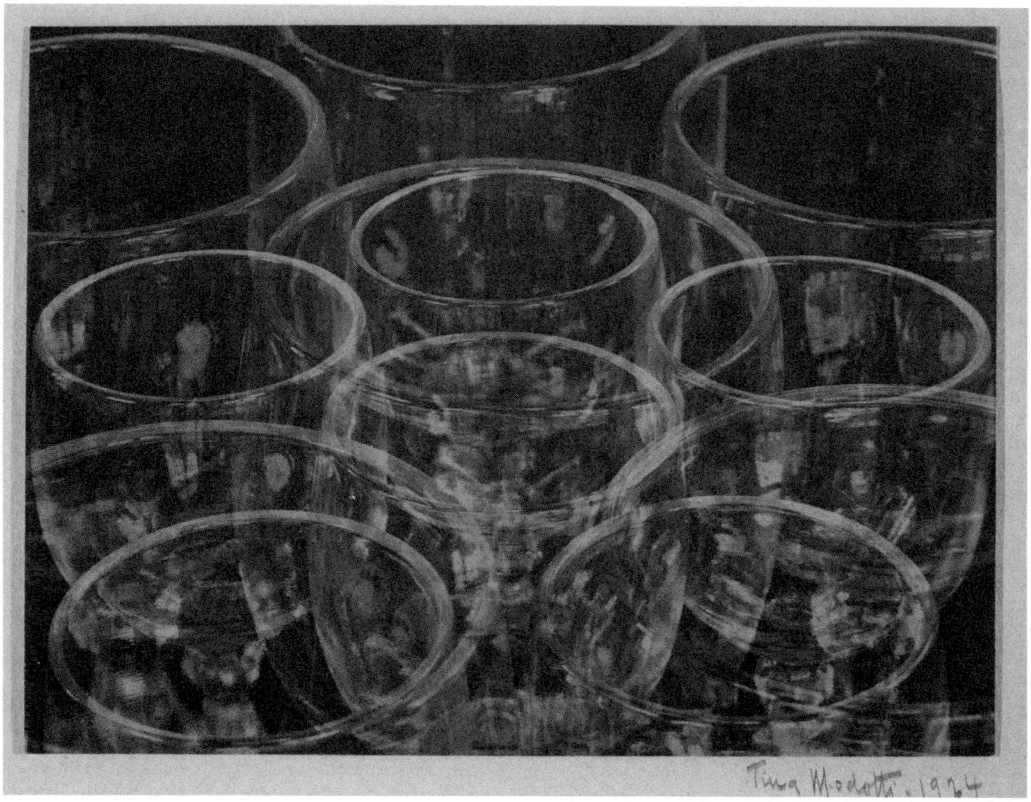

Figure 42. Tina Modotti, *Experiment in Related Form (Glasses),* 1924. Mills College Art Museum, Oakland, California, Gift of Roi Partridge.

Experiment in Related Form is the name of an early photograph made by Modotti in 1924 (with alternate title *Glasses*) (Figure 42). Through a series of multiple exposures, the reflective contours of a thick glass goblet form twelve intersecting ovals and overlapped elliptical rings whose expanding shapes suggest such increase across the photograph's surface that the original referent is rendered visually indistinct. Read allegorically, this photograph identifies our subject. That is, sexual difference need not be visually verifiable for its effects to make a difference, nor is it reducible to any particular point of photographic phosphorescence. The difference Modotti's work makes to modernism is that her photographs struggle with, and leave behind, not a history of purity but a structure compelling less patent internal terms to specific cultural forms. That is, photography began to be photography in the contact zone between visual and rhetorical regimes that inflected outsider standing within the drive to forge a national camera. The operative differences between the works of Modotti and Weston are troubled by the cultural discrepancy or time lag that made image making and representation in the contact zone a visual passage adjacent to other symbolic practices and structures—and for that reason unavoidably partial. In the transitory site of Mexico, Weston and Modotti visually complicated cultural and sexual difference as a limit not unlike those related to the medium of photography itself: never an identical representation, but nonetheless a borderline relevant to both sides of the camera—an experiment in related form.

3. Metropolitan Matters: Álvarez Bravo's Mexico City

The key cultural factor of the modernist shift is the character of the metropolis.

—Raymond Williams, *The Politics of Modernism*

Mexico City tested the forward-looking limits of the camera as a technology for image making, even as modern photographers, Tina Modotti and Edward Weston among them, explored the city's immutable allusions to history, social fractures, and the complex relations between modern and traditional life in the photographic instant. A century-long resident of Mexico City, Manuel Álvarez Bravo (1902–2001), made early use of the capital's material culture—the built environment of the public streets and squares—to frame statements, suggested by the visual relationships he transformed into photographs, about the social and cultural realities of the city's residents. In this way he created seemingly timeless images that can claim their source in "visual culture, spectacle and symbolic codes, and ultimately, the creation of community."[1] If we think of the photographic frame and the metropolitan area as sites of contested space—a location where certain incidents and relations are intensified even as others are excluded—we will have defined a relevant point of departure for thinking about public culture and camera work. In his photographic framing, Álvarez Bravo deployed the metropolis as historic backdrop and as a photographable field for representing material and social markers in relation to time and power at various points of vulnerability. Because the images he made are lyrical, and the visual indeterminacies they activate so lavish, the overall effect of the work often eclipses the constituent parts. From the everyday striving of women and men in their respective social and sexual roles,

Álvarez Bravo rendered complex relations of difference and purpose, assembled with an aesthetic design aimed at interpretive defiance. By looking closely at photographs produced primarily in the 1930s and 1940s, with a view to the political situation and the art movements that gave rise to his unique brand of image making, I demonstrate how this work reflects a critical process that imbricates the material culture of the urban center. A transnational attention to art and culture is critical to the interplay of photography and urban space—as well as to the "unnatural coupling" of photography and European art making—insofar as Mexican modernist photography and French surrealism came face-to-face, in one scene, as a capitalist venture within the U.S. American marketplace for art.

The complexities of Mexico City's metropolitan area served, for Álvarez Bravo and others, as an unqualified visual laboratory, even if its importance in relation to the international movements of twentieth-century modernism has often been underemphasized. Álvarez Bravo relished the unexpected visual joys of the metropolis offered to the passerby perspective, and he capitalized on the disjunction, in modern life, between the meanings of words and images. In *Suspended Fish* (ca. 1930), just one of many examples, the word "emulsión" is written across a mawkishly painted sign of a tin fish so as to highlight the discrepancy between the materiality of the object and representation (Figure 43). An advertisement for cod liver oil suspended over a storefront doorframe, the sign provided Álvarez Bravo with a visual quip about the medium's therapeutic benefits. It offered an opportunity also to show the signifying process itself, photographic or otherwise, as a depth effect in provisional suspense.

These links between representation and metropolitan space compel a brief discussion of the image environment just prior to, and continuous with, the years that Álvarez Bravo came into his own as a photographer, by way of what the critic Raymond Williams has identified generally as the systematic link between "metropolitan perceptions and the emergence of modernism."[2] Within the logic of the Casasola Archive, as I showed earlier, the Mexican Revolution of 1910 overturned the autocratic thirty-year regime of Porfirio Díaz in a sequence of violent upheavals and successive military coups that erupted in various rural parts of the country and in Mexico's capital. It also gave rise to other news photographs displaying Mexico's metropolitan modernity and visual culture, including those collected in the photographic history by George R. Leighton, incorporated in *The Wind That Swept Mexico*,[3] by the Mexican-born writer Anita Brenner, published in 1943, a year following the Mexican government's declaration of war against the Axis.[4]

Carlos Monsiváis has argued that throughout the three decades of the Díaz administration (1880–1911), "that multifarious entity, the Mexican Republic, was to know but a single solitary style: *porfirismo*."[5] The historic period to which Díaz bestowed his name was an era of material prosperity, largely because of the surge of foreign capital that exploited Mexico's natural and human resources. Díaz built roads, railroads, and cable communications, which helped establish financial sta-

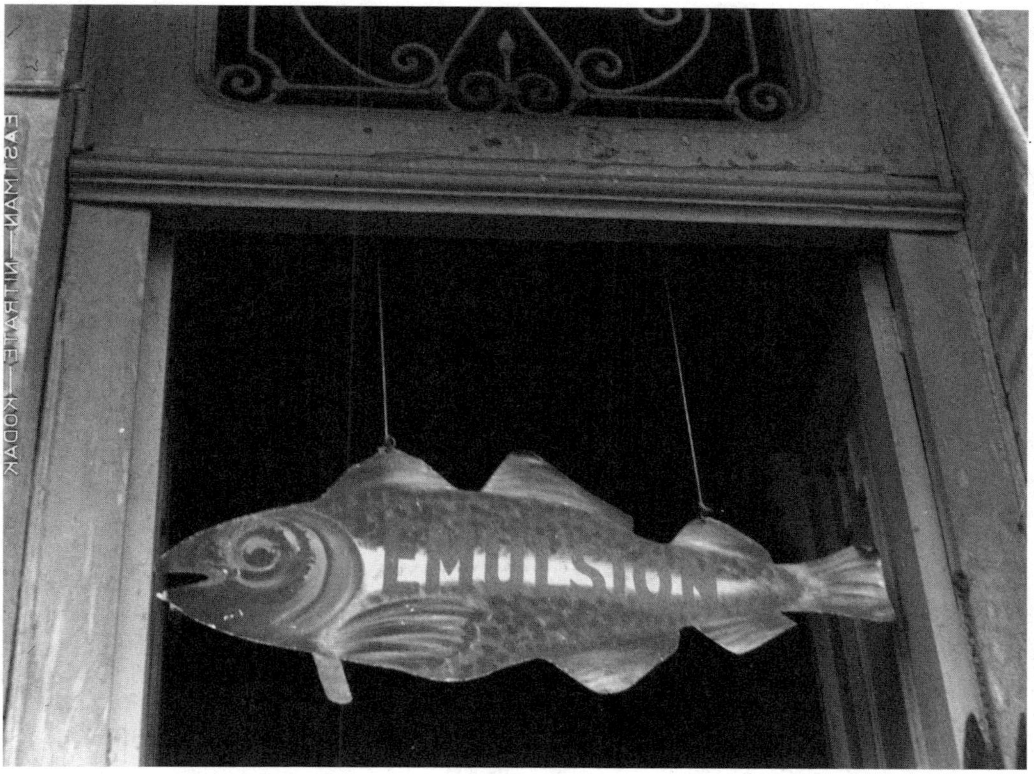

Figure 43. Manuel Álvarez Bravo, *Pez suspenso (Suspended fish)*, ca. 1930. Digital image courtesy of Rose Gallery, Los Angeles.

bility, peace, and prosperity while oppressing the racially differentiated majority of Mexicans who had limited right of access to education or the benefits of social space. This belle époque of the so-called four hundred families is evoked by Monsiváis in a litany of cultural references to class-specific last names and the kind of Spanish spoken by the elite sectors, heavily doused with French and English turns of phrase, a climate teeming with images of garden parties, charity balls, casinos, triumphal arcs, high ecclesiastic pomp, inaugurations—in short, all the materialism and moralizing of refined religious society.

One photograph of Díaz from *The Wind That Swept Mexico* (Figure 44) is representative of the moral and physical attributes that overdetermined the political realm of the time,[6] described by Monsiváis as "imposing, serene, severe, classic, immutable and rotund."[7] Díaz is rendered in a now banal spectacle of power, seated in a horse-drawn carriage, next to an officer in command, chauffeured by top-hatted attendants, and surrounded by a retinue. But Díaz's oppressive authority, which had long been successful in thwarting revolts and rival aspirants, is rendered less certain in this photograph. For all the caudillo's regalia of command, his figure captured at an instant when the show of strength obstructs any view of the very populace that presumably cheers him in the streets, and conveyed in a

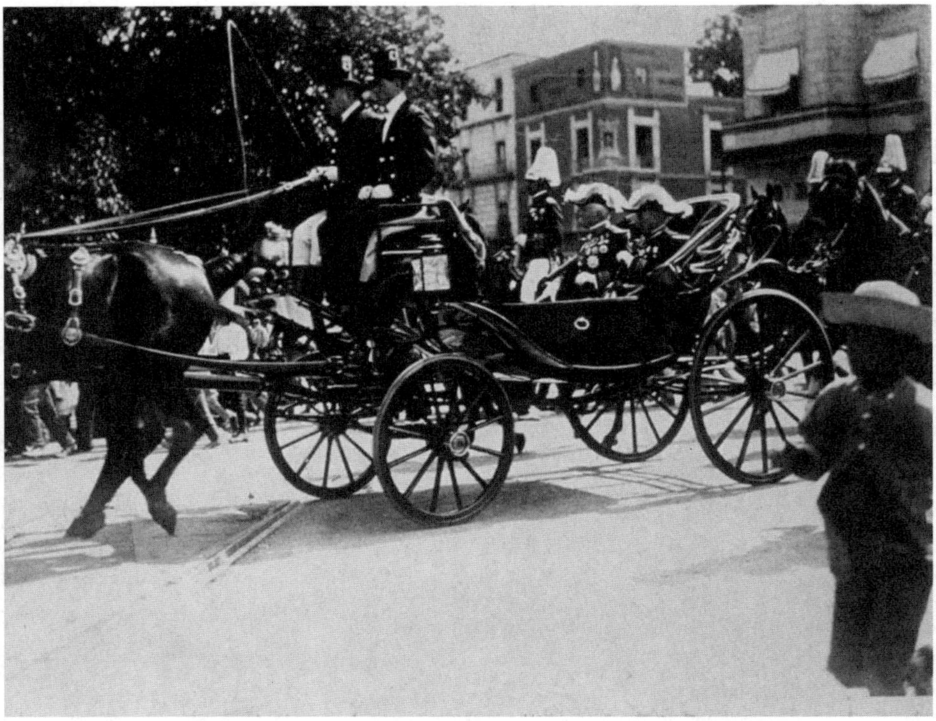

Figure 44. Porfirio Díaz in carriage. Photograph in *The Winds That Swept Mexico.* Image number 36. Photography Collection, Harry Ransom Humanities Research Center, University of Texas at Austin.

vehicle whose technological dazzle was on its way to becoming obsolete, the "cozy little *status quo*" is troubled in the lower right-hand corner by a blurred interruption into the photographic frame: a child from the popular classes captured buoyantly gamboling by—but with his eyes closed.[8] An ancien régime and its artifice *pompier* are unsettled here by the unsuspected appearance of the always already dependent and paternalized, but at an instant when that world of power is shut from the latter's view.

Brenner and Leighton's photographic history, *The Wind That Swept Mexico,* was assembled from many sources—primarily from news agencies but also with images by the Casasola brothers, Brenner herself, and Doris Heyden, Álvarez Bravo's second wife.[9] Brenner was born in Mexico where she lived for many years and edited the magazine *Mexico This Month.* In an energetic, modernist style that blurs the boundaries of personal testimony, journalism, and eyewitness history, *The Wind That Swept Mexico* demonstrates how photography with journalistic intentions and photography with aesthetic aspirations are intertwined in an encounter over the exercise of the public arena and over how that social space is represented.

This is made evident in a sequence of photographs (Figures 45, 46, and 47) that outlines an equation between the morality of the Díaz regime and the imposing and impassive lavishness of the material culture that was its public backdrop. It is remarkable how Brenner and Leighton deftly identified this panoptic sequence: in a partitioning of space, the photograph manages to join the center and periphery, and the hierarchical worlds of above and below, in a "visibility organized around a dominating, overseeing gaze."[10] The captions below the three images read "From the Palace of Chapultepec . . . overlooking Mexico City . . . the Strong Man and Mme. Díaz presided over a brilliant and gaudy society whose mansions fronted a tree-lined boulevard, the Paseo de la Reforma." Monsiváis claims that by 1910,

> with the incredible exception of liberal centers in the provinces . . . and forms of bourgeois and bohemian life in the Capital, a feudal morality reigned with the following equation: defense of the natural right of possession over women, the land, workers and the nation = fortitude of spirit = pillar of society = sexual repression. . . . It was a Mexico at once ideal and tragic, grim and repressive, ferociously cruel and subdued. . . . Splendor and misery, ceremony and crime: the contrasts are obvious, but without the obviousness of contrasts there would have been no Revolution.[11]

Before evoking the political and aesthetic renewal brought on by the Revolution, it is important to pause at this moral and material backdrop that enabled the

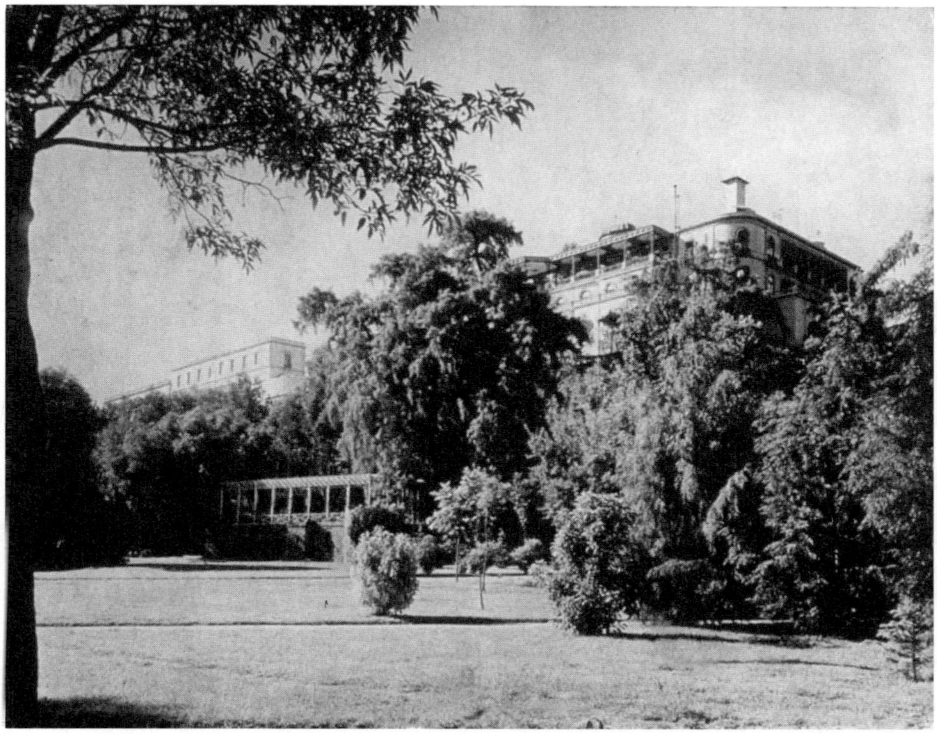

Figure 45. Chapultepec Castle. Photograph in *The Winds That Swept Mexico*. Image number 30. Photography Collection, Harry Ransom Humanities Research Center, University of Texas at Austin.

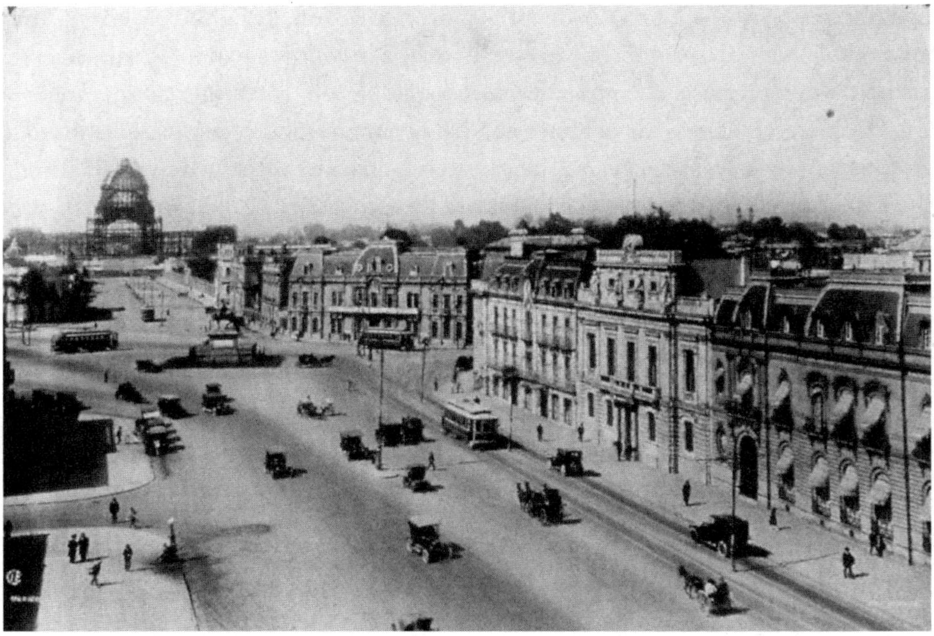

Figure 46. Monument under construction. Photograph in *The Winds That Swept Mexico.* Image number 31. Photography Collection, Harry Ransom Humanities Research Center, University of Texas at Austin.

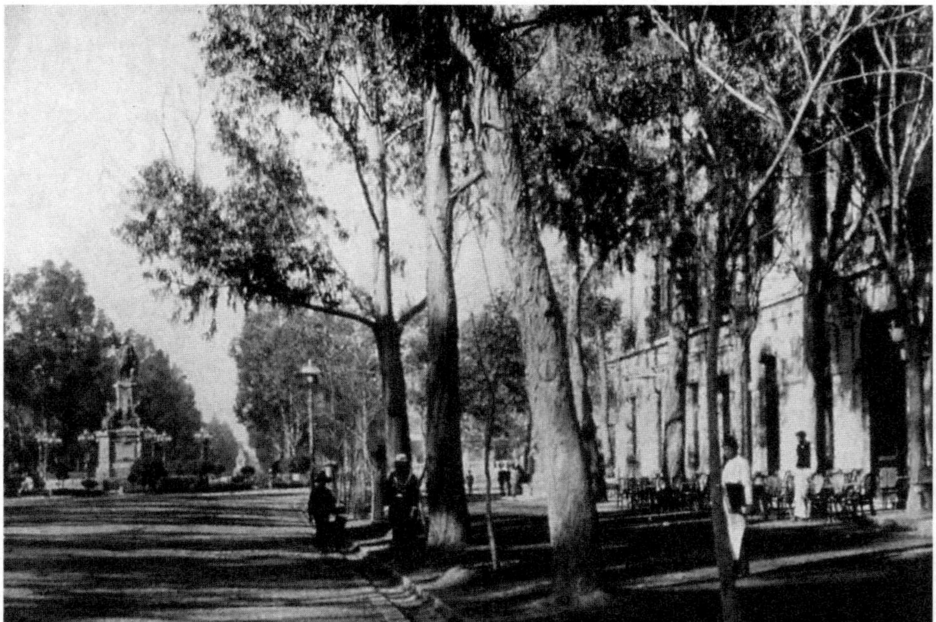

Figure 47. Chapultepec Avenue. Photograph in *The Winds That Swept Mexico.* Image number 32. Photography Collection, Harry Ransom Humanities Research Center, University of Texas at Austin.

emergence of modernism in Mexico. As effected by Mexicans and foreigners alike, modernist practice redirected socially repressive attributes to create formally (and sometimes politically) radical products whose visible features might be described, in an ironic turn, with the very same qualifiers used to modify the political climate of *porfirismo*: that is, "imposing, serene, severe . . . immutable and rotund." It is at this visual juncture that the photographic frame became a locus of inclusions and exclusions effected in the social contest for public culture in Mexico City.

To argue this, I examine the status of Mexico City as a modern metropolis, as the role this metropolis played in matters of transnational modernism is often undertheorized. But throughout the decades that immediately followed the Revolution, Mexico became the setting for one of the most engaging cultural experiments of the early twentieth century, featuring an enormous cast of national luminaries actively forging a revisionist or visionary investigation into their own national ethos: a questioning of inherited notions about Mexico's past that would reverberate in nearly every aspect of the country's social, intellectual, and cultural life.

After ten years of the Revolution's crippling violence, Mexico, now under the presidency of General Álvaro Obregón, was prepared to begin a material, ideological, and cultural transformation of the country. After a five-year exile in the United States, during the turbulent revolutionary decade, the cultural philosopher José Vasconcelos returned to Mexico to form part of Obregón's cabinet as minister of education—gathering artists and intellectuals to contribute to the goals of the "new orientations of art and culture." Brenner writes: "Ideas in progress ranged from irrigation plans to free breakfasts in the schools to serum laboratories and baby clinics and wall newspapers and beggars' hostels and art for the people and cheap editions of Plutarch."[12] If the actual armed conflict and military campaigns of the Revolution had attracted newspaper journalists like John Reed and Carlton Beals, as well as photojournalists from news agencies, then the promise of the post-Revolutionary Renaissance, that joined cultural production to social idealism, attracted a second host of internationals during the 1920s and 1930s.

Ideas about the nation were linked, unflaggingly, to cultural production. In one strand of this narrative—for whose initial impulse Vasconcelos and the muralist movement are largely credited—cultural producers looked beyond the perimeters of the belle époque, whose quasi-comprador gaze was fixed on things external to Mexico in matters of economy and art, to seek roots rather in native tradition. This renewed interest in Mexico's ancient civilizations—there were new explorations at various archaeological sites in the central plateau and the Yucatán peninsula—together with an ethnographic desire for modern indigenous culture, and how both were linked to Revolutionary nation building, is exemplified in the work of Manuel Gamio, public intellectual, pioneer in the modern cultural sciences of Mexico, and author of the influential *Forjando patria*.[13] Mexico was inventing itself, generating an array of icons and shorthand iterations—the murals, the indigenous subsoil, the manual arts, an attention to the ruins and the abrupt landscape, as well as a pantheon of ancient and contemporary mythologies—which, in turn, would lure Mexican and foreign artists alike.

One such foreigner, the Dominican writer and critic Pėdro Henríquez Ureña, wrote a firsthand witness account of the Revolution's transformative effects on Mexico's intellectual life. Published in the mid-1920s, the essay gives evidence of the modernizing enterprise, with its new impulse to establish education for the masses and a philosophical canon that replaced Comte, John Stuart Mill, and Herbert Spencer with Friedrich Nietzsche and Henri Bergson. Not the least of its other appraisals was its attention to the material changes taking place in the city itself:

> The new neighborhoods in the capital, devoted formerly to the cult of the French hotel and the Swiss chalet, are lined with buildings in which the ancient architecture of the country reappears adapted to new ends: buildings that are readily recognizable, thanks not only to the interesting baroque tenor of their lines, but to the Mexican materials employed, the blood-red volcanic stone, *tezontle,* and gray *chiluca,* or sometimes even tiles: these have restored the city to its proper character, in addition to the sumptuous palaces of the older neighborhoods.[14]

Metropolitanism in Mexico City was a circuitry with multiple links to policies of nation building, to the differentiated physicality of the city, and to the influx and contact zone provided by foreign artists who were both observers and participants in the flourishing intellectual climate. The city's social formations, the new links between "center" and (internal) "margin," and a power invested in this new kind of Mexico City elitism converted the rest of Mexico to a serviceable "periphery," if only because the cultural capital of the metropolis was indebted to those links back and forth between a modernizing project and traditional life. In *The Politics of Modernism,* Williams suggests a component relevant to thinking about the developments of photography in Mexico City when he writes that the "most important general element of the innovations in form is the fact of immigration to the metropolis, and it cannot too often be emphasized how many of the major innovators were, in this precise sense, immigrants."[15]

Williams refers to a politically specific kind of displacement, but it is relevant to the double movement at play in Mexico City between modernist expatriate sojourn and the city's changing internal demographics. In the late 1920s and 1930s, when Álvarez Bravo began producing photographs, vast numbers of Mexicans from the provinces began to move to Mexico City. This phenomenon prompted a new kind of metropolitanism, a clash of traditional values and habits as rural folk encountered the urban realities of modern life, making the social disparity of the country increasingly visible. Álvarez Bravo returned to this subject throughout his life, but it is especially discernible in his images from the 1930s and 1940s; his photographs are a rich depository for examining the relationship between the evolving material culture of modern life in Mexico City and the visual challenges the metropolis posed to image making and the limits of representation itself.

Built Environment/Image Environment

Álvarez Bravo was born in the historic center of Mexico City, with its urban latticework of buildings and avenues that intersect around the zocalo, or main square. Material reminders there attest to the indigenous civilizations that existed before the new world encounter, to Mexico's colonial period, and to the Díaz regime. His style developed in conversation, as I've already remarked, with the onrush of artistic production that occurred in Mexico during the 1920s and 1930s, the decades following the ten-year Revolution.

In previous pages I offered an account of how the cultural difference of Mexico troubled the conventional antimonies dividing the present from the past, tradition from modernity, and the avant-garde from the vernacular. In varying degrees, but for both the national cultural elite and the foreigners who took part in its artistic and social cross-purposes, symbolic renderings of Mexico's cultural differences generated a twin representative effect: by pointing to the folk and its traditions to symbolize a collective modernity, a translation or time lag took place, a partial but no less powerful function linked to the representative whole.[16] Relevant then to Mexico's cultural awakening were

> the elements of strangeness and distance, indeed of alienation. But the decisive aesthetic effect is at a deeper level. Liberated or breaking from their national . . . cultures, placed in quite new relations to those other native languages or native visual traditions, encountering meanwhile a novel and dynamic common environment from which many of the older forms were obviously distant, the artists and writers and thinkers of this phase found the only community available to them: a community of the medium; of their own practices.[17]

In 1927 Álvarez Bravo met Modotti, who encouraged the young photographer to pursue his craft. Earlier I examined how Modotti became involved with avant-garde formations and revolutionary politics, including the aesthetics of *estridentismo.* Spearheaded primarily by poets and printmakers with an understanding of Italian futurism, Estridentistas likewise expounded a theory of images controlled by spatial geometry. In manifestos, these artists glorified the electrically powered industrial world of machines, factories, and telecommunications. One of the group's founding members, Germán List Arzubide, spoke of this new aesthetic attitude as "equations of abstractionism." The movement aimed to establish a theory of images as an "infinitesimal calculus controlled by means of a geometry in space" and as "centripetal claims upheld by gravity in the planisphere of manual printing" (Figure 48).[18]

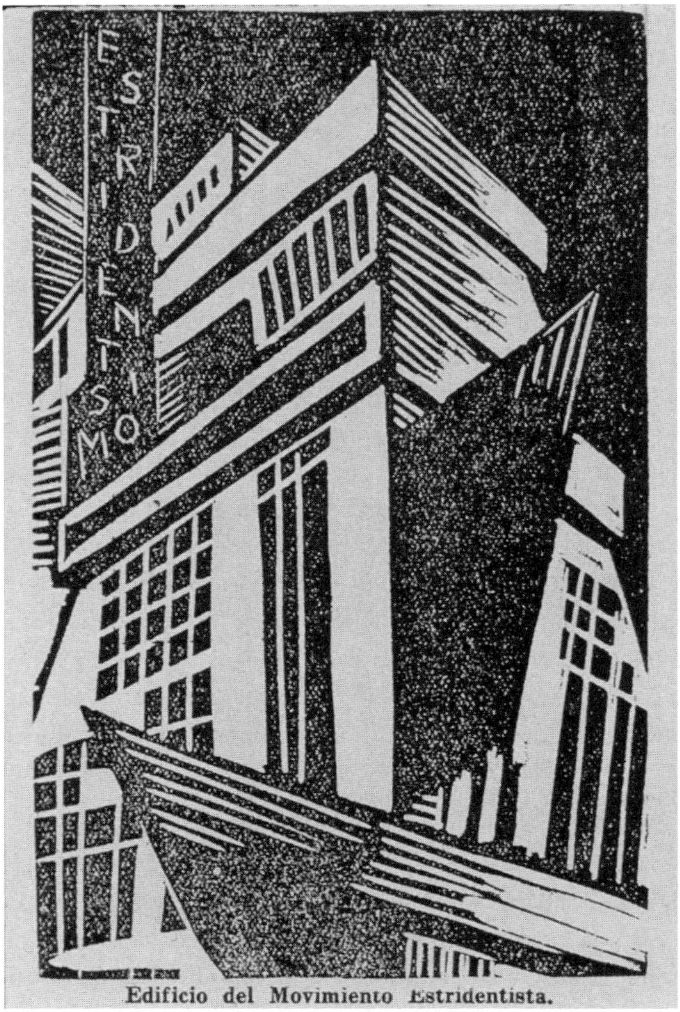

Figure 48. Estridentista building, from *El movimiento estridentista* by Germán List Arzubide, 1927.

Despite the group's overtly masculine tenor and its troubled sexual politics,[19] Modotti was drawn to this avant-garde movement, with its cataclysmic celebration of spatial geometry, thermodynamics, and architecture. To recall, Modotti often made photographs in a similarly austere style, as in a foreboding study of grids and angles formed by open doors inside a Mexico City flat (Figure 27). But to the pure formal studies of lines and planes and confined photographic space, Modotti's photography added a growing involvement in Mexican art and social life; in short, she theorized her practice of the camera as a technology capable of undermining authoritative fields, including those of a nation, which was not one, into redirected force. Álvarez Bravo admired Modotti's work in magazines such as *Forma* and *Mexican Folkways* even before they met in 1927. Another layer can be added to Modotti's composition that year of a worker's caked hands clasping a shovel handle, *Hands Resting on Tool* (Figure 32), when viewed in light of the Mexican photographer's *Study of Tamayo's Hands* (Figure 49), a 1931 negative that lay dormant until the 1990s. Both photographers repeatedly addressed, even in these abstract terms, the purpose of production in agrarian labor and aesthetic manufacture.

Diego Rivera, José Clemente Orozco, David Alfaro Siqueiros, and others led the muralist movement in Mexico, a colossal project that sought to elevate the nation's turbulent history, promote immediate social ideals, and determine a future political purpose.[20] Álvarez Bravo became fluent in the sweeping visual language of murals when he was assigned to photograph a number of pre-Hispanic wall paintings, the country's regional life and manual arts, as well as Rivera's modern frescos, for the magazine *Mexican Folkways* (edited by the U.S. American ethnographer Frances Toor).[21] Like Modotti before him—in the photographs she made on commission of murals by Rivera and Orozco—this experience for Álvarez Bravo also underlined the limits of photography, making conspicuous the medium's inability to represent the epic events of the past. If a photograph is bound to the

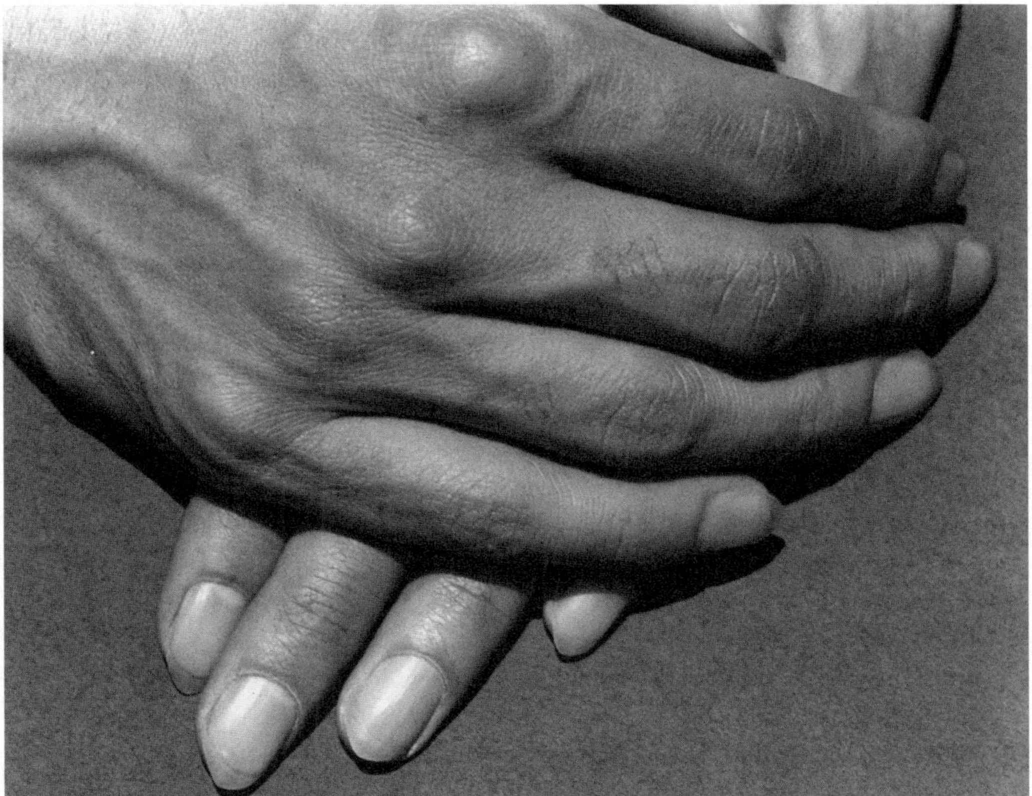

Figure 49. Manuel Álvarez Bravo, *Estudio de las manos de Tamayo (Study of Tamayo's hands)*, 1931. Digital image courtesy of Rose Gallery, Los Angeles.

present, how can the swell of history be represented with a camera? Questions of this kind haunted the relationship between the intents of photography and those of painting with a social purpose, leading the muralist Fernando Leal to write affirmatively of how Álvarez Bravo "crystallize[d] that nebulous state in which the subconscious takes hold of exterior objects and impels them to live an immaterial, embryonic life, almost diluted in the flow of abstract ideas."[22]

Like Modotti, who sought to retain the social content of seemingly abstract forms, Álvarez Bravo learned that one way to mirror crucial historic episodes was to give everyday objects, and imperceptible or possible relations, the heroic tenor of which they are generally deprived. If the political resolve of muralism had stressed the muscularity of events and human forces, the delicate hands captured by Álvarez Bravo emphasize singularity within the larger field of society and art, and they dispute the unapologetically masculine overtones of certain strands of modernity.

The grand project of muralism aimed to depict Mexican history, politics, and everyday life on a monumental scale. Another, less permanent type of mural also gained visual prominence in modern Mexico—the urban billboard. In the 1928–29 photograph *Two Pairs of Legs* (Figure 50), a fragment of signage displays two stylish pairs of legs over the word *inimitable.* Álvarez Bravo explores the contrast between two patterns: the imperfect grid of the advertisement and the rickety slats and windows of the Mexico City building behind it. With characteristic irony, he makes use of the divided plane to create a modern theme: the difference between the concrete world and its copies, as represented in a painted imitation or in the quasi-mirror likeness of a photograph.

Public signage and commercial endorsements in Mexico City contributed to forging what Williams describes as "the new relationships of the metropolis, and the inescapable new uses in newspapers and advertising attuned to it, [which] forced certain productive kinds of strangeness and distance: a new consciousness of conventions and thus of changeable, because now open, conventions."[23] This was especially conspicuous to the foreigner in Mexico: the radical cultural difference made photography more evident as a new medium than as a social custom. Taking his earliest inspiration from the kinds of works created by Weston and Modotti, Álvarez Bravo explored the structure of visible forms otherwise unavailable to the casual eye. In addition to studies of natural subjects, such as tree trunks and leaves, he compared shapes offered by the vernacular arts and those produced by industry and progress.

A photograph of a stack of volumes includes the spine of a work on Picasso, Maurice Raynal's 1922 monograph on the Spanish artist (*Books,* 1930s) (Figure 51). By employing personal effects to analyze the spatial geometry of shape and shadow, Álvarez Bravo was conscious of photography's ability to enlarge details into singular worlds unto themselves, that it was a medium at a remove from painterly

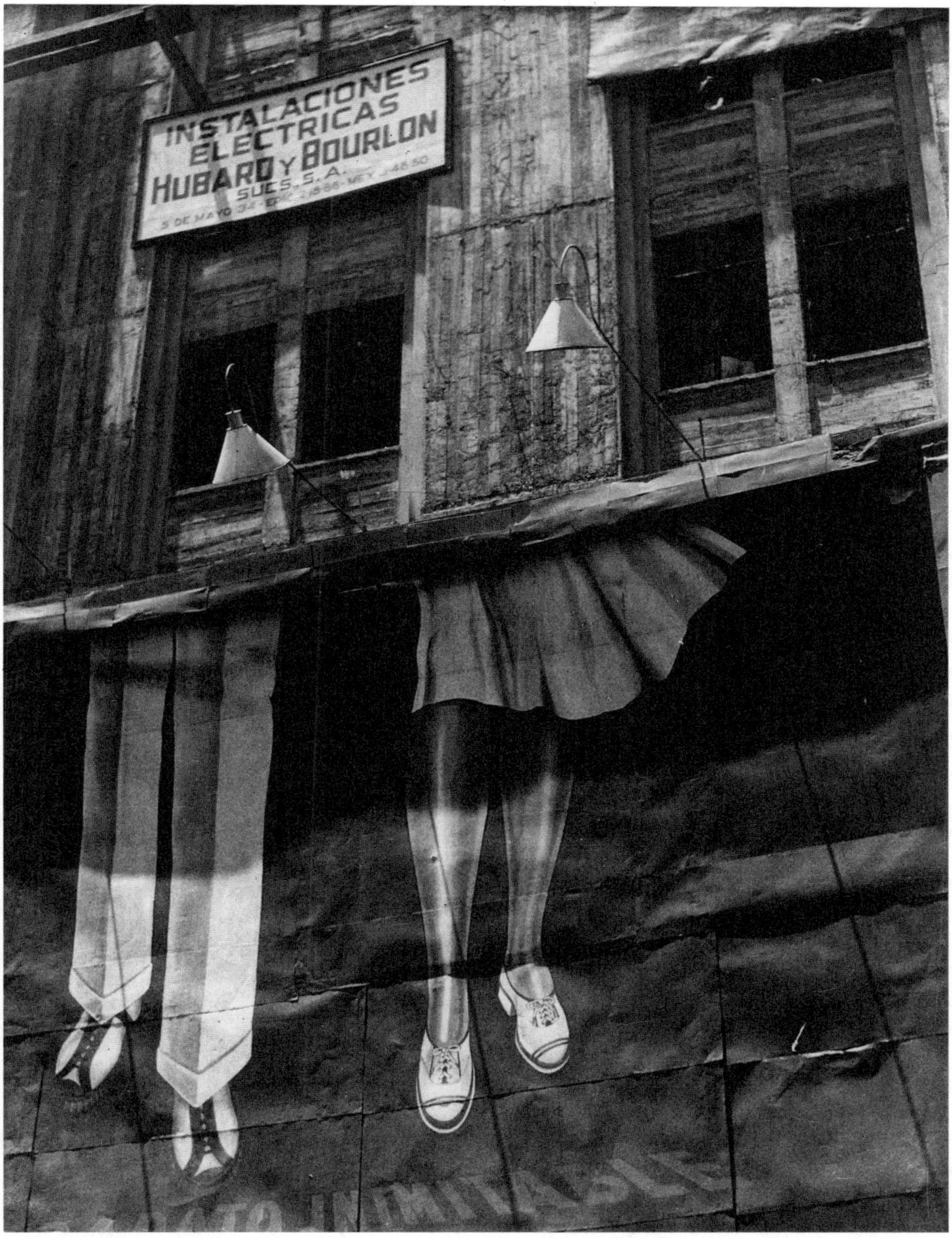

Figure 50. Manuel Álvarez Bravo, *Dos pares de piernas (Two Pairs of Legs)*, 1928–29. Digital image courtesy of Rose Gallery, Los Angeles.

representation but nevertheless an art-related practice of its own. With a reserved nod to the cataclysmic celebration of *estridentismo,* this image is less strident perhaps, but it nevertheless suggests the towering forms of modern architecture and the effects of bringing material and human energy together—as in a building or a book. The image is suggestive of the new ideals and social formations in Mexico's modernizing project described by writers such as Henríquez Ureña, and of their categorical link to a new system of representation, as recognized by Williams:

> Within the very openness and complexity of the metropolis, there was no formed and settled society to which the new kinds of work could be related. The relationships were to the open and complex and dynamic process itself, and the only accessible form of this practice was an emphasis on the medium: the medium as that which, in an unprecedented way, defined art.[24]

Although his work had repeatedly returned to explore the medium itself, the status of the object, and the constructed spaces made visible by the camera, in the 1930s Álvarez Bravo's photography began to focus on the visible social differences in the metropolis, with an eye to the undeniable conditions that separate the haves and the have-nots. These sobering images reveal the grim beauty Rivera possibly had in mind when he recognized the "intimate weave of tatters that clothe life itself," a fabric with which Álvarez Bravo expresses "the class struggle and tragedy over years and days."[25] *For the Sheep's Wool* (Figure 52), of 1932, was one of four images included in the decisive International Surrealism Exhibition organized in 1940 by André Breton, Wolfgang Paalen, and César Moro. In direct appeal to Christian iconography, the sheep lying dead on a curbside appears as if crowned by the tufts of grass growing around an adjoining telephone pole. The title refers to the animal's fleece as well as to money, gullibility, and sacrifice. Made two years later, *The Third Fall* (1934) alludes to the Stations of the Cross, but as linked to the real misery of Mexico: to downfall and defeat. It remains unclear whether the subject of the photograph is unconscious, asleep, or deceased. These photographs point to an important aspect of Álvarez Bravo's vision: in a societal disavowal—using high-angle shots and the logic of "downcast eyes"—the photographer began to collapse direct witnessing and visual metaphors, thereby including viewers as accessories to what often lies vanquished, sometimes directly at our feet.

In a 1934 photograph, *The Crouched Ones* (Figure 53), the framing coincides with the doorway of a Mexico City *comedor,* a type of eatery more commonly known throughout the country now as a *fonda económica,* usually a modest storefront serving a full-course midday meal at a cost affordable to the working and middle classes. The harsh sunlight, together with the straight-on perspective, creates a division of levels: the partly rolled-up metal curtain, the ominous but inviting darkness of the shade cast inside, and the half-obliterated figures of five seated men, their backs to the photographer in a moment of respite from the bustle of the streets.

Figure 51. Manuel Álvarez Bravo, *Libros (Books)*, ca. 1930. Digital image courtesy of Rose Gallery, Los Angeles.

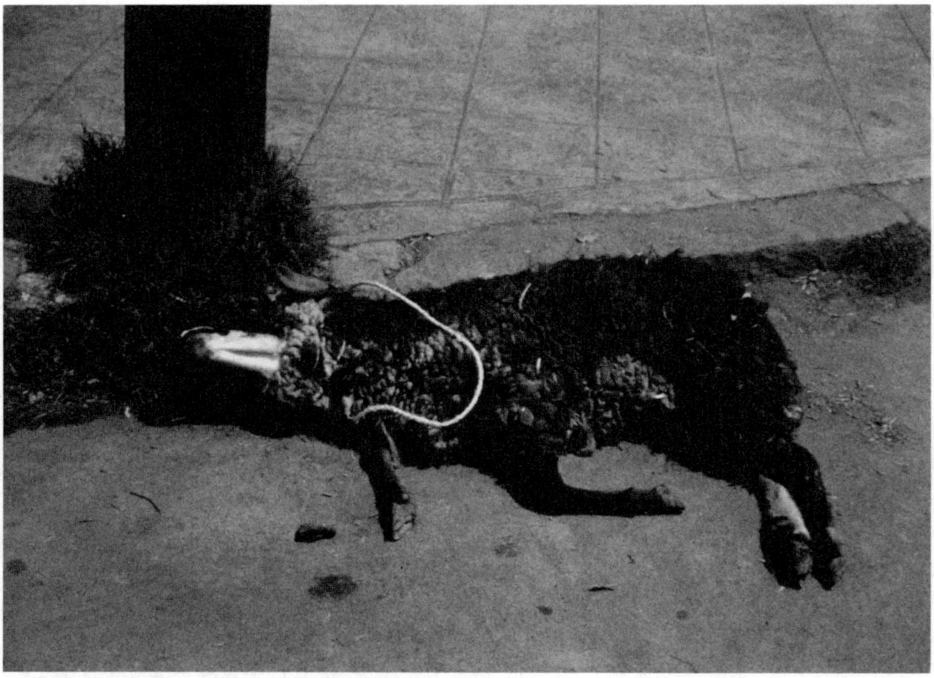

Figure 52. Manuel Álvarez Bravo, *Por la lana del borrego (For the sheep's wool),* 1932. Digital image courtesy of Rose Gallery, Los Angeles.

The African American modernist poet Langston Hughes, who spent significant time in Mexico, wrote about this picture in a review of a 1935 exhibition showcasing the work of Henri Cartier-Bresson and Álvarez Bravo: "Whereas the sun in a Bravo photo almost always has a sense of humor, one cannot be sure about the shadows. . . . The iron curtain is partly down, and the heads of the customers are in the shadow—so one can laugh about the feet."[26] In the following pages I examine the transnational nature of that 1935 exhibition; Hughes was optimistic about the poignant humor in the image, even as he pointed to the undecided status of what it depicted. One could also read the two shoe-shine boxes and the paint-splattered overalls as alluding to the hard manual labor performed by some of the men. The stools are chained to each other and to the counter, suggesting the human constraints of the workaday world and the partial anonymity of those destined to live their lives "crouched over"—as the title clearly suggests. Here, however, the figures are not crouched over but sitting upright: another element that exemplifies the contradictory nature of the scene. Just as the image captures a moment between work and leisure, the viewer is asked to consider the photograph in terms that shift between the social ironies of poetic description and the public space of rhetorical dissent. That is, the picture so confines as to expose self-divisions inside and outside the frame: between the personal, national, and class individual. It submits that the conditions for a citizenry of public culture in

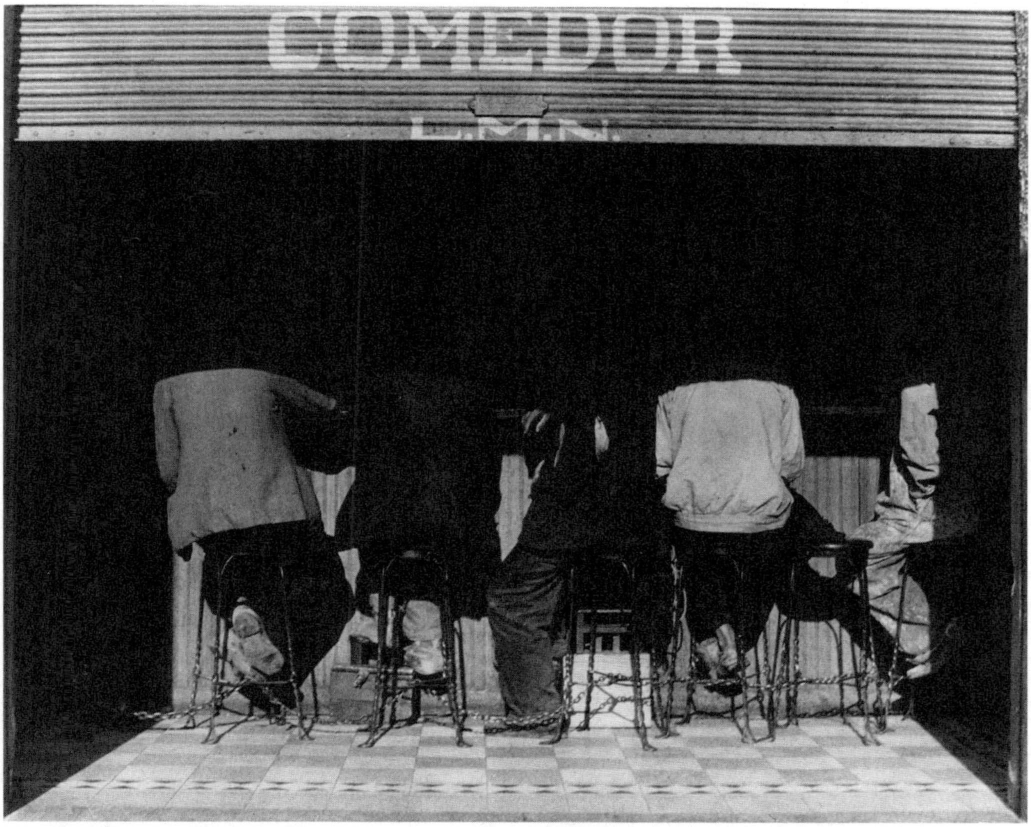

Figure 53. Manuel Álvarez Bravo, *Los agachados (The crouched ones)*, 1934. Digital image courtesy of Rose Gallery, Los Angeles.

Mexico (be it photographic or otherwise) appear only insofar as all subjects are inflected by labor, regardless of whether it can be readily cast into the shadows.

That life conditions appear to be accidental is a perception itself indebted to the bourgeoisie.[27] To view the emergence of class formations at stake in these and other photographs by Álvarez Bravo is to recall important aspects of Mexico City at the material and political levels. A new urban elite, which had benefited from, and capitalized on, the now established revolutionary institutions "embarked on programs of urban renewal, featuring the widening of thoroughfares, construction of diagonal avenues, the creation of new public buildings . . . and the destruction of older working class housing."[28] According to Anton Rosenthal, the metropolitan bourgeoisie indulged in fantasies whose raw material derived from rural attitudes and practices but whose final shape and structure were European.[29] If we consider the visual culture amassed by Brenner and Leighton, there is a sequence of photographs (Figures 54 and 55) that exposes the contradictions made apparent and solidified during the presidential terms of Plutarco Elías Calles (1924–28) and Emilio Portes Gil (1928–30), as evidenced in the material prosperity of the new urban elites. Of the years that led to the 1932 drop in Mexico's economy, linked to a hold on its exports and a worldwide recession, Brenner wrote: "There was a business boom and the Mexico City Country Club, sacred to the foreigner in Díaz days, had a new guest list. The old style roistering generals, accustomed to shoot the nicks off cognac bottles in congenial saloons, were metamorphosed into something more social. They played polo and their cars could be seen drawn up under the Country club awning."[30]

And Monsiváis asserts that there was at this time a mass acceptance of a new meaning to the Revolution—sudden wealth.

> Public morality became secularized and was emancipated of religious sanctions. It then managed to create civil and social sanctions. These included ostracism, repute, the overwhelming sense of lack. The key point in these punitive enterprises became inevitable: patriarchal sexism, and *the idolatry of private property*. . . . To be a nationalist is to do right by one's fatherland, to be fused in solidarity with one's compatriots. Upon discovering the content and shape of the country, the primordial pacts of a collectivity become elucidated and explained. Nationalism is the social morality that the State and the progressive sectors accept and promote alike.[31]

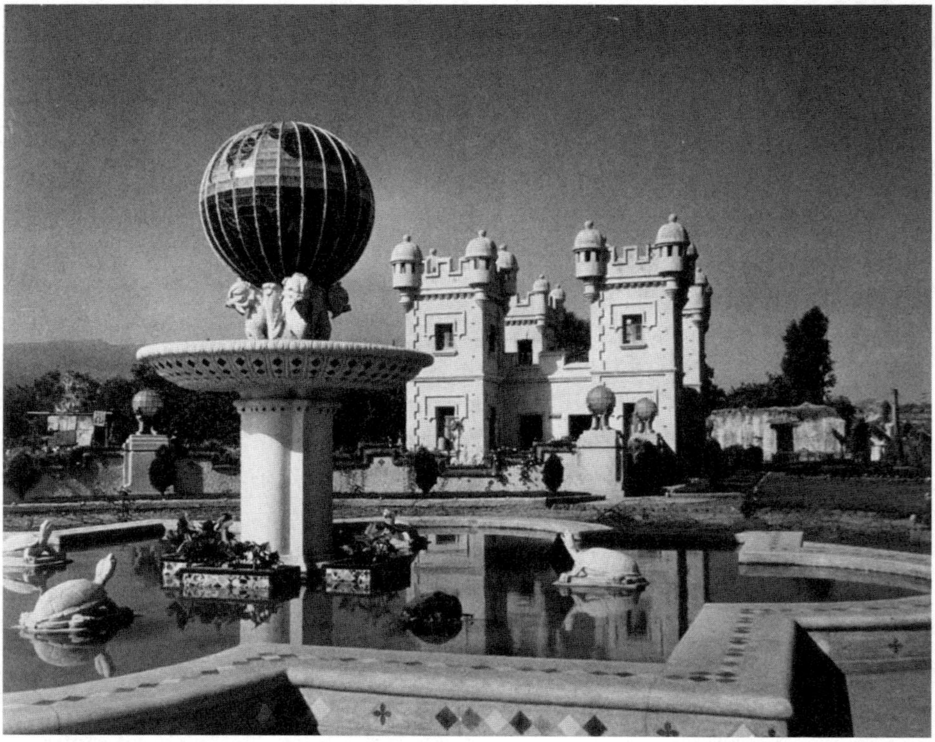

Figure 54. Ali Baba Street (Cuernavaca, Morelos). Photograph in *The Winds That Swept Mexico.* Image number 143. Photography Collection, Harry Ransom Humanities Research Center, University of Texas at Austin.

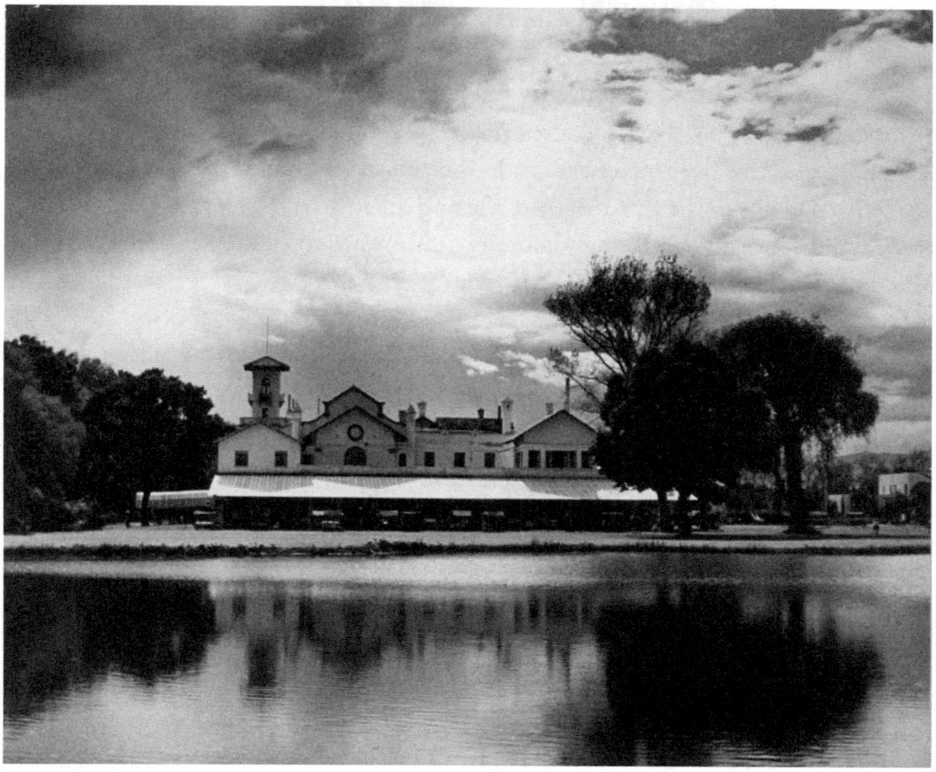

Figure 55. Mexico City Country Club. Photograph in *The Winds That Swept Mexico.* Image number 130. Photography Collection, Harry Ransom Humanities Research Center, University of Texas at Austin.

The metropolis was often deemed sacrosanct as the legitimate center of the nation's cultural legacy, of its residential concentration, administrative headquarters, and the seat of political power—and, no less important, the place where intellectual and artistic practice and socially relevant everyday business transpired. There, it was convenient for the new urban upper classes to maintain the seemingly accidental nature of class conditions in Mexico. Rosenthal reminds us that "in the construction of hotels, monuments, art museums, and new exclusive neighborhoods [was revealed] an elite decision to create a facade of Europeanization and then live within it, *to the point of making the public's space private and the elite's private space a public statement.*"[32]

Álvarez Bravo's photographs are almost entirely devoid of the material or metropolitan markers of political power. Unlike the muralists of the time whose project it was to accommodate representations of history to the current political structure—but far from supplying the patterns of power with a sense of self-identity in terms of the dominant and vacant nationalism to which Monsiváis refers—Álvarez Bravo turned to the differences excluded from Mexico City's public culture and from the political debate writ large. This is to describe what Sara Kofman called—in reference to the camera and photographic function as metaphors of ideology—an "inversion of the inversion."[33] Álvarez Bravo deprivatized public space as enacted by the new revolutionary elites, in order to make arguments about the workaday transit of modern subjects in Mexico, often nameless figures whose labor, "structures of feeling," life forms, and practices made the privatized public space of nationalist discourse possible in the first instance. During the important years of the 1930s and 1940s, he discovered increasingly more complex ways to frame the contradictions of Mexico's urban life into social statements with a distinct lyric vision mindful of precise composition and ironic—hence critical—metaphors.

The metropolis also became a locus for exploring sexual space, in that Álvarez Bravo's photography is indebted to women and to the meanings of feminine representation. In his pictures, feminine identity has a complex symbolic range where sex overlaps with other social identities of everyday life. Insofar as he employed the camera as a cultural tool, but aware that a photograph is a reflection largely cut off from its source, Álvarez Bravo emphasized how representation itself can shape ideas about the real social roles of men and women. In *Daydreaming* of 1931 (Figure 56), and other works like it, the relationship between mood and social content achieves a formal and emotional coherence.

Álvarez Bravo's childhood home, behind Mexico City's Metropolitan Cathedral, was one of many former colonial constructions converted into apartments and flats for Mexico City's working and lower-middle classes. On a visit at age twenty-nine to the courtyard of the building in which he grew up, Álvarez Bravo famously chanced on this adolescent girl immersed in her reverie. He quickly retreated in search of his photographic equipment and returned to discover that the focus of his fascination still remained entranced, oblivious to his presence.

The print is overcast in dark, creamy grays that envelop the figure, in keeping with the theme of reverie. The photographer and subject are separated, physically and metaphorically, by the railing of the upper-level balcony along the building's inner courtyard. The verticality of the bar structure converges at the corner, the handrail forming a horizontal chevron. The daydreamer's right foot rests awkwardly on the bottom rail as if in strained relation to the left hand that sustains the weight of her head. The overall listlessness of the scene suggests an awkward yearning for the future, or at least the disposition of adolescence as a liminal transition from girlhood to womanhood. Indeed, the subject's youth is pitted against the building's weathered state, evidenced by the missing stone tile on the bottom right. The sunlight caressing her right shoulder intensifies the feeling of human pause as interrupted by the camera. Here, daydreaming is embodied as that interval between consciousness and memory, be it personal or collective, even as contemplation and sensuousness convey a political inflection in the Marxian view of them not as lifeless objects but as practical, corporeal human activity. On the one hand, there is room to speculate whether the photographer indulges in a fantasy

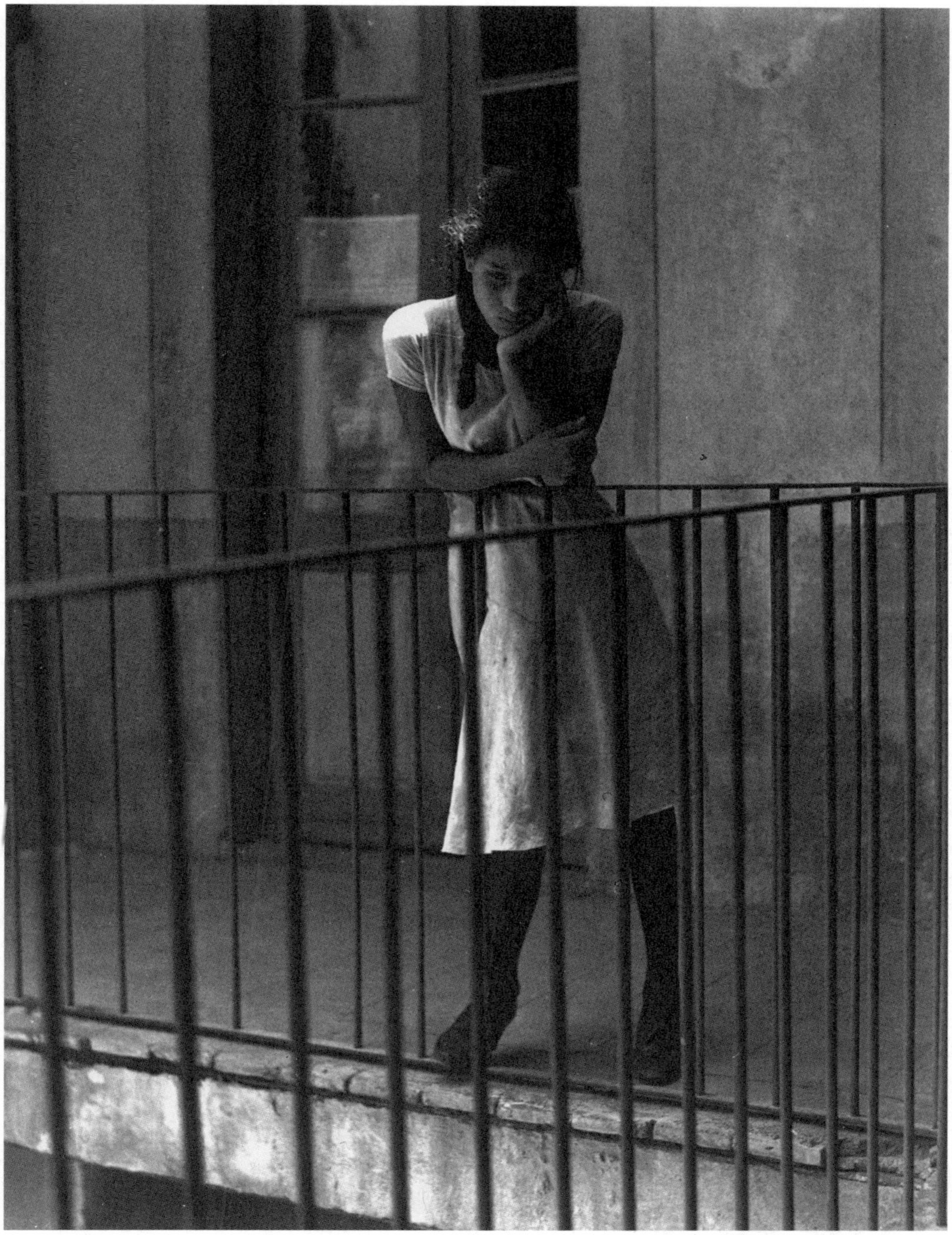

Figure 56. Manuel Álvarez Bravo, *El ensueño (Daydreaming),* 1931. Digital image courtesy of Rose Gallery, Los Angeles.

conflating autobiography with the shifting political geography posterior to the Mexican Revolution. On the other, this singular female subject troubles the assumptions of an exclusively masculine citizenship while reminding us also of the historical process ghosted now in the eroding built environment. On one level, the picture satisfies viewer class-consciousness in that there is no apparent antagonism between this adolescent representative of the working classes and the material living conditions of the private property that contains her. But in other terms, while reverie occludes an understanding of alienation, or makes it invisible, this life situation is nonetheless empowered by the human sensuous activity that is the practice of daydreaming.

Unnatural Coupling

Sexual difference and gender identity are further encapsulated even in those photographs from the 1930s and 1940s in which Álvarez Bravo revisited abstraction and the study of spatial relationships to form. In addition to certain shapes assembled expressly for the camera, there are those that he discovered by chance (or that were made to seem accidental). The distinct patterns produced by identical or miscellaneous objects were often used not only by Álvarez Bravo to achieve sober effects but also by such contemporaries as Agustín Jiménez and Emilio Amero (who reappears below as a link in the shared image environment that emerged in the 1930s among Mexico City, Paris, and New York). Álvarez Bravo especially sought out the conspicuous surfaces of floors and walls as he captured fortuitous encounters of incongruous elements that abound in Mexico, providing further nuance to the claim that his abstract photographs were never other than "exact documents." It is difficult to determine whether an accident occurred or the hand of purpose intervened in *Hair on Tile,* a suggestive image depicting a lock of long, wavy hair on a tile floor with a design of stars or crosses. In the upper right-hand corner, the leg of a chair or table suggests how the extended stage of some ambiguous incident may well have led to the ensuing picture. Whatever else it may allude to, and not without a certain sense of delight in the artifice of the photographic moment, the image of hair evokes a realm of dreams or taboos, of folklore or legend. In theme and form, the photograph is divided between the hint of seduction and that of punishment, between outward signs of the feminine and those of the fetish. Even as women and perversity are cast into a similar logic, the image also ironizes the photographic process: while objects, like ideas, may insinuate the appearance of being self-sufficient or distinct, they are never entirely detached from the chain of their own genesis.

Following a structure of affirmation and overturning, Álvarez Bravo made two iconic photographs, one in 1934, the other in 1938, inciting dissonance between what an image contains and what a title conveys, that is, between appearance and identification. Accordingly, this juncture compels the discussion put forward by

Rosalind Krauss in her various writings on corporeal depiction in the uncertain undertaking of surrealism in photography. Surrealist methods were a function and effect whose origins are found in the *informe,* a term distinguishing thought when, at the limit of categories, its features restrict but cannot entirely delimit the terms of its composition.

Georges Bataille—whose journal, *Documents,* I discuss below—activated this concept for the "removal of all those boundaries by which concepts organize reality, dividing it up into little packages of sense."[34] To the degree that thought can be conceived as unstructured—a nakedness that bourgeois society window-dresses into ill-fitted fashion—Krauss identifies the appearance of surrealist differences in a photographic technique. To rotate the (chiefly female) body and to undertake its alteration is to produce a desired effect: disorientation, perplexity, confusion, or bafflement. Body parts are presented in the *conditional* mood—as though breasts were horns and arms ears—to create extravagant and unexpected metaphors of excess, amazement, and wonder. This conditional signature—made by means of the camera's *hold* on its object: an axial rotation from vertical to horizontal—releases a syntax of inversion, of radical low angles, foreshortening, and close-ups.

It also inaugurates a spatial device, a "doubling," that causes human subjects to resemble—that is, "decline" into—the condition of animals: "The camera automates this process, makes it mechanical, a button is pushed and the fall is the rest."[35] Disintegration is favored over the manufacture of form, so that human subjectivity in surrealist inclination is no longer seized by internal reflexivity. (It is in this sense that Álvarez Bravo depicted reverie in *Daydreaming.*) Instead, bodies are assaulted from the *outside in,* that is, the visual formations that psychoanalysis and surrealism describe are a "mastery from without, imposed on the subject who is trapped in a cat's cradle of representation, caught in a hall of mirrors, lost in a labyrinth."[36] Dispossession is the outcome of any enticement to merge, and loss of selfsameness is the price paid after the allure of incorporation. A subject's relation to space is constitutive of the image environment in that it structures the site and setting for representation.[37]

At variance with the Paris of his European counterparts, the space of the metropolis in Mexico City was for Álvarez Bravo the locality of lopsided social relations born of first- and second-order economies that mirrored each other in a surrealist doubling of their own. Both in the political seat of the city and the rural spaces that constituted a national narrative, Mexico was the subject of a capitalist venture where the body politic was seized by metropolitan space as caught between differences doubled in the interval from peripheries to their center. In the following pages I return to Bataille's *Documents,* and its relevance to the photography of Álvarez Bravo and others, activated in terms of the commercial art-market economy, namely, in the figure of the North American entrepreneur Julien Levy. For the moment, however, I turn to two images where sexual difference is distributed between a rural and urban violence, between an actual and simulated death.

In *Striking Worker, Murdered* of 1934 (Figure 57), the photographer makes viewing an act rendered wordless to the degree that a camera has the capacity to capture in one sense the unspeakable reality of a death—in this case, an unapologetic and brutal one. The story leading to this image has often been remarked, and it was Álvarez Bravo himself who situated the incidents within the Lázaro Cárdenas presidential administration beginning in 1934, the year of this photograph. Álvarez Bravo was taking film footage in the Isthmus of Tehuantepec, "a place highly prized by the muralists and painters" as well as by foreigners like Cartier-Bresson, Sergei Eisenstein, and Paul Strand.

> I was [filming and making photographs in Tehuantepec] when all of a sudden I heard sounds I thought were firecrackers or rockets, and so I turned to aim my movie camera at a group of striking workers. I filmed and then with my still camera continued to capture other scenes; I was in no hurry. I stayed in one spot to see what would happen, and even with nothing about to take place, I'd have waited for something to happen. . . . Soon I heard the firecrackers again and saw someone darting away. I asked him where the festivities were taking place, and

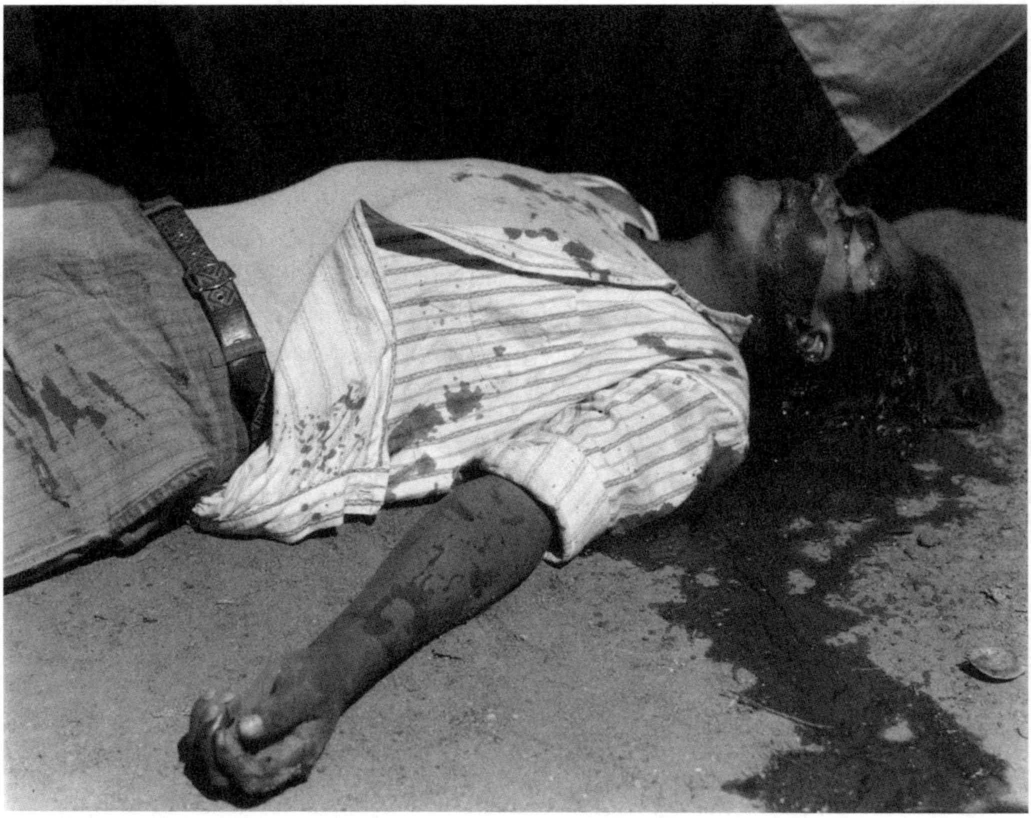

Figure 57. Manuel Álvarez Bravo, *Obrero en hulega, asesinado (Striking worker, murdered)*, 1934. Digital image courtesy of Rose Gallery, Los Angeles.

> laughing out loud he cried, "Near the train station, hurry!" On my shoulders I strapped the wind-up film camera (with all but a hundred feet of film) and my Graflex. On the way, I ran into a young man who was staying at the same hotel I was. He was one of those scoundrels who made money reselling gold from women in Tehuantepec. I asked him to help me with the camera in order to get there faster. What firecrackers? They were gunshots! Upon arriving I came across the man in my photograph *Striking Worker, Murdered.* He was a laborer in the sugar mill owned by a woman who was a personal friend of the local elected official. When I began to make the picture, someone vehemently warned, "Beat it, you have no idea what you're getting yourself into"—to be sure, one has no idea of the dangers in this line of work.[38]

With two frames left in his Graflex camera, Álvarez Bravo took this image very close to the corpse, low enough to the ground to render the murdered worker's arm as if in muralist foreshortening. This photograph is rightfully celebrated for its angle and framing, which suggest the photographer's apparent dissolution. The image certainly contains a critical detachment or political imperative, even as it underlines a brutal crime. It also achieves its effect without denying the victim's handsome features. (Álvarez Bravo: "He had a very youthful body, face and hands. I think his name was Rosendo.") Further, while noticeably absent from the photograph, other figures are ghosted in this image. In his verbal account, Álvarez Bravo makes present the indigenous women of Tehuantepec and the wife of a political boss who was responsible for the encapsulated crime, such that crucial to the photograph's meaning are these agents or subjects in the power relations connecting historic subjects in a violent political landscape of the national.

One of Álvarez Bravo's classic female nudes—arguably among his most celebrated and emblematic images—can be reexamined, especially in regard to what it has to say about canonical surrealist conventions regarding woman and feminine physical beauty as a projected masculine locus and shifting convention, especially the eroticism in fixed or "lifeless" renderings of the female body. This 1939 image, *La buena fama durmiendo* (Figure 58), is not without its difficulties in terms of sexual politics, beginning with its title, translated as *The Good Reputation Sleeping.* In it, the smooth naked body of a young Mexican model—lithesome light-brown skin in black-and-white—lies on her back, face to the sun, with eyes shut and her left hand as a pillow beneath her head, her right leg slightly crossed over her left knee. In a reclining position, she is almost completely nude—but for the white bandages around her left ankle and around her waist and thighs—and her pubic hair is left exposed. She lounges across a dark blanket whose pattern is composed of alternating bars and stripes. In contrast to the concrete floor and textured wall (a veritable abstract expressionist landscape behind her) are four star cacti strewn along her left side, the sharp needles alternately blurred and in high contrast. A visual–linguistic sexual pun is established between the subject's closed eyes, crossed

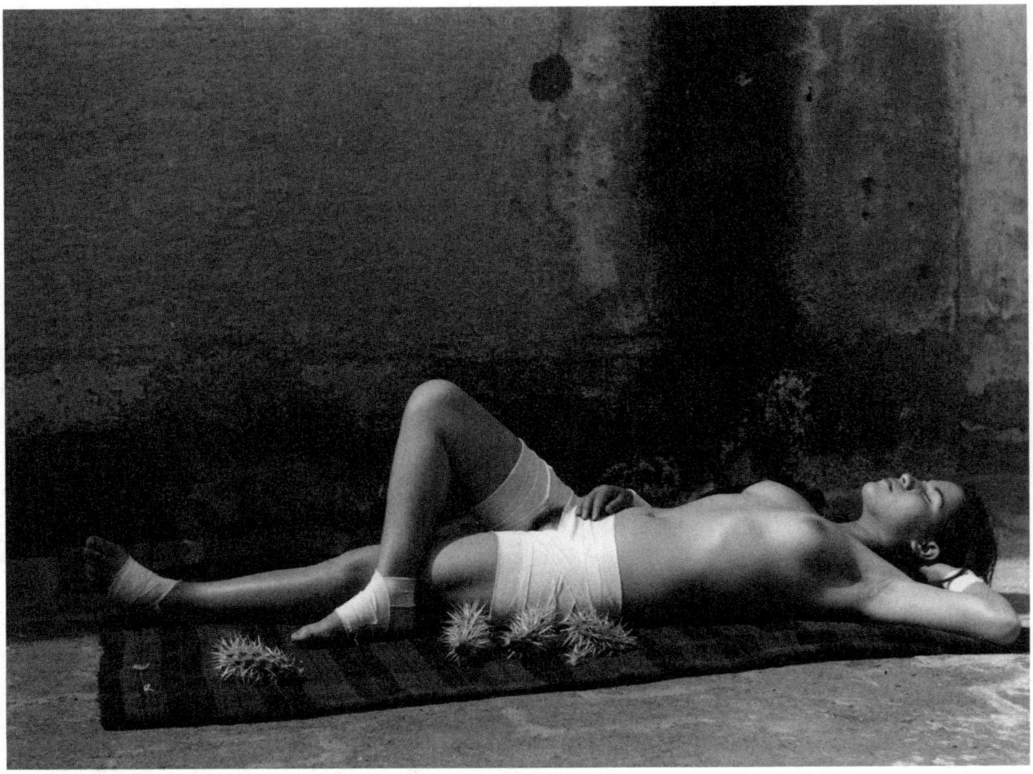

Figure 58. Manuel Álvarez Bravo, *La buena fama durmiendo (The good reputation sleeping),* 1939. Digital image courtesy of Rose Gallery, Los Angeles.

legs, exposed pubis, and these four star cacti, whose name in Spanish is "abrojo," suggesting, by slight elision, the word "abreojo," which might be loosely translated as "eyes-wide-open."

The image is the result of an abrupt, now famous telephone petition on behalf of Breton while Álvarez Bravo was at the Academia de San Carlos in Mexico City—awaiting his paycheck.[39] The image Breton sought was to be the cover photograph of the catalog to accompany the International Surrealist Exhibition. In a sudden convergence of happenstance and inclination, the thirty-seven-year-old Álvarez Bravo immediately went to work on staging the subsequent mise-en-scène, employing the services of the young academy model Alicia and the help of his friend Dr. Francisco Arturo Marín (who provided the bandages).

This dialectic of chastity, beckoning, menace, conquest, and violation is, not surprisingly, in perfect keeping with the canonical masculine-centered perspective of French surrealism: what Walter Benjamin identified with regard to Breton's Nadja as "a world that borders not only on tombs of the Sacred Heart or alters to the Virgin, but also on the morning before a battle or after a victory."[40] The *Good Reputation Sleeping* demands to be read side by side with other portrayals of women in Álvarez Bravo's visual production, images that testify to the interaction between photographer and subject, a dance of command and seduction as she undresses and applies or removes the bandages herself on the rooftop of the Academia de San Carlos. Together, these and other images make discernible the imposing spaces between sociosexual content and anonymous transit, the jarring angle between living figure and lifeless object.

If a photograph is always more than it frames at any moment in time, then a first-order viewing of this image and its masculine-centered overtones may well surrender its authority under extended examination. Does a viewer's gaze deny the photographer's voluntary or involuntary purposes, the very fixity of the image, to prevail? Is it beside the point, my looking at this model, this Alicia sublimated into the patrimonial value of a "good reputation"? Or does my regard belie the conventional equation of woman with the telluric? Can my viewing bring latencies out of immanence to counter Alicia's *to-be-looked-at-ness*? Does Alicia's face, relaxed and untroubled, persevere in the pleasures I attribute to her luxuriating in the Mexico City sunlight? Is the mood a menacing one—or a pleasure independent from the act of image making that brings Alicia now into being before another viewer looking? Is there further unease dormant in the photograph to be underlined? And if so, whose reputation and whose gaze are thereby in question? Can a claim of ambiguity be made regarding Alicia's right leg gently crossed over her left thigh, as though in that gesture she were released from the endless visual chain of formal conquest and possession into a kind of virtual self-command? And on whose volition will this depend? Is an optimistic view necessarily a privileged one, a latency that is the other side of determinacy in Alicia as an image? Can these considerations on the logic of the visible and the politics of the image fully acknowledge their debt to the actual body—now unattainable except by analog—of Alicia as she once posed for the photographer in 1938?

These questions offer an alternate reading of this image despite the power relations inherent between photographer and sitter, with Alicia as virtual cocreator of what has become one of Álvarez Bravo's most iconic images. The photographer complicates the codes of visual and erotic impact by staging a contrast between the dynamics of overall viewing—the sexual difference on both sides of the camera—with the mutuality of the photographic subject involved in a series of possible defiance to the camera's would-be totalizing eye. This is very likely why fabrics or bandages are a leitmotiv in many of his photographs. By framing the figure of a woman with various drapes that cover and disclose, Álvarez Bravo disputes the idea of a photograph as "reality unveiled," affirming instead the fabricated nature of appearances. As Kofman claims in *The Camera Obscura of Ideology*: "An idea is a reflection cut off from its source, engendering phantoms, fantasies, simulacra and fetishes."[41]

Side by side, *Striking Worker, Murdered* and *The Good Reputation Sleeping* betray an alternate surrealist affinity than that which equates eroticism and physical demise. Together as renderings—factual or fabricated, male or female—they complicate distinctions between the body as vital subject or potentially lifeless object, and they underline the difference between the surface of appearance and the less visible workings of perception, both sexual and social. In so many images by Álvarez Bravo, weathered walls are the backdrop to fortuitous encounters or incongruous elements—physical labor and language play, sensuality and brutality, injury and redress, social eye-witnessing and ironic metaphor—all these elements are suggested in these two photographic icons. A transfiguration of things "above and behind appearances" was the phrase Rivera used to describe Álvarez Bravo's photography.[42]

Álvarez Bravo had already come into contact with surrealism long before the making of *The Good Reputation Sleeping,* possibly through such magazines as *Minotaure,* where Breton later published nine images by the Mexican photographer along with a text that recognized the lyric quality of the pictures and what he referred to as a "fate seen only in clairvoyant glimpses."[43] Álvarez Bravo acknowledged that the surrealist movement may have led him to produce work under its influence, and one could reasonably argue that the photo-collage titled *Sympathetic Nervous System* (ca. 1930) was so inspired. Pointing to fashion as a standardizing process or as sexual subordination, Álvarez Bravo comments on the sociology of taste in this picture of an advertisement for women's slimming corsets, over which he has affixed, with the actual clasps used to attach seamless stockings to a garter or corset, a cutaway view of a male torso in profile. These elements speak of power and desire between the sexes, even as the picture suggests how aesthetic styles, like fashion itself, are often abandoned when they become generalized and commonplace. This suggestive conjunction raises the issues of photography's role in the mass media of magazine design and advertising, social patterns that lead to "improving" feminine appearance—as he did in *The Good Reputation Sleeping*—and the acute pleasures at stake in the fetishistic act of looking at the slightly forbidden.

This brings us to the function and effects of looking (fetishistic or otherwise) in the photography of Álvarez Bravo. A remarkable aspect of his work, especially clear in many of his classic photographs, is the way he draws the viewer—and the very act of viewing—into the image. As observers attempt to decipher the cultural or formal elements depicted in certain pictures, observation itself comes under scrutiny. His work is an extended meditation on the nature of looking and the medium of photographic reproduction, as evidenced in images that abound in references to sight and visibility.

Difference and discontinuity are two hallmarks of Álvarez Bravo's photographs, especially as such discrepancies and fractures relate to the sexed phenomenon of looking and the shifting boundaries of vision and voyeurism. For psychoanalysis, the split between the eye and the gaze constitutes a dialectic in which "there is no coincidence, but, on the contrary, a lure." *Optical Parable* of 1931 (Figure 59), made from the perspective of a passerby looking up from a city sidewalk, shows an optician's shop with an oval hanging sign, but the picture is reversed. Because Álvarez Bravo claims to have originally printed the negative normally (Figure 60), this version invites speculation about its origin and whether the transposition was deliberate or the result of a felicitous accident in the darkroom, a question that further enhances the meanings of these two images.

The name of the business, "La Óptica Moderna," literally means "the modern optician," but it can also be read as "the modern viewpoint." The Spanish title of the picture, *Parábola óptica,* is also a play on words: *parábola* denotes parabola and parable, as if to suggest the mutual connection between shapes and their meaning, no matter how disjointed they appear. In this mood, the reversed names on the sign and glass—E. Spirito and A. Spirito—refer not only to the two opticians, who, in keeping with the two versions of this image, are presumably related to each other. Their last name, which can be read as *espíritu* (spirit)—evoking the Latin blessing "spirito, spirito sancti"—becomes an irreverent quip about the material vehicle that contains the otherwise ghostlike photographic image. With actual references to the human eye, the "parable" of the picture is about the unreliability of looking, about visual afterthoughts or the alteration of viewpoint, and therefore about the nature of photography itself. Exploring the difference between design and metaphor in this and other images, Álvarez Bravo made visible reference to the undersurface of what we see and to our overconfidence in appearances.

Like the photographic process itself, where positive and negative values are flipped to be inverted once again, Álvarez Bravo proposed not a negative view of the historical (as in the case of muralism, which sought present legitimacy in the artifice of the former or archaic) but a positive appraisal of the undervalued, even in the new contradictions of the post-Revolutionary period.

> The point of view [that] sees relations as inverted is that neither of error or illusion. It is that of a certain kind of mind—an anti-artistic one—which wants to see reality without veils, naked, from the point of view of indecency. Naked, in broad daylight, outside of the dark chamber of consciousness. It is the perspective of those who are unaware that, behind the veil, there is yet another veil. It is the symptomatic unawareness of the instincts' loss of virility. To seek the unveiling of truth is to reveal that one no longer knows . . . about—or doesn't want to know about—the differences between the sexes: fetishistic denial. The inverted point of view is that of perverse judgment, by instincts neither strong enough nor fine enough to love appearances for appearances sake.[44]

Álvarez Bravo did not see relations as inverted but as inversions of an inversion through the political and formal process of representation. His achievement was one of engaging public space, the working classes, and sexual difference while resisting the post-Revolutionary state's ideological commitment to depoliticize, by

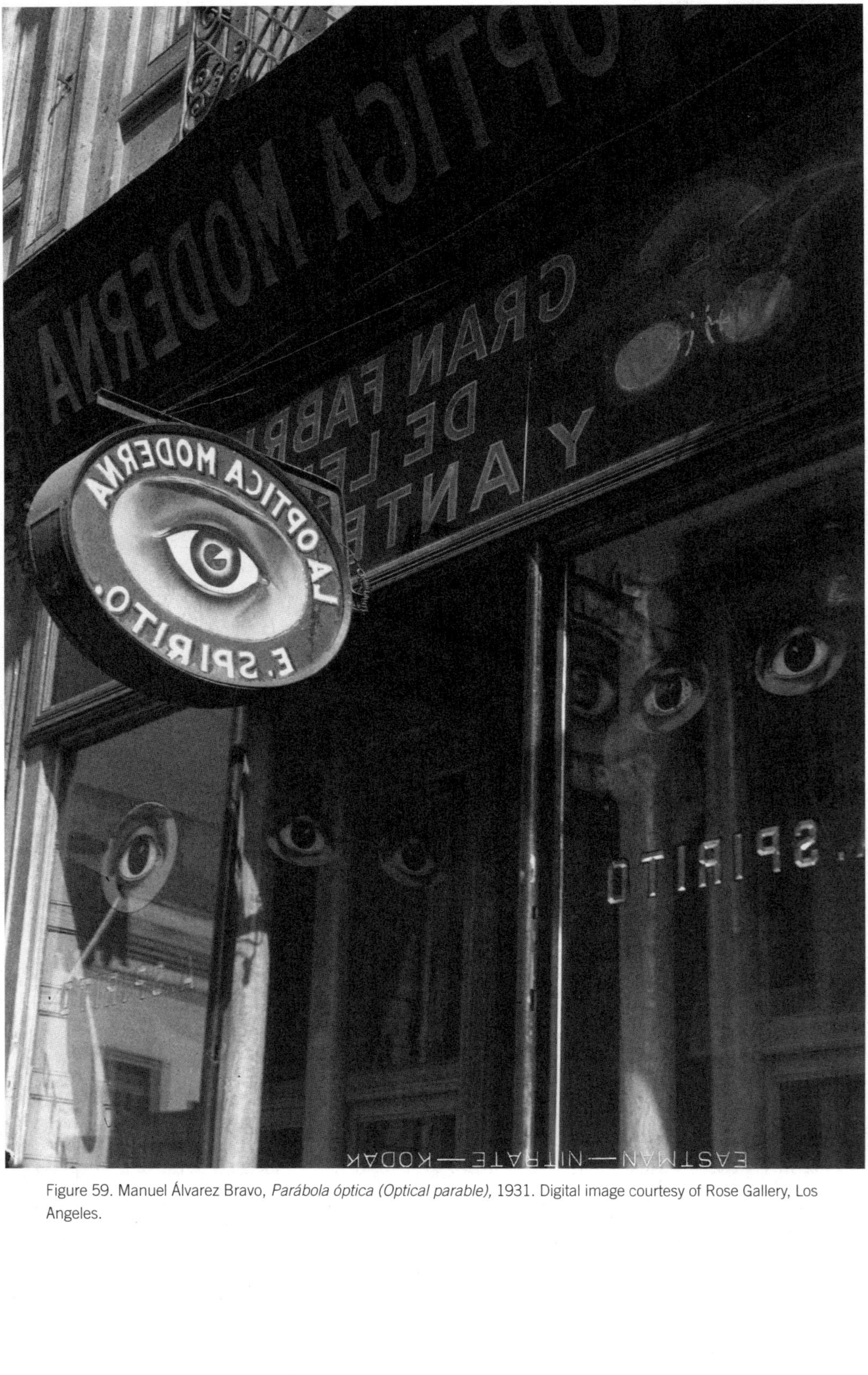

Figure 59. Manuel Álvarez Bravo, *Parábola óptica (Optical parable),* 1931. Digital image courtesy of Rose Gallery, Los Angeles.

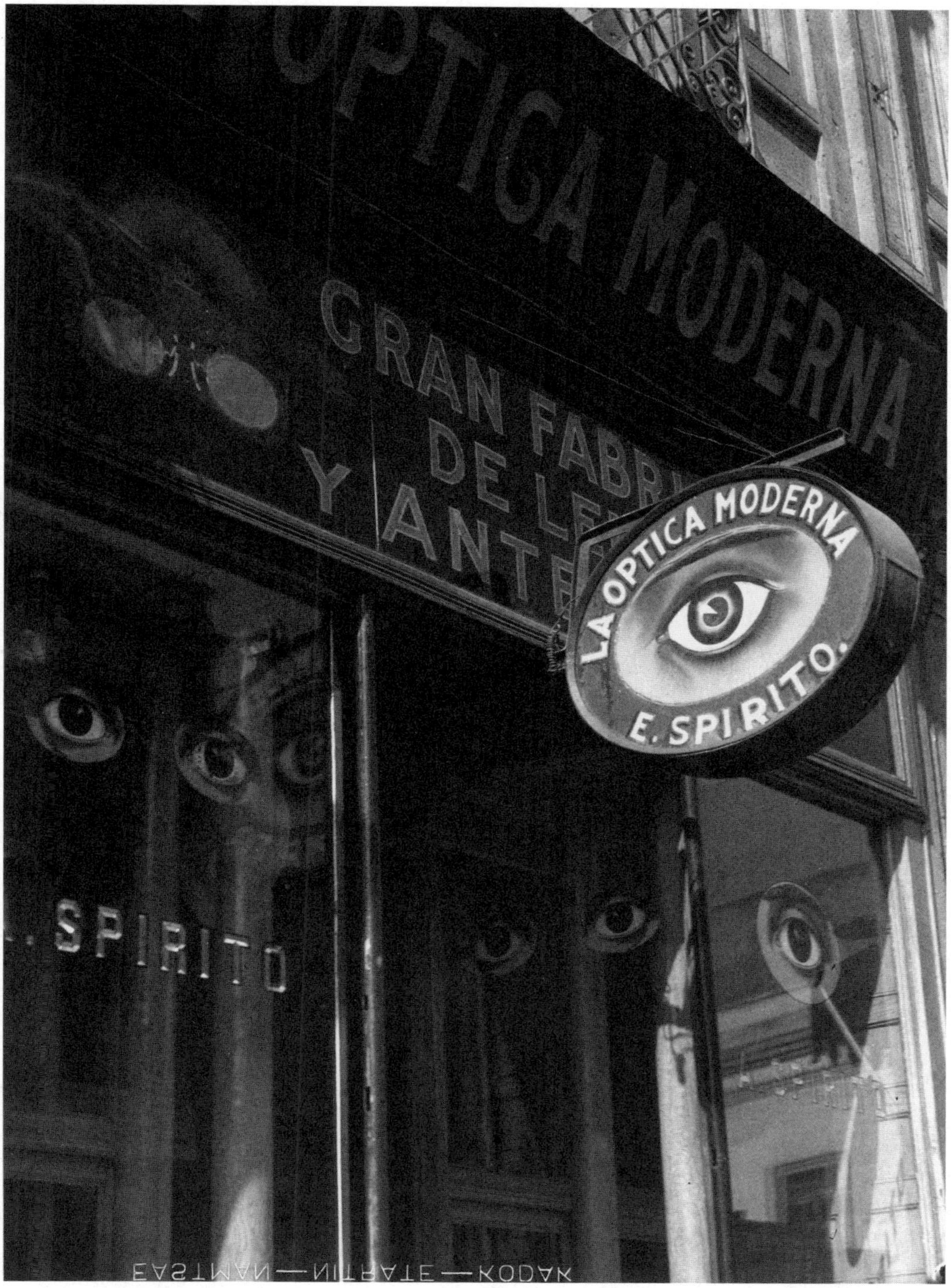

Figure 60. Manuel Álvarez Bravo, *Parábola óptica (Optical parable),* noninverted photograph. Digital image courtesy of Rose Gallery, Los Angeles.

replacing politics with morals and the rhetoric of nationalism. Álvarez Bravo's "inversion of the inversion" is established through material culture and the spectacle of the public space, hence the importance of representation (in the sense of constituency, display, semblance, and mimesis) against the kind of nationalism that sought to blur the social contradictions long after the Revolution. Through his lens, Mexico City becomes a site not of moral, or heroic, but of social relationships and material clashes. His lyric temperament elevated many images into icons that capture the unexpected combinations of everyday existence in urban and rural Mexico. This work has lent aesthetic insight into Mexico's actual and imaginative headwaters of history, landscape, and contemporary reality. Álvarez Bravo examined how photography, as a form of memory, is forever a modified fraction cut out of duration and also a meaningful cultural depository. The tension between this pursuit of timelessness and that of exacting a portrayal of society is a central quality of his work.

In this attention to physical, metaphoric, and ideological contradictions, Álvarez Bravo conveyed his inverted visual analogies of the always already inverted—of the social body as an idealized and actual life-form suited for expressive acts yet with a material substance at base. Side by side with his portrayal of female nudes, his pictures of laboring male bodies reveal how social effects are not always outwardly visible at the intersections of class and gender. By making other corporeal comparisons and contiguities, by portraying the ephemeral and finite nature of the built environment in contrast to the open-ended quality of photographic meanings, the photographer documents how actual and metaphoric figures advance together in a network of practices and events, both social and cultural. From this exchange between ordinary life and photographic perception, Álvarez Bravo rendered highly profitable returns from the social energy set in motion between the pleasures of visual appeal and the political promise of semantic ambiguity.

Equivocal, Ambivalent, Antiplastic

I want to give final cadence to a brand of transatlantic surrealism by placing photography not at the margins of the market economy but at its center. For this, in effect, is what occurred as made effective by a focal art-gallery enterprise. Álvarez Bravo recalled how Amero had "lived for extended periods of time in New York [where] he taught photography and print-making. . . . In all likelihood—I don't know if it was before or after his own solo show—he arranged the Levy exhibit of Cartier-Bresson, [Walker Evans,] and myself."[45] In a letter written during the mid-1970s, Álvarez Bravo referred to the mid-1930s link between his own work, Amero's, and—of particular importance to what follows—the influential Julien Levy Gallery in New York. I submit that Álvarez Bravo's photographs cannot be contained too readily, for his work historicized visual links in excess also of the boundaries defined by the social and cultural formations in Mexico at the time. As a participant in the double movement that was modernist image making and its alliances with public or commercial agencies, Bravo can also be linked with an important American cultural promoter to provide an additional view of the diverse links between surrealism and photography. These associations are marked with historic resonance, especially as they coalesced in the 1930s and 1940s around the Levy Gallery. Not only was a singular brand of exhibition practice inaugurated at this dynamic art space and creative center, where spheres of artistic production, previously seen as incompatible, were overlapped and transvalued. As a case study of the ways cultural power shifted from Paris to New York, it also made visible the contours of an often excluded term—that of Mexico's parallel modernity. To look then, even briefly, at the Levy Gallery's 1935 exhibition that connected Cartier-Bresson, Evans, and Álvarez Bravo is to trace one of numerous diagrams in the history of surrealism that might join it to the questions I want to explore here of transcultural relevance.

Recent scholarship has uncovered the complex role Levy played as one of modernism's crucial entrepreneurs.[46] Equal parts public personality, private collector, *marchant,* and disinterested cultural promoter of the avant-garde, Levy is a link between so many of the protagonists of the cultural movements that emerged between the two world wars.[47] Significantly, he also happened to be the son-in-law of the extraordinary modernist poet and visual artist Mina Loy. Both as an in-law, friend, and arts mentor, Loy was an important figure whose guidance and sponsorship cannot be overestimated.[48] With radical taste and affinity added to her beau monde savvy, Loy communicated her modernist values to Levy as she likewise won his entry into the salons of bohemian and expatriate Paris during his 1927 sojourn. When he finally opened his New York gallery four years later, Loy continued to serve as his Paris representative.

Levy had been an early collector of works by Marcel Duchamp, the friend who first compelled him to visit Europe. In Paris, already a self-professed (if ambiguous) admirer of Alfred Stieglitz,[49] Levy soon became an unconditional enthusiast of Paul Nadar and the surrealist idol Eugène Atget. ("One of Atget's photographs appearing in Breton's magazine *Surrealist Revolution,* had caught my eye. 'Pass by and knock on his door any afternoon at all,' Man Ray urged. 'If he is in you will be welcomed.'")[50] Levy attributed his uncommon acceptance of photography as a fine art, preceding these personal encounters and connections, to his early training at Harvard University.[51] In his published memoirs, Levy wrote: "I became seriously interested in cinema as an art form and combined with my art history courses some work in the physics of optics and the psychology of vision. . . . when I opened my gallery of contemporary art, one of my initial interests was to promote the recognition of photography as a form of modern art."[52]

"American Photography: Retrospective Exhibition," a kind of homage to Stieglitz, was Levy's 1931 inaugural launch at the gallery's first space on 602 Madison Avenue (November 2–20). On display were images by Matthew Brady, Strand, Charles Sheeler, Steichen, Clarence White, Gertrude Käsebier, and Stieglitz himself. In what remained of that year, and during the immediate ones to follow, the Levy Gallery hosted successive exhibitions that comprised photography, either prominently or exclusively. These included the 1932 "Surréalism" show,[53] a dual exhibition of Nadar and Atget, and solo exhibits of Ray, Berenice Abbott, Lee Miller, George Platt Lynes, and Amero, as well as group retrospectives such as "Modern European Photography"[54] or others that included antecedent figures such as Julia Margaret Cameron or David Octavius Hill.[55]

Levy's art world affiliations and breadth of curiosity ranged widely, and indiscriminately, through popular culture, fashion, entertainment, the decorative arts, performance, and the art of the cartoon. This eclecticism was reflected not only in gallery exhibits but in "his own line of photo objects, *trompe-l'oeil* wastebaskets and lampshades" that he sold alongside the more elevated artworks.[56] This sensibility was further reflected in his embrace of all forms of the new photography, from the "objective" image or the photomontage to Ray's rayographs, Miller's solarized pictures, and Cornell's daguerreotype portraits, together with stock newspaper images and film stills. The heterogeneity of photographic practices legitimated by Levy at his gallery was destined to contribute to the debates at the time about the vexed location of photography with regard to the other visual arts, not to speak of its status today as an object for acquisition by collecting institutions. (This last point is especially conspicuous in the next chapter, of a recent archive of "souvenir photography" from the 1970s on the U.S.–Mexico borderlands of Nuevo Laredo.)

Techniques in photographic modernity had distorted conventional habits of reading an image or frustrated governing assumptions about a picture's potential meaning. Parallel to the formal method of dadaism, constructivism, and surrealism, another kind of image making began to surface. Its analogous social realism belied a new objective relationship with the world, the complexity of positions within it, and invisible allegiances to the unconscious—all of these effects often represented in the single instant captured by a camera. Following the legacy established by Atget—lensman as modern observer of the city streets—certain image makers had set out on "a search for particular, transitory, minute signs, in the [concretizing] of the unexpected, in the strangeness of the moment."[57] One of these photographers was Cartier-Bresson. The man Levy later described as "unquenchably eager, shockingly optimistic, wide-eyed with wonder and naïveté" had been a practicing photographer for little over two years.[58] Levy nonetheless recognized the "'snap-shotty' miracles" produced by Cartier-Bresson and organized an exhibition of his prints from September 25 to October 16, 1933, titled "Photographs by Henri Cartier-Bresson and an Exhibition of Anti-Graphic Photography." There is insufficient documentation to affirm exactly which photographs by Cartier-

Bresson were on display in that exhibit. But we do know that Levy employed the apocryphal persona of "art critic" Peter Lloyd to frame the curatorial proposal of the show in the form of a letter that served as the announcement essay. Disguised as Lloyd, Levy wrote:

> Why don't you show the photographs of Cartier-Bresson in one, and the innumerable, incredible, discreditable, profane photographs that form a qualifying program for his idea in the other room? Septic photographs as opposed to the mounting popularity of the antiseptic photograph? Call the exhibition amoral photography, equivocal, ambivalent, antiplastic, accidental photography. Call it anti-graphic photography. That will demand the greater courage, because you have championed since the beginnings of your gallery, the cause of photography as a legitimate graphic art.[59]

Again, we can only surmise the content of those images that constituted the "qualifying program" for the Cartier-Bresson exhibit—although we do know their tenor as that of news agency or press photographs. If the septic is characterized by decomposition, Levy equates this corruption with graphic aspirations that reiterate the always already organized. Levy seemed to have viewed these anonymous images not as subordinate or incidental to Cartier-Bresson's project but as imperative to the image environment at large, which is capable of producing legitimate, if unwitting artifacts—an "anti-graphic" register that disavows the accepted premises of what we know by what we see. If these stock images were at all continuous with those of Cartier-Bresson, something about them must have betrayed the camera as the accidental glimpse into the psychology of social space as carved from a fraction in time.[60] Whether by mere verbal correspondence of the "anti-graphic" or by some invisible thread of fact, the foregoing suggests related concerns as they unfolded elsewhere—in the pages of *Documents,* the short-lived magazine of 1929–30 edited by Bataille.

The Levy Gallery and *Documents* are linked concretely by photographers whose work appeared concurrently on the walls of Levy's 602 Madison Avenue place and on the pages of the Paris journal—Eli Lotar and Jacques-André Boiffard, among them. It seems highly improbable that Cartier-Bresson would have been unaware of *Documents* and its axioms of *"Doctrines | Archéologie | Beaux-Arts | Ethnographie."* The magazine had circulated in ways significant as to contribute to the complex links between ethnography and surrealism that were to form part of a general twentieth-century cultural disposition.[61] Not unconnected to the impetus that led Bataille to fashion himself a student of Aztec or Mexican art so as to interpellate in its religious economies, in 1934 Cartier-Bresson spent a year in Mexico, where he made images of the underlife of the country's urban capital, the town of Juchitán, Oaxaca, and the state of Puebla. Between a kind of exhaustion of the already known, and a pervasive postwar uncertainty, the turn to Mexico can be viewed as forming an important piece in the assemblage of European and American cultural modernity, and its institutions of the visual. Regardless of their differing media, intentions, and results, both Cartier-Bresson and Bataille produced from that cultural contact zone what Michel Leiris later described as a convergence of "eroticism, cosmogonic lyricism and the philosophy of the sacred."[62]

The foregoing connections are meant to be suggestive in general, and relevant in particular, to "Documentary and Anti-Graphic Photographs by Henri Cartier-Bresson, Walker Evans and Manuel Alvarez Bravo," organized by Levy in 1935 (April 23–May 7). Because no checklist survives of the exhibit, to speak of it is to traverse the uncertain but no less alluring topography of speculation. There are, however, some records and materials worth pursuing. A month prior to this exhibit, pictures by Cartier-Bresson and Álvarez Bravo were featured briefly together at Mexico City's Palacio de Bellas Artes (March 11–20), suggesting a possible connection or resemblance between the Palacio and the later Levy exhibits. An even earlier show at the Levy Gallery of paintings, watercolors, drawings, and photographs by Amero (January 5–31) suggests the additional importance of this Mexican modernist in his role as New York champion of Mexico's vigorous artistic climate and its cultural avant-garde.

For the Palacio exhibit, Langston Hughes—who not only spent significant time in Mexico but who even shared an apartment for a time with Cartier-Bresson—wrote a critical text, presumably for the accompanying catalog.[63] Titled "Pictures More Than Pictures," Hughes makes reference not only to specific images by Cartier-Bresson and Álvarez Bravo but also to the difference between the documentary and the antigraphic,[64] when he begins the essay: "A picture, to be an interesting picture, must be more than a picture, otherwise it is only a reproduction of an object, and not an object of value in itself." In this way, Hughes calls into question the role of the photographer as a subject both continuous with, and at a remove from, the people or public spectacle recorded, so as to identity a relevant photograph as being somehow in excess of itself.

As for the 1935 Levy exhibit, it is tempting to imagine Cartier-Bresson's 1934 images of Mexico as having figured side by side with Evans's 1933 series produced in Havana, Cuba. However, based on what seems to be the sole surviving review of the exhibit—it passed otherwise unnoticed—Evans was represented, at least in part, by the architectural series he had recently completed in the American South. The anonymous critic for the *Sun* wrote: "Walker Evans's 'documents' begin to be well known, but the better they are known the better they are liked. The present series of Southern facades with iron-grilled balconies are among his most enchanting."[65] The same critic spoke in contrast of the "happy accidents" produced by Cartier-Bresson and Álvarez Bravo, which suggests the contraries intended by the title of the exhibition—as if the antigraphic were that which makes visible the impossibility of a one-to-one relation between the world and its various analogs, photographic or otherwise.

The design of the gallery announcement invitation—the name of each artist forming typographic upper and lower eyelids—alludes inevitably to Álvarez Bravo's now iconic 1934 image *Parábola óptica.* Even as it linked Paris, New York, and Mexico City as sites of modernity, the exhibition also pitted optic viewpoints involved in activating new formations, both cultural and formal. Cartier-Bresson's Mexico may have been constructed through a lens of the exotic, but no less so than Evans's American South or the familiar made strange in his New York City pictures. Similarly, there is no reason to assume that Evans did not also exhibit, in addition to the images of New Orleans and elsewhere in the South, some of his New York photographs, as he had done previously at the Levy Gallery for the show "Photographs of New York by New York Photographers."[66] (In the journal *Documents,* Leiris had written: "Like everything which has about it a prestige of exoticism, the tall buildings of America lend themselves, with an insolent ease, to the tempting amusement of comparisons.")[67]

To imagine the Levy Gallery exhibition of 1935 is thereby to think the differential relationship produced between the work of Cartier-Bresson, Evans, and Álvarez Bravo as historic operations still active in the present. To the monumental promises made by the perspective and spatial division that modernity gave rise to—especially in New York as recorded by Evans in his images of skyscrapers, bridges, billboards, subways, aerial views, and neon advertisements—there surfaced in response what Benjamin identified as "a dialectical optic that perceives the everyday as impenetrable, the impenetrable as everyday."[68] And it was Ortega y Gasset who, already in 1925, had identified surrealism or infrarealism as a change of perspective in the "natural order" and its "definite hierarchy." As a critical relation to the categories of metaphor and taboo, or all that which is resistant to representation, Ortega y Gasset viewed surrealism as equipped with the negative force of aesthetic expression and irony's "unexpected grimace of surfeit or disdain." He wrote that it was possible "to overcome realism by merely putting too fine a point on it and discovering, lens in hand, the microstructure of life."[69]

The borderline relation of these three photographers to surrealism might be summarized best by the uncanny resemblance in their individual images describing the quotidian ceremony of public eating—the distinct but inscrutable expression on the faces of the suit-and-hat office men looking out through the storefront counter in Evans's 1929 depiction of a New York City lunch counter (Figure 61) and the two portrayals, one by Cartier-Bresson, the other by Álvarez Bravo (Figure 53, *The Crouched Ones*), of Mexican workers, respectively, at an outdoor and indoor *comedor*—with backs turned, oblivious to the onlooker. (Gastronomic practices are relevant in the transnational comparisons by Octavio Paz in pages that follow.) If the descriptive terms of *documentary* and the *antigraphic* are meaningful today, it is as Levy might have envisioned such prescriptive effects—as joining forces to make visible that "lack of organic connection between art and society which is characteristic of the modern world." Like Herbert Read, Levy suspected "the fault lies in the economic structure of society." As a surrealist himself, Levy knew that "no satisfactory basis for art can be found within the existing form of society."[70] Had they been included together at his gallery in 1935, these three images would have sufficed to say as much.

Are photography and surrealism such an "unnatural coupling"—as one view has so suggested?[71] If the legacy of the surrealist enterprise endures, like the effects that led to many of its photographic artifacts, as a series of inexhaustible practices, then Levy's injunction against "the mounting popularity of the antiseptic" survives as a relevant formal and social residue from the 1935 exhibition. In the lapse between the way it might have existed in an actual historic past and how it may be useful in the variable present, "Documentary and Anti-Graphic Photographs by Cartier-Bresson, Walker Evans and Álvarez Bravo" provides us with a meaningful theoretical wager with regard to one aspect of photographic surrealism and its systems of value and representation. Even as these three photographers seldom destructured the photographic plane into the *informe,* or rarely distanced the image from its referent, they nevertheless saw beyond the descriptive function of the photograph. In this, Levy preferred to see the documentary and the antigraphic activated as incisive surrealist techniques. Not at all opposing forces, the documentary and the antigraphic presented mutual intensities—as with Álvarez Bravo

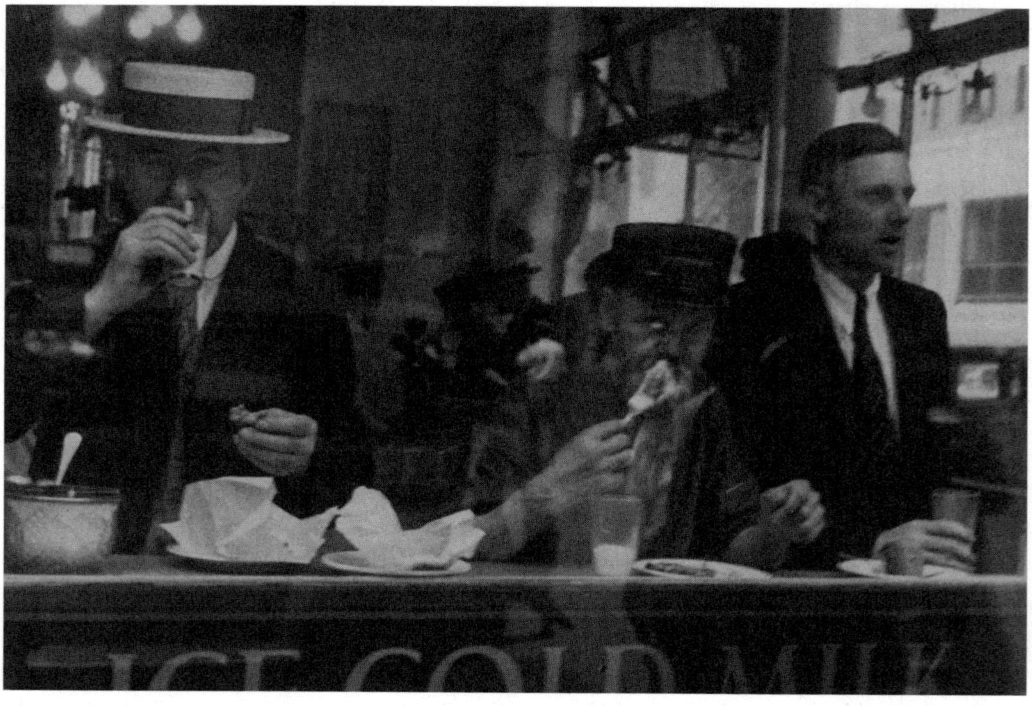

Figure 61. Walker Evans, *City Lunch Counter, New York,* 1929. Copyright Walker Evans Archive, The Metropolitan Museum of Art. Digital image copyright The Museum of Modern Art. Licensed by SCALA/Art Resource, New York.

in terms of public culture and camera work, between power and desire, taboo and metaphor. In the image environment established between Mexico City, Paris, and New York, Álvarez Bravo made visible the pressure wedged between bourgeois pathology and its idealization of the working classes; with the help of Levy and these final images of consumption, it was so interconnected as to make the material life of the senses productive of a social order.

4. For History, Posterity, and Art: The Borderline Claims of Boystown

The body is the sign of difference that exceeds the body. The modern concept of race is therefore predicated on an epistemology of visibility, but the visible becomes an insufficient guarantee of knowledge. As a result, the possibility of a gap opens up between what the body says and what the body means.

—Samira Kawash, *Dislocating the Color Line*

To conclude, I return to the place where this book began, the Texas–Mexico border, and to the period in which the Casasola Archive became national patrimony as bestowed to the Mexican state. The 1909 photographs that depict presidents William Howard Taft and Porfirio Díaz meeting across the Ciudad Juárez–El Paso border represent an important episode of that photographic record, gifted to the Mexican government in the mid-1970s. To close with this decade is to revisit matters arising from the international transit of photographic commodities, but in ways that differ manifestly from the art-market venture of the Julian Levy Gallery in the 1930s. In this latter-day entrepreneurial effort, restricted cultural capital and sexualized mass-media fantasies fuel the invention of another sort of archive, even as these forces defy the public trust associated with state-funded collecting institutions, thereby compelling questions of image ownership, national heritage, copyright, and fair use.

I refer to a photographic archive fraught with cultural, artistic, and ethical uncertainty—a rarified process, as well, that runs the risk of rendering these images devoid of historical content. These pictures convey an everyday life that is the realism of many Mexico–U.S. border towns: in Nuevo Laredo, this quasi-legal compound of restaurant-bars and bordello bedroom-cells is known as the Zona de Tolerancia (zone of permissiveness); its telling name in Texas, and elsewhere in the United States, is Boystown. The vast archive comprises images produced by a handful of "anonymous" itinerant photographers within the walled premises, and it chiefly depicts female sex workers (alone in single portraits or in the company of their associates) and the clientele who employ their services: single males, groups of adult and adolescent men, or hypothetically heterosexual couples in casual or official groupings. But in this rehearsal, the logic of first sight gives way to a second visibility that reverses matters as they appear.

Insofar as I examine the erasures that ensue when pictures are developed into aesthetic objects and cultural commodities, the political promise of these photographs is aided by the philosophy that views bodies as raw material for experience on both sides of depiction. In short, I uncover my own stakes on the meeting ground between the mode of image production and the potential terms of viewer reception. Inasmuch as anxieties about art engender private fantasies of real political consequence—they establish ambivalent values about sexual, national, and ethnic identities that vex the visual account—I link documents of a prior visual culture to contemporary photo-based practice. Even as certain "anonymous" photographs index social realities of a particular historical moment on the U.S.–Mexico border, I question their alleged truth status as popular souvenir mementos by foregrounding the desire that brought this archive into being, and, in the process, I lay bare my own wish: to configure another onlooker for these images, a viewer who informs these pictures with the methods of contemporary art.[1]

The Boystown record is in excess of the contradictions that structure its visible content and the partial view of its provenance. To imagine the Boystown microcosm of 1974–75, with only these images as evidence, is to recognize the incommensurable gap that opens up between the act of photographic viewing and the webwork of an everyday reality or "structure of feeling," even as it gives way to "more than its separable parts."[2] Raymond Williams suggested the documentary terms that can define a culture while stressing the compromised integrity of visual or written confirmation provided as support of authenticity. To approximate the organization of a culture is to allow also for the unsuspected channels of connection to make available the flesh and second visibility of photographic viewing when "actual life" betrays itself as the input production for fetish and fantasy alike.

Insofar as Stuart Hall has demonstrated how it is preferable to go beyond the dialectic of "positive" or "negative" images in affirmative or stereotypical systems of representation, I submit a counterstrategy within the "complexities and ambivalences of representation itself [that] tries to *contest it from within*."[3] A major concern of this book has been the challenging but changeable relationships between the discursive and visual regimes. My use of parallel and subsequent image environments has been both literal and metaphoric to the extent that an *interface* is located *between* discursive practices and photographic performances. This interface constitutes a blueprint for a larger sociopolitical system that is the "shared image environment" of meanings that otherwise could not have found exchange. It is plausible to read some of these Boystown photographs as "documents" in the conventional sense before complicating their provenance and status as an "objective" archive, while keeping in mind the real and representational distinctions between that Nuevo Laredo of the mid-1970s and the archival reference that reads "Photographer Unknown, Boystown: La Zona de Tolerancia, 1974–75."

Like the gap between "what a body says and what a body means," a chasm opens to remind us that the whole organization—between the elusive past and our attempts to make meaning of its residual artifacts—can confound any culture conceived in narrow documentary terms. To this effect, I appeal to the writing of Maurice Merleau-Ponty, and to its reception and currency in Mexico and the United States during the mid-1970s. To complicate the sexed gaze in La Zona, I turn to the work of contemporary Mexican and U.S. Latina photo-based artists who employ strategies that relocate or challenge the patrimonial regime by staring point-blank at the intended effects it is meant to perpetuate.

Promissory Pictures

The above-mentioned gap also comprises a difference of twenty-five years between the historical time of production and posterior occasions of display. In 2000, *Boystown: La Zona de Tolerancia* was published by the Aperture Foundation "in association with the Wittliff Gallery of Southwestern & Mexican Photography at Southwest Texas State University" (now Texas State University at San Marcos). A writer–producer of westerns for Hollywood films and television *(Lonesome Dove, Red-Headed Stranger, Good Ol' Boys),* and an aspiring fine-art photographer himself, Bill Wittliff edits a series of handsomely designed photography books produced and published jointly with such institutions as Aperture and the University of Texas Press. Texas State University's Alkek Library and its Special Collections division currently houses the Boystown archive of negatives and prints, and an exhibition of these photographs was displayed April–September 23, 2001, to coincide with the publication of *Boystown: La Zona de Tolerancia*. The book features over one hundred images from an archive of seven thousand negatives that Wittliff has capably printed since acquiring them, and has placed approximately six hundred of these 16 x 20 and 11 x 14 prints in the public trust, under the state-assisted stewardship of the Texas university system.

These images further produce an incommensurate rift that marks the literal and figurative intercourse between women and men; they convey social relations between Mexico and the United States as imposed by the lopsided relations specific to the economies of power and pleasure ensuing from the traffic of commodities within such strict perimeters. In sum, the pictures comprise a largely after-hours portrait whose setting is a notorious area in the city of Nuevo Laredo, in the state of Tamaulipas, Mexico. Figures are depicted in the posed or candid preludes to sex for money—largely under the influence of alcohol in unbridled exchanges, hostile menace, or eye-shut stupor. Subjects are rendered innocently kissing or blatantly groping, in aggressive recognition of the camera or otherwise engaged in the photographic moment by dint of a grimace, leer, or other displays of unambiguous behavior. The subjects encompass a microcosm varying in age, sex, class, nationality, and ethnicity. Insofar as some images were meant to serve as souvenirs for clients, at times imposed by the photographer in question, women are portrayed at work in the various cantinas and night clubs that make up Boystown—and on rare occasion, at least in this assemblage, also depicted are their transgendered counterparts. But a strictly souvenir intention is betrayed in that they capture sex-worker leisure time in the company of associates, friends, and family, or in the austere quarters where many of the women live on the grounds.

I take up the hazy souvenir status of these photographs after some remarks about the packaging and content of the book *Boystown: La Zona de Tolerancia* (Figure 62). From the band of vivid pink that, by descending order, blurs into swathes of fire-flame orange and yellow, and again into deep green and blue at the lower edge of the book's horizontal format, there appears the well-worn typography spelling out "Boystown" in all caps: threadbare signage against the palette of a Mexican serape. A photograph hovers above the bold title. Depicted against the backdrop provided by a wood-paneled wall, a seated light-skinned man throws back a cackle that so distorts his bearded face as to render his open mouth the focal point of the picture. His missing upper right-side tooth provides visual connection with a loose electrical cable—perhaps to an unseen window-unit air-conditioner—dangling above the lavishly ornamented mariachi sombrero fixed on his head; concentric forms reiterate the aura of light above the hat, as in the round Formica table bearing a trio composed of a *Coronita* beer bottle, an empty glass, and—prominent for the purposes of the entire series—a wallet. Awkwardly draped across the man's lap—arms around his shoulder, hands gripped at his neck—a blondish woman appears to swivel her shapely figure; she wears a light-colored short-sleeved midriff and high-rise shorts that accentuate her bare legs in full-length boots. The lower right-hand corner of the photograph is coincident with the definitive proceedings of the picture: an unidentified knee interrupts any transparency to reinforce the spectacle on public display in this corner of a cantina, insofar as the client–sitter firmly rests his right palm over the woman's crotch.

Inside, the title page bears the place-name "Boystown" again in mammoth bold font next to the following photograph: a man and woman of bronze complexion huddle closely, drinking from respective beer bottles, seated side by side at an aluminum foldout table over which is inscribed the logo *Carta Blanca* (Figure 63). On the table and in full foreground is a toolbox with a small padlock, presumably owned by the man in the picture, and an indication of the class to which

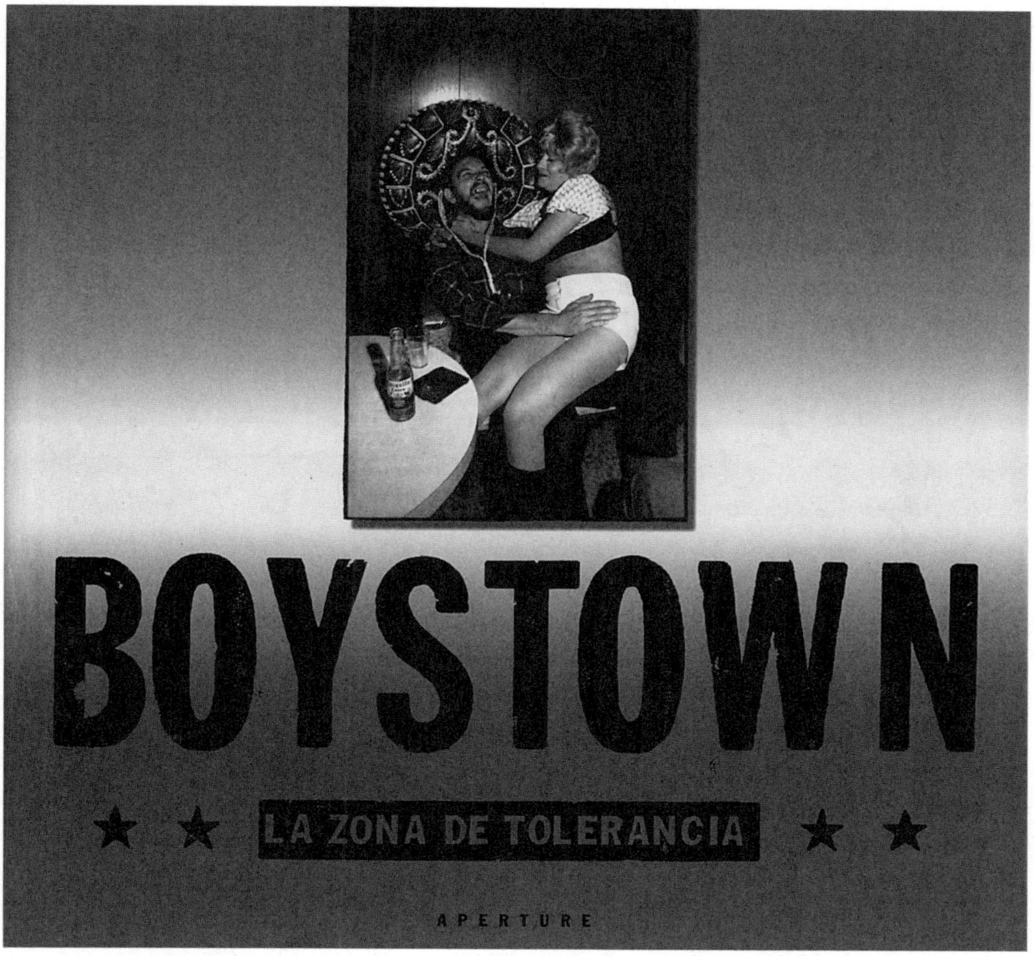

Figure 62. Front cover of *Boystown: La Zona de Tolerancia* (New York: Aperture Books in association with Wittliff Gallery of Southwestern and Mexican Photography, 2000).

he belongs. A small jar that formerly served as a baby food container—its lid having been punched with holes—now provides the table with a saltshaker. The man wears a neat button-down shirt; the woman, what appears to be a modest knit blouse under her cardigan sweater. But any tender slice of life is violently betrayed by the forcefulness with which the man grips his hand around the woman's shoulder, his smile hidden as he presses closer as though to whisper some boozy endearment. The woman's half-closed eyelids are caught by the click of the shutter in an expression that seems to swell from a look of detachment into the beginnings of a snarl.

In blunt contrast to these scenes is the framing device of the blurbs provided by the actors Tommy Lee Jones and Jessica Lange. Hollywood fantasy doubles over into the fine-art aspirations that generated this archive, reiterated insofar as Jones compares the efforts of Wittliff with the blue-chip art historical reference that is

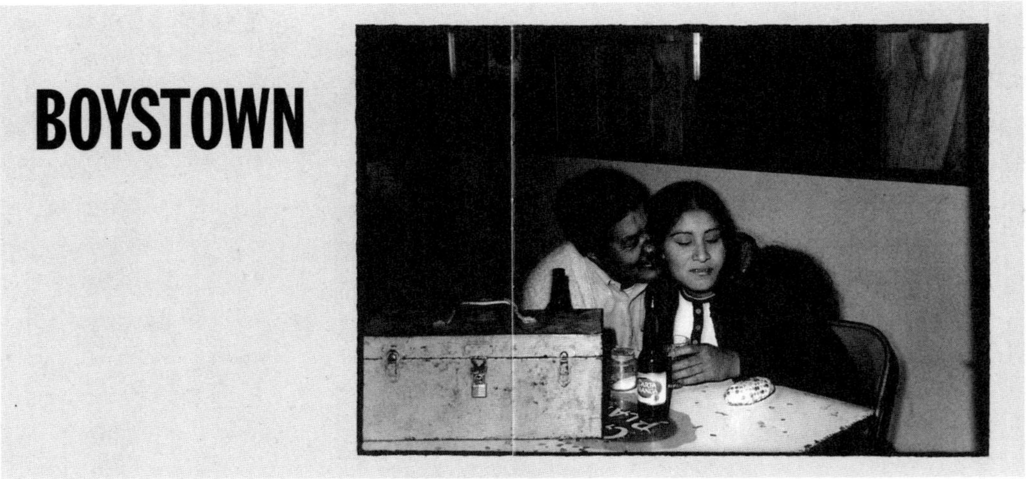

Figure 63. Frontispiece, *Boystown: La Zona de Tolerancia.*

Pablo Picasso. "[He] has accomplished a similar feat," claims the blurb writer, "by collecting and preserving a bunch of whorehouse souvenir photographs, which explain to us quite clearly that the Rio Grande Valley is a separate culture." Regardless of the hyperbole, Jones makes an insightful claim when he suggests that anyone's place in a country, real or otherwise, is "as parts, not embodiments, of culture," to which the Boystown archive bears unequivocal witness.[4]

Lange does her piece to bolster the archival verity of these pictures when she claims that Wittliff "has compiled a collection of images from a world we'd otherwise never know; a record of a time and place—mysterious and hidden—provided by anonymous photographers who were an integral part of that world." She, too, offers antecedents in comparing them to photographic images made by Horst P. Horst (Horst Paul Albert Bohrmann) and the Hollywood portraiture of George Hurrell. Lange persuasively nominates these photographs as part of a "familiar iconography—poses made famous by movie stars . . . —only here the light is a little harsher, less forgiving, and there has been no retouching."[5] The photographic effect of *Boystown: La Zona de Tolerancia* rehearses a familiar haunting: formulas from the realm of social documentary and specters of Hollywood fantasy disturb the real and symbolic levels insofar as historical preservation trumps the archive's unearthing, and tactical contaminations threaten any idealized purity. In what follows, I further peer into such irresolvable gaps.

These photographs speak volumes about the anxiety and desire of their originator, Bill Wittliff, in that to trace the difficulty of the photographs and their ultimate implications is to examine their provenance and to scrutinize how this archive came into existence. This leads to questions of anonymity, vernacular photography, U.S. American exoticism, purchasing power, visual power relations; how film fiction intertwines with these photographs; and how the anxiety of art and the concern for its unique status resemble the unease of dependency. First, however, is the actual practice that led to the documentary and virtual nature of this archive.

In his *Boystown* essay, the renowned Texas-based photographer Keith Carter renders his reflections on these artifacts; the resulting account provides a useful approximation of the routine performed by the itinerant souvenir photographers in La Zona. To be brief, on any given evening, a cluster of photographers, ranging in number from five to eight, presumably Mexican and male, stalked the Boystown cantinas with their cameras primed to render a hasty portrait in exchange for pay. The lensmen for hire shared a makeshift studio with drapes, backdrop curtains, and some semblance of lighting equipment. There are also portraits made against a bare stucco wall, like the one featured on the back cover to *Boystown,* bearing witness to the integrity of this particular convention (Figure 64). Austere quarters provided the darkroom for developing these pictures. Insofar as the 35 mm film roll could be cut into single frames, photographers worked at nimble speeds so

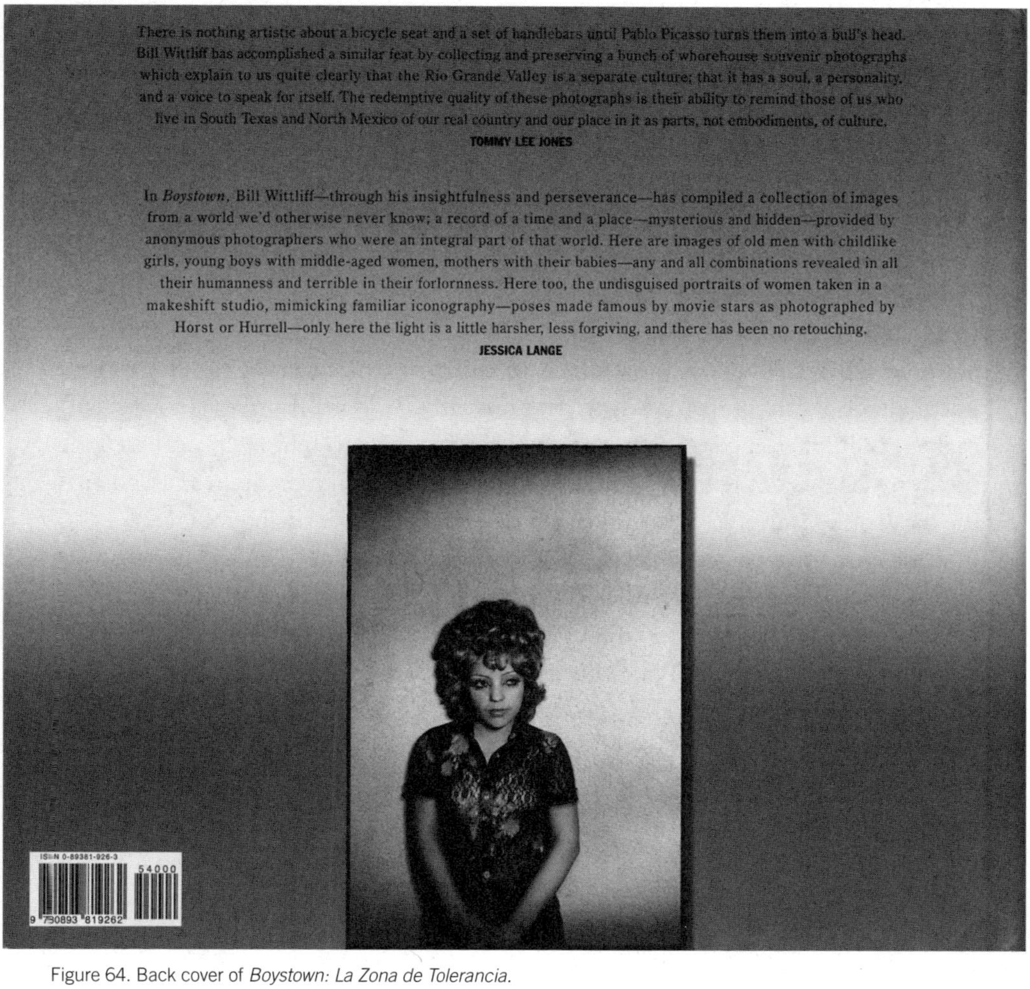

Figure 64. Back cover of *Boystown: La Zona de Tolerancia.*

that, on returning from the nighttime din and liquored bordello pitch, they could work together with a technician, around the enlarger and chemical tray, to develop a single negative at a time. The resulting product was a 4 x 5 print that photographers sold to the willing or persuaded customer: "The single damp negative was then discarded onto a growing pyramid of previously discarded negatives."[6]

Provenance is at the center of the debate today in terms of national patrimony and institutional collecting practices; it is also the origin story for meanings whose end result is intended to appear as a kind of inevitability.[7] Open to question is the authenticity narrative as currently constructed by the archive's originator. The outline of a story emerges not only from Carter's article but also from essays in the volume by the Texan art writer Dave Hickey and the Mexican journalist Christina Pacheco. In addition, the book includes a personal statement by Wittliff himself. We know that in 1974, the filmmaker traveled to La Zona hoping to capture the borderland compound and its human subjects as atmospheric research for a screenplay: "I went down there thinking Boystown might be a good location for a movie I was writing. I took my cameras with the vague notion of maybe running across a good image or two."[8]

Aims were soon foiled for this Austin-based writer and photographer, in that enforced no-flash regulations frustrated his attempt to take pictures in nocturnal *situ.* Inspired to return the next morning, the cameraman was certain he might find his subject more tenable in the watchfulness of dawn: "Such was my gringo arrogance, I thought I might even be welcomed or at the very least tolerated."[9] Wittliff's misassumptions are hardly exceptional to this occasion. His narrative confirms a tradition that fuels U.S. American art and literature. A self struggles to establish democratic (often eroticized) inclusiveness and the overwhelming boundaries set by the drive that aims "to equalize citizens by being blind to the unequal goods" that fortune "distributes unfairly."[10] Wittliff's magnanimity conceals a conflicting appetite that longs to identify, so as to find reciprocal recognition, even as this desire betrays an imperialist compulsion to contain at all costs—the totalizing resolve, so to speak, that appears in the guise of an embrace.

For an origin narrative to have effect, nationalist hubris must therefore endure a cruel rebuff: "I was wrong," Wittliff continues. "Walking down the street I turned and took a single picture of a prostitute sweeping out her little streetside cell. She heard the click of the shutter and cut loose with a string of curses, all *impugning my masculinity* and condemning me to fiery hell. Up and down the streets other prostitutes emerged from their doors. In a second they were all shouting curses. Then they began pelting me with rocks and sticks, having recognized me for what I was: an exploiter and a thief, there to steal fragments of their lives that were not for sale until the sun went down."[11] Following this logic, it isn't long before the sentimental education becomes the cover story for a transaction. Having identified the transient photographers within the Boystown premises, and approaching them as colleagues to talk shop about cameras, Wittliff gains informant trust and accepts an invitation to visit their darkroom. There, he spots a pile of castoff negatives—selecting one from the soggy heap to hold up to view. If Wittliff had entertained vague notions about the images he was trying to make himself, these negatives were in excess of every conceivable expectation, as though—in the dream that conflates subject and object—no barriers stood between the photographer and the Boystown sex worker.

Wittliff recalls making an initial agreement to buy the stack of "about forty negatives." "I asked if they'd sell them," Wittliff ponders, underpinning his bid by showing these now anonymous photographers a series of black-and-white images he produced on Mexican *vaquero* or rodeo culture, to legitimize his ethnographic and humanistic concern.[12] "My friends made slicing motions across their throats, saying it was too dangerous and the authorities wouldn't like it. I said yeah, but for history, for posterity, for art—and I meant it. They said, yeah, yeah, okay, but for money, too."[13] In his desire for a portrait without artifice or refinement, acknowledging the insider status and mobility of these photographers, Wittliff returned the next evening to negotiate the continued acquisition of images. As a result, the Nuevo Laredo cameramen began sending negatives to Wittliff's offices in Austin, from July 4, 1974, to August 1975: in sum, over seven thousand negatives.[14]

Open to speculation are the specific images that comprised those original forty negatives. (To be sure, a handful of prints with marks and stains originating from emulsion damage on the negative comprise some of them, but few if any of these, unless radically retouched in the printing process, feature in the Aperture selection.) It is safe to assume, however, that these originals must have been similar in kind to the ones discussed above on the front cover and title page of *Boystown: La Zona de Tolerancia*: that is, of couples and groups at tables, or of a Boystown sex worker in the photographers' studio.

It is not unreasonable to suggest that a conversion occurred the moment those photographers conceded to the paid proposal, complicit in the knowledge that any subsequent images they produced were for purchase by a U.S. American—and at a critical distance from the desire "for history, for posterity, for art." It is not impossible to contemplate that this additional expertise radically altered the potential range of the itinerant photographer's practice into what I want to call the *promissory content* of the images. The Nuevo Laredo photographers were attentive to the fact that (1) any and all their negatives would be acquisitioned, and (2) the resulting pictures would circulate and be viewed in environments never intended for this kind of image making. It is not unrealistic to suggest that all subsequent photographs were enhanced by this intelligence—resistant to the transparency and purity of Wittliff's visual appetite.

How does a viewer otherwise account for images of the Boystown women gathered in their private quarters, sometimes alone, other times bearing a child in arms or in groups? How does a viewer account for photographs of an outdoor carnival scene, the portrait of the Boystown warden or of the girl lying in a bed recovering from what appears to be a now-bandaged injury to her head, the wound an accident or the aftermath of some hideous exchange? These and countless images cast doubt on the explanation or analysis that interprets these images as simply paid mementos or souvenirs. To allow the photographers this promissory practice and its critical agency is to afford those depicted therein access to a posterior subject effect otherwise lacking in the manner by which this archive has been turned into a printed commodity and—not excluding my own account—into the object of research.

I submit that the Nuevo Laredo photographers and their subjects, in various degrees of appreciation and intent, employed tactical measures to upset facile first-order understanding; built into the structure of their image production, the photographers "contaminated" the intended conceptual destination and so overturned the ideology that would sublimate the means of this image production into artifacts of a so-called vanished culture. At times, a subject herself will deploy the complicit gestures of defiance or impulsiveness; other times, the photographers will make use of vantage point as an informed subject, perhaps foregrounding those aspects they believed might please their patron on the other side of the border; in the last instance, these makers were alert to the "second visibility" that a camera can awaken.

There are examples of photographs from La Zona that stage these kinds of potential effects, and image analysis knows how to speak to this. However, the paucity of Boystown illustrations in this discussion owes to the fact that Wittliff claims copyright ownership and has denied permission to reproduce any images on these pages—inexplicably, insofar as readers can freely consult the published Aperture publication. Perplexing, too, are the efforts that a publicly assisted institution like Texas State University at San Marcos has invested in the taxing and costly stewardship of an archive whose content demands critical attention but whose availability to the debate at large has been so restricted. Insofar as the parameters for fair use involve interconnected factors of not-for-profit educational use, the "amount or substantiality of the portion used in relation to the [purportedly] copyrighted work as a whole" and "the potential market for or value of the copyrighted work,"[15] in the case of the Boystown photographs, a convincing argument links copyright as private property to the chiefly female bodies that circulate among men as commodities of exchange.[16] This is to speak of the ever-increased calculus by which labor-force expansion is to global capitalism as large-scale image management is to the privatizing of knowledge. As evidenced in the Casasola collection, archival structures are open-ended, and insofar as the seven thousand negatives made in La Zona constitute Mexican cultural property, broadly defined, any authority of copyright in relation to those images is a questionable claim at best.[17] This dubious international legality further complicates the by-now-contested "purity" of the pictures' origin. A further residual force effect: never identical to the donor's desire, these photographers and what they photographed endure in the archive as proprietors of a knowledge to which no viewer gains right of entry. The images not only betray Wittliff's appetite for a homespun epistemology; they inform as well on his self-styled legal exemptions to confirm allegations the archivist would rather renounce: a liability to his subjects of representation.

If this appears belabored, there is more. To recall, Wittliff had already imagined Boystown, prior to the negatives in question, as "a good location for a movie [he] was writing." His drive did not lay dormant, for such aim found its object, together with the archive in progress, as a screenplay that, after undergoing drafts that date back to 1974, became *A Night in Old Mexico* (1988), a motion picture currently in production. The release date appeared scheduled for 2008, allegedly with Robert Duvall and the Mexican pop star Thalía in the leading roles, and directorial charge rumored to be at the reigns of Dennis Hopper or, alternately, Walter Hill.[18]

A Night in Old Mexico is a lament for a world no longer,[19] told in terms of two narratives that lead to an intramural crisis point in Nuevo Laredo's Zona de Tolerancia. On a South Texas dirt road, J. T. McAdams, a small nervous man in his early thirties, and a slightly older Moon Phillips, a film noir Texas thug, together plot a nighttime drug deal as a charade to murder Ramon, a Chicano portrayed in coat, tie, and groomed hair. With the double-cross accomplished, the two Texans abscond with the ready money and, as per the convention, make their way south of the border. Before long in the story line, Panama Corrales—a Chicano described as having a malformed eye glazed white—seeks the service of an assassin, Cholo Fuentes, in reprisal for Ramon's death and in search of the stolen cash.

Elsewhere, the aging representative of a Texan prior order, Red Bovie, faces a future in a nursing home or the prospect of taking his own life. Red has been forced to sell his longtime family ranch land, and bulldozers already make way for the tract development that will be Clear View Estates. At this crucial juncture, Red, a man well into his sixties, receives a timely visit from his grandson Gally. The nineteen-year-old in Polo shirt, slacks, and sneakers has abandoned college in a quest for connection to his family lineage and its original Texas settlement, even as Gally's father and Red's estranged son, Jimmy Bovie, has become a prosperous New York stockbroker. References to Jimmy produce in Red a brief soliloquy about the honor and timelessness of the homestead, and the outburst draws out the political map of Red's consciousness. Persistent in Red is the umbrage of the settler whose lineage, founded on a colonizing violence, commandeered land belonging first to Native Americans, and later to Mexicans. Despite initial antipathies between the family connections, Gally helps his grandfather Red in a frenzied getaway from the Morning Glory Nursing Home, and so inaugurates the Cadillac road trip to Nuevo Laredo. To Gally's geographic probing, Red replies that they are headed down the highway, about two hundred miles to Old Mexico. Along the road, Red and Gally reluctantly offer a ride to Moon and J. T., whose own vehicle has left them stranded at a gas station. To the degree that the two story lines overlap and conclude in Boystown, another kind of coupling speaks to the question of kinship that worries this narrative.

As the first gestures of a bond surface between Red and Gally, the elder indulges in a bit of erotic nostalgia about his first incursion into Mexico. He recalls that, as a young cowboy on his first visit to Mexico, he spied a Mexican girl with long hair and an alluring body. With the softening of Red's asceticism, Gally ridicules by inquiring whether his grandfather had "screwed" the girl that haunts his memory. Bluntly, Red unleashes a rejoinder to the crass insinuation: he *married* the woman Gally had equated with an ordinary hussy, Gally's own grandmother.

Opportunity gives way to what a body means as being contrary to what it says, insofar as Red's descendants have been heretofore oblivious of their transnational bloodline and mixed ethnic heredity, as if to verify that race is irreducible to facial or bodily markers, or to descent strictly defined. Hence the fiction that is *A Night in Old Mexico* links the Boystown archive back to the structure of kinship. In his essay "The Erotic Zone: Sexual Transgression on the US–Mexican Border," Ramón Gutiérrez makes visible the cultural meanings that regulate ethnicity and sexual coding as national forms of distinction. He submits that U.S. American self-descriptions are founded on who is and who is not kin by blood and marriage. These conventions shape a legacy "of nature and law [that] explains how Americans project their hysterias and anxieties and thereby symbolically construct Mexicans."[20] Citizenship in the United States is based on natural and legal grounds that make possible the "moral community" of the nation, and sexual intercourse, insofar as it is state sanctioned by marriage, establishes the dichotomies that differentiate the national from the foreign body, the male or masculine from the feminine or female, the pure from the contaminated, the biological from the cultural, the entitled from the dispossessed—and so by extension, the subjects of history from the objects of representation.[21]

What remains after the predictable portrayals of prostitution in *A Night in Old Mexico* is the confounding and disavowal of the maternal, hence part Mexican, Bovie line. Sputtering his words before long from the boozy context of the Boystown brothels, Red repudiates the devotion he had earlier entrusted to Gally about his grandmother—after all, she was just something he'd picked up on the streets of Old Mexico. In the end, the narrative allows Red to attach this denial at last onto the body of Patty Wafers, the heart-of-gold prostitute who, by the narrative's end, Red pretends to make legitimate.

If sex work corrupts the conjugal identity convenient for the state, then women at the limit of patrimonial labor are consigned to the extreme fringes of national status: a sexual workforce that is the surrogate citizenry to a phantom matrimonial state. Insofar as the Hollywood film industry is unparalleled for gauging the desire of capitalist and national structures of power, and to the degree that the economy of sex work and the specter of kinship loom large in *A Night in Old Mexico,* the image archive engendered in La Zona begets another type of progeny. Paternity of this kind indulges two forms of national masculine rank so imposing as to be giantlike metaphors of conceptual opposites. The shifting social field relevant to Mexico and the United States during the 1970s is reflected in the meeting ground enabled by the changing daylight of sexual and national politics after the would-be absolutes of a night in Old Mexico.

The Indiscreet Mirror

To associate the anxiety of art status with the compulsion that bestows unique standing to photographic identity is to tread in the uneasy regions of dependency. To claim that a photographic archive and Hollywood invention are alone in shaping the image environment complicit with the political and sexual economy of Boystown is to obscure the role of the Mexican state in its equally negligent misrepresentations. This is finally to turn from Hollywood social fantasy to the political theater of Mexico's political class and intelligentsia as framed by one protagonist.

In a writing life so often concerned with the national and its zones of relation to the United States, the preeminent Mexican poet and intellectual Octavio Paz published a collection of essays in 1979 titled *El ogro filantrópico: Historia y política (1971–1978) (The Philanthropic Ogre: History and Politics [1971–1978]).* The volume gathered earlier articles in large part featured in the pages of two journals of which Paz was publisher, *Plural* (1971–76) and *Vuelta* (1976–98). Well positioned in terms of a general readership, possessing distinct cultural capital, and whether endorsed or contested along ideological lines, the contribution of these media venues to Mexico's national debates cannot be overestimated. My points will not allow for an extended discussion of this print culture or of its broader implications for the nation's political life. However, *The Philanthropic Ogre* appears at this juncture in that the publication history of its essays is consistent with the years that furnished the Boystown archive with raw material to produce that photographic U.S.–Mexico image environment.

Paz's title essay provides one of the book's major themes, namely, the "peculiar physiognomy" of the Mexican state whose colossal bureaucracy he saw constraining the country in a structural holdover, as much from the nation's colonial history as from the untimely progress of its modernity. To this end Paz knowingly embraced a long-confirmed tradition of literary political critique in Mexico, with prose of personal and social conviction previously typified by such figures as Fray Servando Teresa de Mier in the late eighteenth and early nineteenth centuries, and Daniel Cosío Villegas in the twentieth. *The Philanthropic Ogre* argues with Mexico's political present in a self-styled language alternately "diagnostic" and "therapeutic"; it comprises a sequence of reflections on the history and society of Mexico, its status with respect to other countries in Latin America and in connection to the United States.

Paz's impassioned standpoint ponders themes as varied as they are suggestive: the role of the new Left in Mexico and Latin America on matters related to political pluralism; the function of democracy in a socialist society; feminism, labor-union rights, and the civil liberty of minorities, be they political, ethnic, linguistic, religious, or sexual. Linking the essays is Paz's skepticism of, and complicity with, Mexico's own intellectual elite, whose enchantment with the working people is so often a waiver of its own liability to interrogate "the value system that serves as the foundation to the edifice of the ruling classes."[22] For Paz, scores of intellectuals on the left in Mexico are no more than uninspired apologists of "historical socialism" in its contradictory configurations, from Joseph Stalin to Leonid Brezhnev, insofar as the Mexican Communist Party was laying claim to democratic pluralism without renouncing the "democratic centralism" of Leninist inflection. In this respect, Paz betrays his own troublesome relationship with the writings of Jean-Paul Sartre and Merleau-Ponty, in that the opinions of these philosophers circulated so widely as to hold sway on the attitude of the Left in Mexico and Latin America. Even as he was compelled by the events of 1968 and the subsequent critical philosophy associated with the "school of Paris," Paz remained largely disapproving of its antecedents owing to earlier alignments with the Communist Party and, perhaps reluctantly, applauds Sartre's and Merleau-Ponty's latter-day renunciations of Marxian orthodoxy. (In a moment I examine the later philosophical writings of Merleau-Ponty, about which Paz, remarkably, makes no reference.)

Perhaps less evident at the time of its publication, to read *The Philanthropic Ogre* today is to find it squarely framed within a postcolonial critique. The essays look to the remainders of Mexico's viceregal period and to the contemporary state's ability to "rectify history" in favor of disavowals productive of national amnesia. Paz scrutinizes Mexico's "patrimonial regime," whose legislative structure shapes the terms of private and public life, insofar as its colonial layering maintains two variant moral codes: in the home and on the streets. Effects deriving from the family patriarch form a circuit back and forth to engender a brand of masculine performance (machismo) that functions as a powerful representation in art, social fantasy, and politics, or that alternately symbolizes the image of the caudillo (local political boss) or of executive leadership for the nation—the varying shades often conflated into one figure.

Paz diagnoses a severe crisis in the Mexican political system at the very moment that a government commensurate with the state—namely, the Institutional Revolutionary Party (PRI)—claims to seek legitimacy in pluralism. His critique of the Mexican state counterbalances a dissection of the United States, whose democratic social contract often conceals its religious foundation, such a puritanical pact between men and God as to render impossible any separation between morality and religion. Exposing the contradictions inherent to an ethics based on the appearance of sobriety, measure, and moral reason, Paz anticipated the troubled prospect for a multiracial democracy compromised by repeated U.S. imperialistic rehearsals and government eagerness to comply with elite and corporate interests.

This logic of disconnection impinges on all aspects of U.S. American everyday life, especially its culinary, hygienic, and sexual practices. Paz sees the traditional preparation of meals in the United States—to recall: the reflection dates to the mid-1970s—as being devoid of mystery: food that is "simple, nutritious, and deprived of condiments." Even as he takes pleasure in the alternate vocabulary of U.S. "gastronomic cosmopolitanism," Paz uncovers a correspondence in his comparisons of the United States and Mexico in terms of hygienic pedagogy, where cleanliness rivals godliness, and culinary practices hesitate between two extremes: "The glass of milk and the tumbler of whiskey." Evidence of this is reflected in the 1929 photograph by Walker Evans of a city lunch counter on whose storefront windowpane is inscribed the signage "Ice Cold Milk" (Figure 61). Moreover, for Paz, a U.S. obsession with the antiseptic reflects a disjointing at the level of sex, race, and ethnicity, based on an alleged "purity of origin." Admittedly based on empiric observation and suggestive association, in lieu of systematic analysis, Paz's accounts of North American self-techniques establish cultural comparisons in the unambiguous mirror reflective of the differences between the neighboring nations. In the process, he addresses perspectives at variance on sexual difference and the normative roles attributed to masculinity and femininity.

Paz also harshly assesses the Mexican state during the administrations of Luis Echeverría Álvarez (1970–76) and José López Portillo (1976–82), particularly of the structural negligence regarding population explosion; Paz uncovered how the state's inability to recommend birth control, planned parenthood, or the legality of abortion hinged on a symbolic menace to Mexican masculinity.[23] Most remarkable and relevant to this rehearsal is Paz's metaphoric staging of the two nations as masculine giants, reflective images along the U.S.–Mexico borderland. In the essay "El espejo indiscreto" ("The Indiscreet Mirror") Paz describes the United States as "a generous oversized oaf, a sort of simpleton."[24] He builds on this metaphor to say that the United States is a credulous "dupe, unaware of his own strength, easy to fool, but whose wrath can destroy us."[25]

The Mexican state, too, is portrayed as a munificent leviathan: both openhanded and corrupt. Sometimes charitable, other times fraudulent, Mexico's public administration—"a scandal to the nation and foreigners alike"—allows a zone of tolerance for the persistent residues of the colonial experience: "Persons of irreproachable private conduct, mirrors of morality in their home and neighborhood, are bereft of scruples in disposing of the public trust as if it were proper to them. This is less a question of immorality than it is a matter of the unconscious currency of another morality: in the patrimonial regime, vague and unpredictable are the *borders* between the public sphere and the private arena, family and State."[26] Paz's critique of the difference between the two nations serves not only as a metaphor but as the geopolitical groundwork for relations between the United States and Mexico and their opposing versions of an impending globalization—especially as they were staged on the real and spectacular divide between the daydream and nightmare scenes along the borderlands.

A glance at the indiscreet mirror reflecting the adjacent nations gives onto a vision of masculine transcendence where capitalist manpower meets face-to-face with bureaucratic virility. U.S. capitalist masculinity instructs in its celebration of "competition and emulation," values that regulate any advancement secured by women, who make gains only as "subjects under the law," that is, as "neuter or abstract entities, as citizens, not as women."[27] Paz and Wittliff converge in their mutual misrecognition of Woman within the national project. Wittliff's Boystown archive betrays an aim to "rectify history" in a mirror doubling: by "disposing of the public trust," the archive performs a cruel parody of the philanthropic ogre that is the Mexican state, with U.S. generosity that constrains subjects to a logic that is not disinterested. Wittliff's desire is to transform the archive into a bureaucratic institution itself, generously donor related and stewarded, but with authoritarian limits to its admission. To think these images dialectically is to account for the complicity of the Mexican state. It is as well to see Wittliff's image in the indiscreet mirror: his acts of liberality conceal the desire to subdue and dominate, even as they expose a bureaucratic masculinity drunk with leverage only over the most vulnerable.

Paz was eager to imagine an economy of abundance and generosity between the sexes as being irreducible even under political domination. In his view, freedom was that particle of the self that escapes all determinisms, the indivisible residue that we cannot measure: "True mystery does not reside in divine omnipotence, but in human liberty."[28] But Paz was unmindful of his own "national amnesia" on the subject of an overly centralized government. During the important changes taking place during the decade in question, Mexico's social architects and ideologues, Paz included, neglected to account again for the workforce discrepancies and sexual–economic conditions at stake in the northernmost reaches of its national domain.

Flesh and Second Visibility

Insofar as the philosophy of Henri Bergson was instrumental in overturning the positivist ideology that prefigured Mexico's modern state, Merleau-Ponty was strategic for artists and intellectuals of the 1970s, in Mexico and elsewhere in Latin America. Merleau-Ponty's original works, as well as Spanish-language commentaries and translations, appeared widely in a transnational framework, principally between Spain, Mexico, Venezuela, and Argentina. Even as Paz objected to the early political thesis of *Humanism and Terror,* he acknowledged the importance of this French intellectual to such Mexican writers and philosophers as Luis Villoro and Leopoldo Zea, who hailed Merleau-Ponty within the framework proper to the Americas.[29] Claiming the author of *Phenomenology of Perception* to advance an authentic Latin American philosophy, Zea submitted that, even despite underdevelopment, a genuine critical tradition could emerge "out of our capacity to confront the problems facing us, down to their very roots" with a means to enable "the new man."[30]

If Merleau-Ponty's writings bear on the production and consumption of visual meanings, in terms that speak to Woman, it is because potentiality abounds, especially in the posthumous work *The Visible and the Invisible.* The unfinished manuscript, particularly its culminating chapter, "The Intertwining, the Chiasm," is remarkable on many accounts, not the least of which is its compelling metaphorics of the body: a writing rich in regard to the meanings of the visible and the act of looking as they are found and confounded in an unfolding logic of the flesh. This marriage of somatics and visuality has been a salient aspect discussed by many of Merleau-Ponty's commentators—Luce Irigaray, Iris Marion Young, Elizabeth Grosz, Alphonso Lingis, Joan Copjec, and Judith Butler, among others. Some of these writers have pointed out the primary omission from this phenomenology—that it constitutes a body thinking that universalizes the corporeal and makes no distinction as to sexual difference, and that it exploits a language of production that does not acknowledge its reliance on the female body. Nevertheless, some of his critics point to still other possibilities made available by the openness of this unfinished work. On account of its engagement with and complication of the terms by which the visual is rendered, Merleau-Ponty's "Intertwining, the Chiasm" demands to be read in light of the photographic image and canonical art historical representations of the female body (namely, the patriarchal institution of "the nude" in various visual cultures), as through a lens that might account for the ethics and politics of sex-specific image making and viewership. To this end, I unravel some of the closely woven filaments in this suggestive tract regarding corporeality and bodilessness pursuant to the duplicity of display and the ultimate reversibility that is the flesh.

Pertinent to my ongoing argument is the view in "The Intertwining, the Chiasm" whereby what-there-is-in-the-world and what-we-know-of-it are both established, albeit precariously, through bodily substance and the perceptual senses as they move, of a piece, in the material environment of space and in interaction with other bodies. Each body is both "subject" and "object" to itself: for inasmuch as a half profile cannot successfully cancel its other out, neither can the body perceive itself at once as subject *and* object, except through a kind of reversibility, a "certain node in the woof of the simultaneous and the successive."[31]

In the fact of the body, ontology and epistemology are conflated, because neither contour—of the body as activity or passivity—can entirely exclude the other; they are "two systems applied upon one another."[32] Although the "visible around us seems to rest in itself,"[33] the objective world, including other bodies, is contingent on the gaze of the viewer if it is to wax into visibility. It is a covering that clarifies or makes transparent, a look that envelops what it locates at the endpoint of a gaze. "How does it happen that my look, enveloping them, does not hide them, and, finally, that, veiling them, unveils them?"[34]

This twin effect suggests a prior nakedness of matter and the posterior garb of intentionality as granted by sight. Like Bergson before him, Merleau-Ponty sees the body as an image unto itself and as an image that undergoes and produces major changes in contact with other objects. Sight becomes the privileged modality of experience and perception. Neither the objective world of matter nor the subjective world of a perceiving and lived body constitutes a blank page, a void, or nakedness. Instead, Merleau-Ponty suggests the agreement of mind and matter by way of vision, inasmuch as the gaze provides that nakedness with flesh.[35]

This relationality involves endless and ever-changing movement. Merleau-Ponty argues that there is a duality to perception: to the perceiving mind and its bodily matter and to the perceiving subject and its relation to an external horizon. This compels a porousness, a mutability, and an unceasing commencement in the interplay of inside and out—for Merleau-Ponty, always an interdependent plenitude and an ambiguity. If there is an anterior term to the relation of seer and seen, it might be considered, provisionally, as color, for example.[36] It is at these straits—*straits* in the sense of a narrow space or passage but also as a situation of perplexity and distress, at this productive difference, then, between the thing seen and the seeing subject—that Merleau-Ponty locates the latency of being-to-the-world. This latency he calls the "*flesh* of things."[37] Sight and touch are sense giving and form providing. But there is more: "It is in that the thickness of flesh between the seer and the thing is constitutive for the thing of its visibility as for the seer of his corporeity; it is not an obstacle between them, it is their means of communication."[38]

Merleau-Ponty nominates the flesh—albeit as latency or virtuality—as that which constitutes reversibility itself; it is matter with a view to mind. That is, the thing I see is an object that regards me; it somehow comes into contact and impresses its hue on me and, in so doing, shapes my perception insofar as I give aspect to that very thing on which I allowed my gaze, momentarily, to rest. For this intertwining to occur, for this ceaseless ebb and flow to exist—between my body and the surrounding material sphere against which I actively press by looking—requires something other than the somatic.

In "The Intertwining, the Chiasm," Merleau-Ponty comes close to describing a photograph as the metonymic function of what he calls a visible. Because each separate cut-out of visuality is in a differential, comparative relationship with all else in the surrounding visual field, any arrest, halt, or stammer of the gaze constitutes a "certain node in the woof of the simultaneous and the successive."[39]

In chapter 1, I turned to Bergson—despite his photographic disavowal—to argue that a photograph seizes and detains the intersection between a lived body and the outside world at an ephemeral passage or stress point in time and space: a duration, that it makes manifest the frame of two-way transit between exterior and interior horizons and that it accentuates the differentiation between the two at a provisional inflection or quiver. With Merleau-Ponty, we can consider the photographic still image also as that set of colors or gray-scale, that surface depicting a profundity, the material optic counterpart to the flesh; this double movement back and forth between seer and seen establishes "identity without superposition" as well as "difference without contradiction." In short, this is a "divergence between the within and without that constitutes [the] natural secret" of those surfaces haunted by a touch or vision.[40]

Between all visibles and all viewers there spans an *untouchable* "connective tissue"—that productive illusionistic intertwining, neurologically performed in the body by the optic chiasma, that X-shaped partial decussation on the undersurface of the hypothalamus through which the optic nerves are continuous with the brain. It is this bodily operation that in turn provides continuity with the material world—perceived and experienced in accommodated cinematic effect. Merleau-Ponty gives this gap, this openness between the seer and the seen, the tactile connotations of *flesh.* But this flesh is always latency, that is, the flesh is *photographic* insofar as it constitutes reversibility itself, matter with a view to mind as it may be awakened in the present tense of viewing.

The photographs commissioned to encapsulate the borderland practices of Boystown during 1974–75 unite the time zone of relation to the critical questions articulated at this precise moment in the medium's history, as well as its troubled relation to sexual difference. Merleau-Ponty's "The Intertwining, the Chiasm" ignites photographic viewing out of mere one-sidedness and explodes it into multiplicity. For Merleau-Ponty, flesh is as much latency as it is a relation. For photography, flesh is that connection between photographer and subject, between image and viewer, between the preterit of the photographic in relation to the present of its viewing. Flesh is not the shadow of the actual but its principle.[41] It, too, is reversibility in that "the seer and the visible reciprocate one another and we no longer know which sees and which is seen."[42] The surveyed–surveying is a virtuality that beckons the actual. Whereas an image can be regarded at a distance, it can, perhaps less perceptibly (indeed, invisibly) gaze back—at the very least we might imagine an ethical or political world *whereby it does in fact reciprocate our sight.* Does difference *preclude reversibility* and, similarly, does reversibility *deny difference*? If flesh is to reversibility as sex is to difference, can these terms—flesh and sex, reversibility and difference—exist internal to each other? Is the notion of universal flesh in Merleau-Ponty the view that there are always manifold systems and incommensurable sexes?

Merleau-Ponty's own omissions of difference cannot go without remark. Throughout "The Intertwining, the Chiasm" all references to the body and the flesh assume the masculine body of the author himself. Siding with Irigaray, Grosz takes issue with the unacknowledged language of Merleau-Ponty, indebted, on the one hand, to the productive nature of women's bodies and the maternal but that, on the other hand, views the feminine as a shortcoming or lack. In an ontology that takes the male body as the universal standard, the status of flesh is a cover story for the function of the feminine and maternal continuity.[43] To be sure, his language of cavities and folds describes attributes of the male body as well, but the metaphors remain ambiguous in a discussion that makes no specific reference to sexual difference. With the exclusion of women in this text, one cannot overlook an implicit homoerotics in Merleau-Ponty's engagement with the other as a male seer seen, at least as he is embodied in one particular passage.[44]

On the other hand, this twofold nature is availability to other landscapes in excess of one's own; this "intercorporeity" of fusion and exchange is a provisional place always open to other visibles; this secrecy, latency, and a concomitant logic of appearances meet at the intersection that is the flesh. This flesh invites what might be called a *second visibility*: a double take, at cross-purposes, a twofold vision—a skepticism. On the one hand, the viewer produced in light of Merleau-Ponty can recognize a sexual, psychological, and historic projection implied in spectacle; on the other, this observer is awake to standardized or deviant forms of gender formations, or of the female-in-the-male regard and the male-in-the-female view. A photograph gives way to a view as the photographer might have envisioned it within the historical context and the ideological climate of the time; to the sexuality the image assumes as its viewer position; and to how I inflect the image with my own sexed body, particular sexual dispositions, fascinations, fantasies, perversities, and pleasures as well as my personal vocabulary and cadence, my habits, anxieties, and blind spots, my involuntary gestures and deliberate ceremonies both private and public. This particular manner of movement and being-to-the-world and my own form of looking comprise a syntax.[45] Because it is never complete, the photograph *sees me* in this articulation. In excess and never self-identical, the photograph contains a virtuality that is never reducible to its viewing position, or my own, even as it is that which prompts its interrogations.

Is failure an inevitability when looking at images made in La Zona? Can my viewing bring latencies out of immanence to counter a structural "to-be-looked-at-ness"? Is there further unease dormant in the photograph to be underlined? Can these considerations on the logic of the visible and the politics of the image fully acknowledge their debt to the actual body—now unattainable except by analogic image—of these now anonymous subjects as they posed for the photographers in 1974–75? Are these questions themselves not a quiver of the universal flesh about which Merleau-Ponty speaks?

From Flesh to Figure

In *The Practice of Everyday Life* Michel de Certeau allows for the unseen drama wherein assigned meanings are contested: "Only then can we gauge the difference or similarity between the production of the image and the secondary production hidden in the process of its utilization; . . . how . . . silent technologies determine or short-circuit institutional stage directions."[46] In this respect, Certeau differentiates between "strategies" and "tactics"—the former being an autonomous and self-sufficient location of "force-relationships" that make up "political, economic and scientific rationality."[47] The tactical, however, because it has no identifiable place or site, hovers in the realm of those opportunities that can be "seized." Certeau points to the almost invisible practices of everyday life where information is received or consumed. In this sense, Certeau turns his attention not to the inescapable (and equally totalizing) prison house of sign system production where latitude is scarce for individual engagement. In a turn of poetic justice and visual irony—yet without turning a blind eye to the power relations in *La Zona*—we might also reverse viewing many of the images so that the photographers and subjects, aware of the "process of utilization," are entitled themselves, in principle if not in demonstrable fact, to yield claims.

If there is value to the viewing of these images, it is in the document of individuation in the nearly boundless range of facial expressions: faces that reflect realities of race, class, and gender; faces that span the emotional ambiguity wherein laughter and impassive blankness are of a piece. Though they exist today outside their original frame of intent and meaning, these images cannot be reduced to individual desire of their production and consumption. The force relations in the Boystown photographs can be unleashed—and a certain subject agency successfully rendered—if we consider that, on some level, many of these female subjects, though certainly not all, were involved in a kind of constitutive performance, by means of a not-unlikely knowledge or recognition of eventually being "looked at" by a specific gaze "outside" the actual conditions of Boystown. But, in a double movement, our present viewing of these photographs raises individual ethical decisions as to whether we should be gazing at these images at all or, alternately, looking away. There is no small uneasiness about transforming the actual lives and bodies of the women and men in these images into photographic subjects for our consumption. However, these images can be read against the totalizing grain of their origin with reversible purpose of making room for legal speculation that would question actual ownership of these images: they are, in principle, the political (if not precisely the cultural) patrimony of the Mexican public trust. It is no small claim to submit that although one individual may claim to own the rights to their use and reproduction, their present and future meanings will elude the domain of private property. The Boystown archive reflects, even as it is in excess of, the ideology or "grid of intelligibility" that structures the social order between the United States and Mexico as it existed in 1974–75—indelible, and so beyond the scope of any archive.[48]

A curatorial desire drives my aim to situate these Boystown images as they might otherwise activate a relation to contemporary art practice, insofar as I find forceful but incomplete any tendency to level the subject effect of those portrayed into allegories of the border as brothel or as a "penetrable effeminized Other."[49] Paz described the mirror on the transnational U.S.–Mexico dividing line as unsubtle and unseemly. Despite the ideological recklessness to Wittliff's handling of these images—and perhaps, more important, on account of it—to discredit them totally is to refuse the affirmative effects they endorse and activate. Photographs are an opportune medium to test the relation between an image and the material conditions of historical production. By distinct manufacture, a photographic image summarizes a material expression and encapsulates a practical genesis that the final object largely conceals. With Merleau-Ponty again, photography provides forms of experience and action in the world. The art theorist Paul Crowther has turned to this philosopher for what, disapprovingly, he sees as a division between "medium- and practice-based historicity" and an "external relations" model of art history. This overturning has shifted the "productive energy of the art world into the curatorial sphere,"[50] a wide domain of cultural institutions and practices. In the curatorial view wherein concept overrides specific manufacture—or qualities of form and expression—to limit visual experience to the unique status of art is to effectuate a conclusive wedge. In terms of photography, this "closure," or essentialism of the medium, so defines the practice as a unique form of meaning. In terms of the pictures made in La Zona, this closure has an additional effect in that—with Wittliff insisting on such inimitability—the archive consolidates a class-consciousness that guarantees a regional geography of exception and immunity in terms of history, posterity, and art. The filmmaker and his archive lay claim to artistic status, but despite all philanthropic intentions, Wittliff remains complicit with the phenomenon of external relation he refutes, paradoxically, when he speaks of transparency and purity.

To counter this essentialism of the medium itself, one that does not view La Zona as a place of exhausted or self-contained social representation, I'd like to wager some final remarks that compel a shared image environment of my own design: a conversation between the Boystown photographs and the aesthetic and theoretical issues at stake in a commitment to contemporary Latina and Latino art making, visual culture, and the image environment at large, in terms of both practice and effect. Across the private–public divide, the shape of meanings attributed to—or inscribed on—individual and cultural bodies conspire together with other markers that render visible, at the level of representation, a powerful historic network in terms of sexual and social difference. As transitory sites on—and through—which various forces intervene, bodies can be registered, detained, or made to appear natural in representation, but equally transformed or reframed so as to unsettle, cause disruptions, and effect change.

Two rejoinders to La Zona emerge in a C-print image from the 1996 series "Interior Cartography" by Tatiana Parcero (who divides her time between Mexico City and New York) (Figure 65) and an Ektacolor print, "Untitled #127," produced in 2000 by the Los Angeles artist Ken González-Day (Figure 66). Reaffirming Álvarez Bravo and Rosalind Krauss on surrealist technique, these artists explore two distinct entry points into the corporeal mappings of body images—that is, either from the inside out or from the outside in, tattoos and scarifications across a multihued, collective epidermal gridwork or pages from a Mexican codex as projected on Parcero's own bodily surface—in either case, what the novelist Severo Sarduy called "an archeology of the skin."[51] In this sense, Parcero and Gonzalez-Day address what the critics Norma Alarcón and Coco Fusco, among many others in the debates of the late 1980s and 1990s, located as omissions in the making of literary studies and art theory.

Along with other subject positions of sexuality, race, and social standing, Alarcón and Fusco pointed to an elision or oversight of the Latina–Latino subject in the politics of progressive cultural criticism, and the importance of these debates cannot be underestimated. But I want to move from what Alarcón recognizes as the problematic of oppositional thinking when she acknowledged a discrepancy whereby "on the one hand, women [and queer persons] of color are excluded from feminist theorizing on the subject of consciousness and, on the other, that though excluded from theory, their books are read [or their artworks are discussed] in the classroom and/or duly (foot)noted."[52]

As far as production itself is concerned, Coco Fusco has claimed that "[no] longer bound to a sense of having to restrict one's focus, materials, or genre, many contemporary artists of color move back and forth between past and present, between history and fiction, between art and ritual, between high art and popular culture, and between Western and non-Western influence. In doing so, they participate in multiple communities."[53] As Alarcón cautions, we should be alert to the pitfalls of venturing a "shared consciousness" that obfuscates differences in the name of unity, but I think it's also possible to think today in terms of a shared image environment to which varying subject positions can respond not as a unified field but as one that activates multiple reading strategies or that renders complex and intertwined the supposedly distinct categories of Latin American, Anglo-American, or U.S. Latino art production together with other forms of cultural studies and gender criticism. We can turn to postcolonial theory and continental philosophy, for example, to coincide with the "plurality of self" as rendered by Latina/o artists and writers or to fashion a "politics of varied discourses" (as per Alarcón) that might allow us to discover the interconnectedness of historical subjects and material artifacts belonging to a greater system of mutual power and

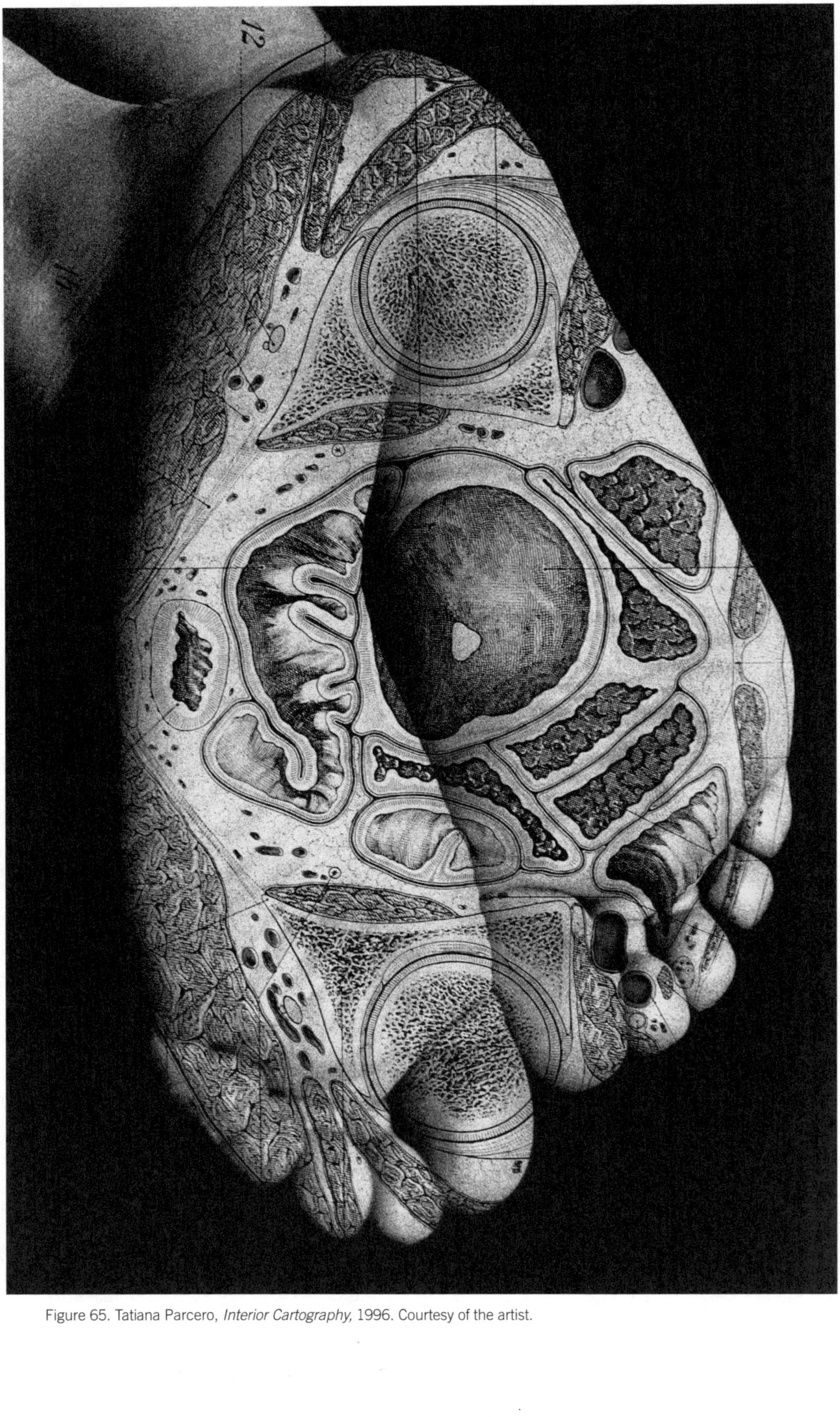

Figure 65. Tatiana Parcero, *Interior Cartography,* 1996. Courtesy of the artist.

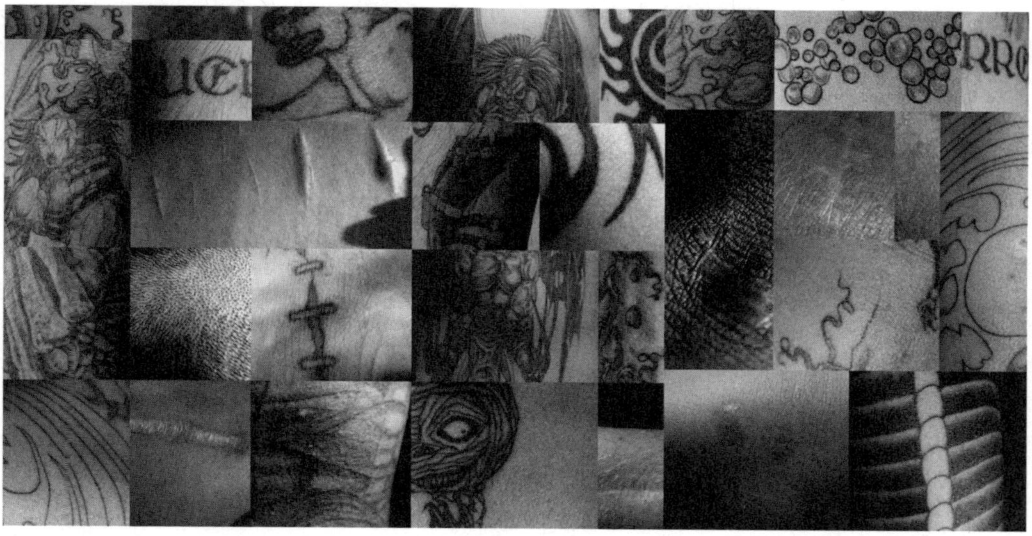

Figure 66. Ken Gonzales-Day, *Untitled #127,* 1999. Copyright 1999 Ken Gonzales-Day. Courtesy of the artist.

desire, without ignoring the powerful machine of representation and its political effects.

Previously we looked at reflections on the actual and virtual relationships that exist between Mexico and the United States, in terms that address the imbricated spheres of history, geopolitics, rhetoric, and representation. These relational effects between the United States and Mexico have come together in singular and revealing ways, especially since the latter half of the twentieth century, to create, under visible force relations, this shared image environment between distinct national cultures, though not exclusive of internal distinctions or of intertwining experiences of the modern and postmodern. This has become increasingly relevant to the boundaries and differences between the visual and the rhetorical—between what can be seen and what can be said. W. J. T. Mitchell has brought this point to bear as follows:

> The domains of word and image are like two countries that speak different languages but have a long history of mutual migration, cultural exchange, and other forms of intercourse. The word/image relation is not a master method for dissolving these borders or for maintaining them as eternally fixed boundaries; it is the name of a problem and a problematic—a description of the irregular, heterogeneous, and often improvised boundaries between "institutions of the visible" (visual arts, visual media, practices of display and spectation, and "institutions of the verbal") literature, language, discourse, practices of speech and writing, audition and reading.[54]

It is my desire that an investment in this problematic has been embodied in the objects under discussion up to this point, and that again it will be performed in the brief rehearsal of contemporary artists from Mexico and the United States, largely photo based, but all working within widely differing idioms, practices, and legacies. Prior chapters addressed the onrush of artistic production that occurred in Mexico during the 1920s and 1930s, the decades immediately after the social turning point of the ten-year Revolution. I sought to analyze those points of vulnerability and excess residues in the ever-unsettled relationship between art and society, between material culture and the built environment and the often less visible or fleeting phenomena of public social space and spectacle. Artworks and artifacts, of course, even despite certain tenets of modernity, are anything but self-evident or autonomous. The conditional nature of art as valid inquiry into the public sphere—even in its most pleasure producing of guises—allows for aesthetic meanings to circulate.

If, as Sara Kofman claims in *Camera Obscura of Ideology,* that "an idea is a reflection cut off from its source, engendering phantoms, fantasies, simulacra and fetishes," then photographic difference is always already at a crossroads where a politics of location and the modes of image making intersect. Recent critical efforts have underscored the imminent power relations that are successively staged between photographer and subject—who looks at whom and with what authority? This condition of the medium, however, must account for interpretive strategies that, without ignoring such a dynamics of power, allow us to discover points of underachievement or junctures by which an image is in excess of its medium and maker. One strategy made available to many artists, Mexican and U.S. Latina, has been the use of corporeal self-representation as a site by which to bring viewers into "contact" with remote and otherwise untenable sexual, social, and political realities.

Especially relevant to the Boystown archive of 1974–75 is the work of Graciela Iturbide, as brought to bear in an early photograph. Iturbide has sought to explore the kind of severed optics with regard to the possible meanings given shape through images of women. Her photographs not only inquire into the division of private and public life in terms of sex but subvert those attributes or motifs that have been designated by convention to female transcendence. It is in this respect that many of her pictures address the other side of Mexican femininity. Pressing against the dubious "authority" of her camera, Iturbide offers a sly comment on Mexico's sexual and social contradictions—with women as the appearance by which representation and culture are said to coexist on two utterly incompatible planes.

Witness the photograph titled *México D.F. (Mexico City)* of 1972 (Figure 67). Supporting her weight with elbows firmly resting on the round wooden table in front of her, a woman leers at something beyond the frame of the picture. Her eyelids struggle with drowsiness or the effects of alcohol: an empty shot glass glimmers under the smoldering ember of her half-consumed cigarette between the index and middle fingers of her right hand. Bold mascara and eyeliner accentuate a look of disdain, desperation, or knowing abandon. In a floral-patterned short-sleeve dress, she sits on a chair whose wrought-iron back forms an arabesque behind her, under the wall mural depicting the vague outline of a human skull. In the skeletal orbits are scenes of a hotel room with an empty bed and night dresser, as well as an infirmary, with three beds, one empty, and two female subjects convalescing under a crucifix on the wall. A tombstone with the obligatory R.I.P. rounds off the moral to this cautionary account. Iturbide situates sex and cultural specificity, however, between actual experience and the no-less-real effects of depiction, at least as this scene endures in the photograph: it captures the artifice of a tableau in a Mexico City wax museum. In this picture, Iturbide belies the masquerade of feminine performance in the national camera of patrimonial desire. Similar references to sexual difference and the nation are staged by comparing contemporary practitioners from Mexico and the United States.

An image environment is established between the Chicana artist Amalia Mesa-Bains (*Cihuatéotl,* earth sculpture, 1997) and the Mexico City artist Silvia Gruner, in their use of the precolonial past toward a present-day politics of memory (Figure 68). The imagined nation space of Mesa-Bains's 1997 "Cihuatlampa, The Place of the Giant Women" (a third episode in her *Venus Envy* project) and the sexual and national politics referred to in Gruner's video-screen-grabs, provocatively titled

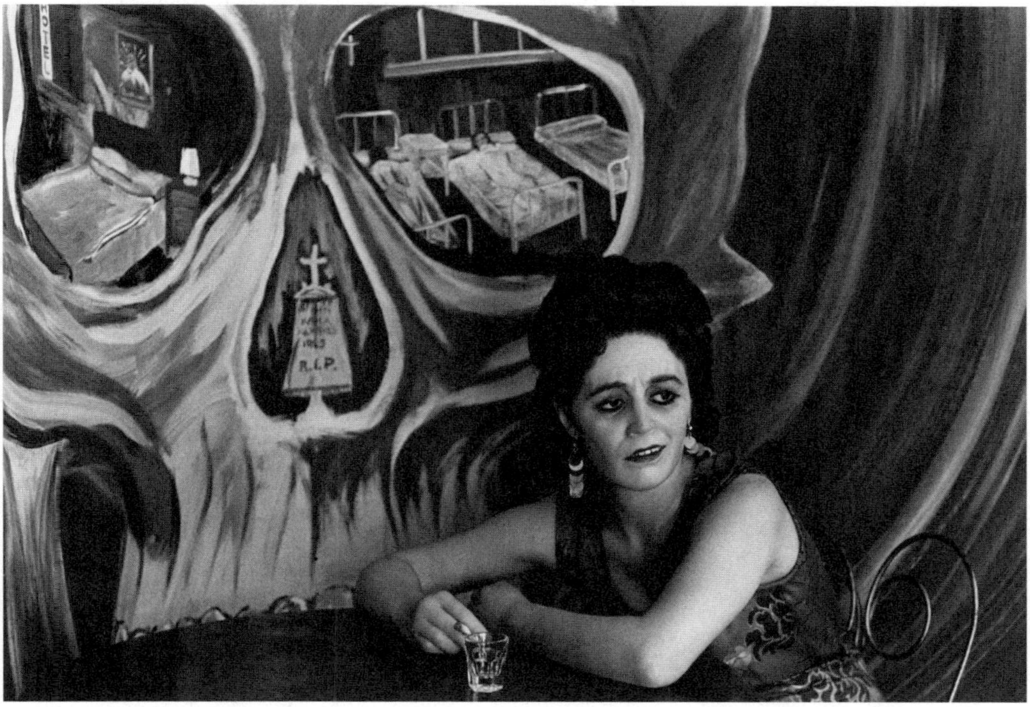

Figure 67. Graciela Iturbide, *México D.F. (Mexico City),* 1972. Digital image courtesy of Rose Gallery, Los Angeles.

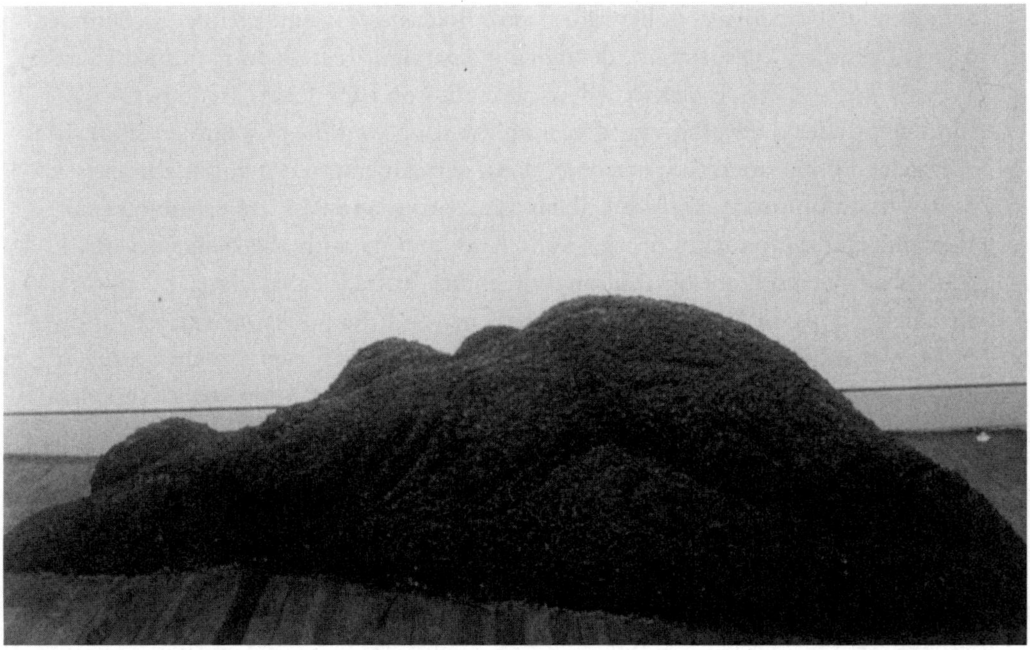

Figure 68. Amalia Mesa-Bains, *Cihuatéotl,* 1997. Earth sculpture. Courtesy of the artist.

"Don't Fuck with the Past or You Might Get Pregnant" (Figures 69A, 69B, 69C), can be read across one another as alternately optimistic or less auspicious statements about the degree to which the precolonial can serve as a site to think new, hybrid, or syncretic identities—at best, with a political purpose in light of actual or possible prohibitions, uncontainability, and menace.

Lost steps are retraced in the work of the Los Angeles Chicana artist Christina Fernández in her 1995 series *María's Great Expedition,* with images like that titled "1930, Transporting Produce, Outskirts Phoenix, Arizona" (Figure 70). Alluding to the traveling cultures of modernity—to its diaspora and migration—Fernández restages the local history of her grandmother's displacement from Mexico to the United States, with Fernández herself in the identifying role, and with text also that anchors the photographic images to "a specific location and the socio-political context of the time"; images which, according to the artist, betray "subtle anachronisms, via props, to bring the images to the present." Next to this image we can view one by the Mexico City artist Claudia Fernández from her 1996 series titled *El alimento (Nourishment)* (Figure 71). In this image and others, Fernández has painted a throng of (mostly women's) footwear to resemble the patina known as peltre, a glaze found on a kind of metal dinnerware and utensils widely used by the working classes of Mexico. By placing them on the steps or at the foot of the Pyramid of the Sun at Teotihuacán, Fernández questions the degree to which a large majority of Mexican men and women have access to citizenship and to social space in contrast to the degree to which a history of monuments and the so-called

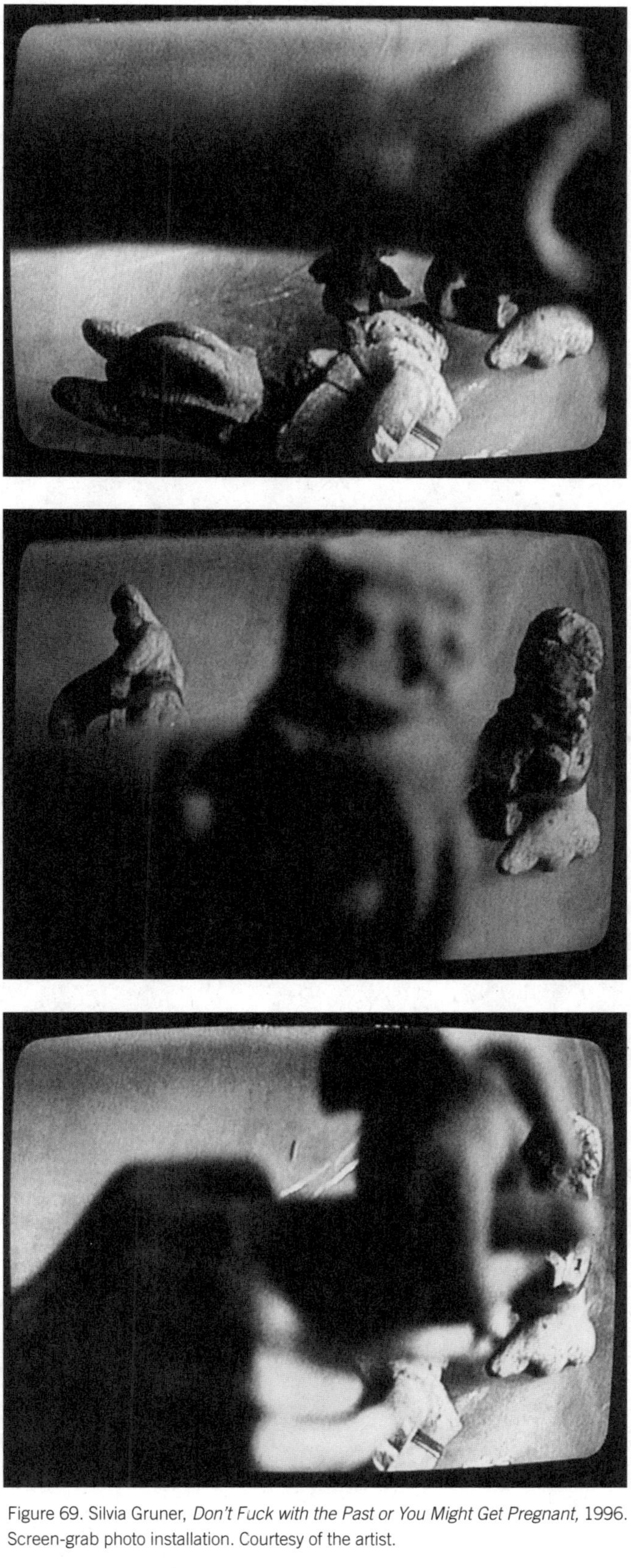

Figure 69. Silvia Gruner, *Don't Fuck with the Past or You Might Get Pregnant,* 1996. Screen-grab photo installation. Courtesy of the artist.

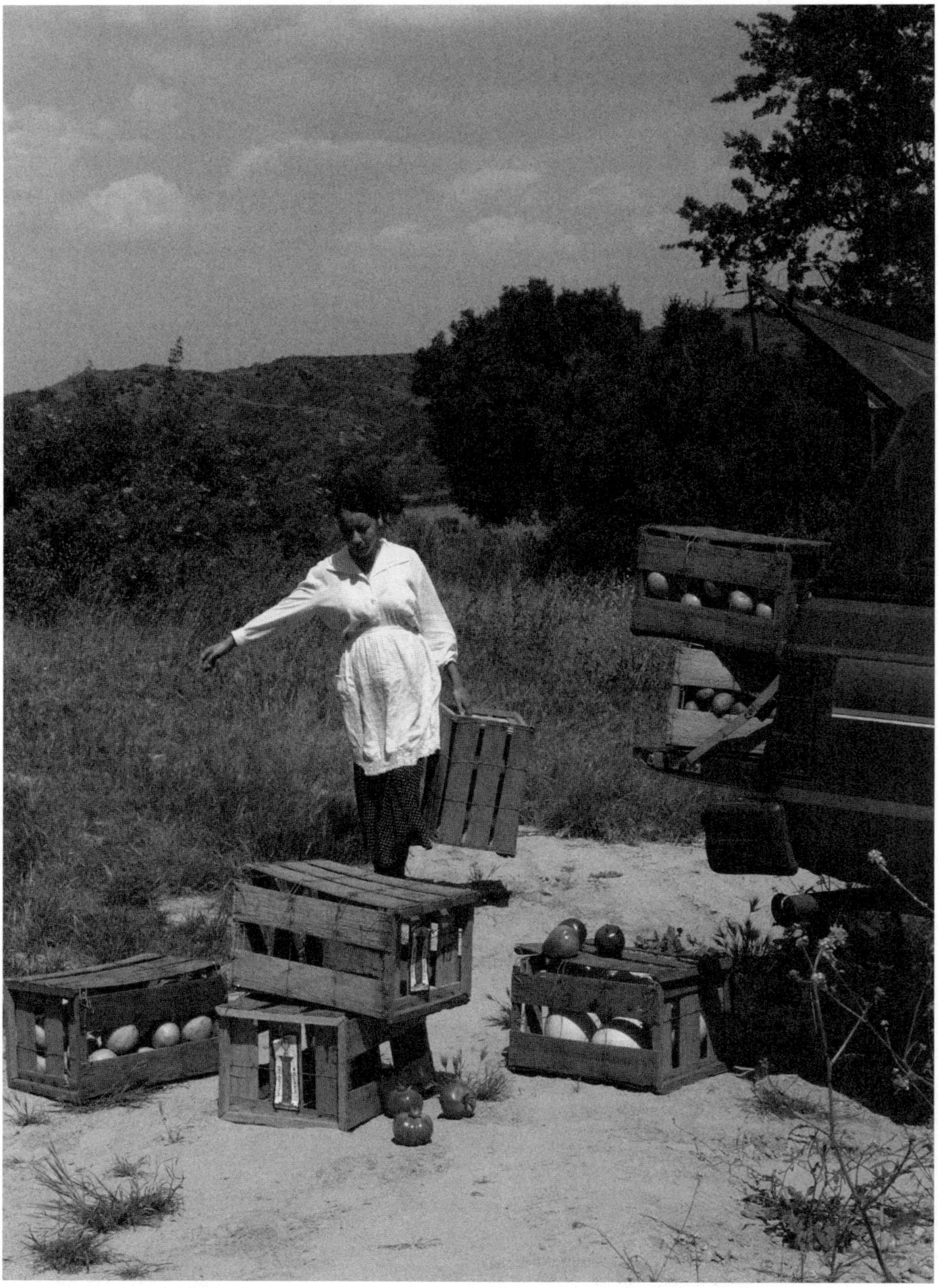

Figure 70. Christina Fernandez, *María's Great Expedition,* 1995. Courtesy of the artist.

popular classes are deployed and conflated in official constructions of Mexican identity. Both artists interrogate the limits of making visual assertions about local histories, which have been rendered partially invisible by looming material reminders that support certain narratives of nation.

The centrality of the body as a material site for artistic practice can be critically examined under the phenomenological lens of Merleau-Ponty. Judith Butler charges rightly that Merleau-Ponty's "subject" perhaps denotes "a given history of sexual relations which have produced [a] disembodied voyeur and his machinations of enslavement." But she also admits a debt to a work that allows framing the gender-specific and socially located body as a legitimate "scene of cultural struggle," a site in which "the intimate and the political converge, and a dramatic opportunity for expression, analysis and change."[55]

In *The Visible and the Invisible* Merleau-Ponty claims that because each separate cut-out of visuality is in a differential, comparative relationship with all else in the surrounding visual field, a photograph constitutes a "certain node in the woof of the simultaneous and the successive."[56] This recalls the "double writing" of the Casasola and Wittliff archives, for example, where a subject is intelligible only in the passage between the "many-as-one" and the "one-by-one," between displayer and displayed, between a present juncture and somewhere else. Because representation seizes and detains the relations between a lived body and the outside world as an ephemeral passage (or stress point in time and space), it is in two-way transit

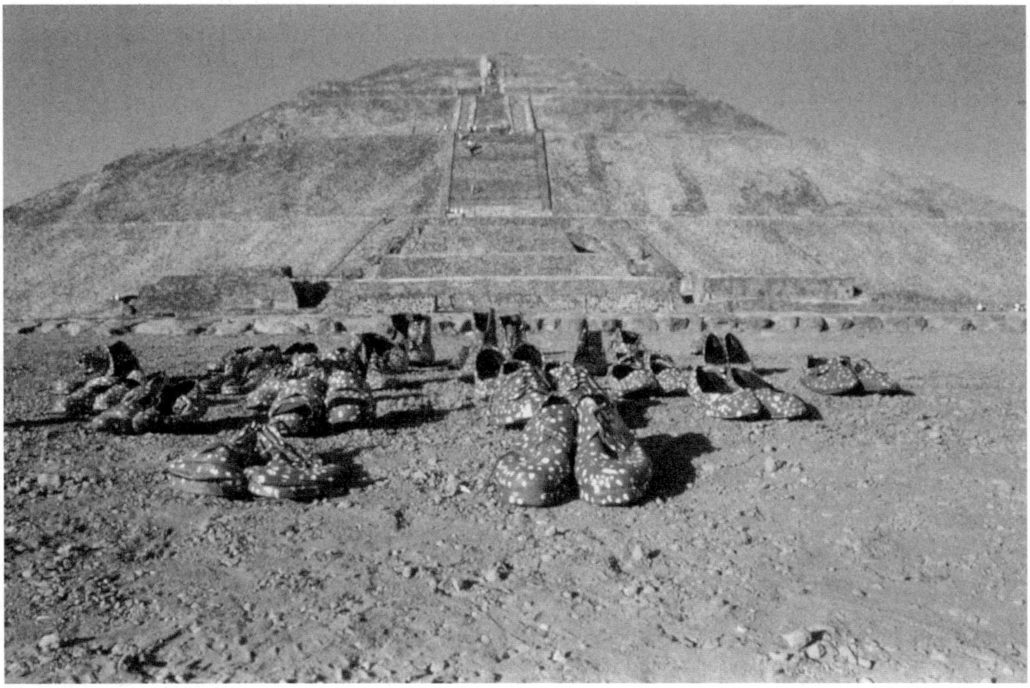

Figure 71. Claudia Fernández, *El alimento (Nourishment)*. Courtesy of the artist.

between exterior and interior horizons. We might consider the image environment as that shared surface depicting a profundity, as the material representative counterpart to the double movement back and forth between seer and seen. A photographic image can be viewed as a "divergence between the within and without that constitutes [the] natural secret" of those surfaces haunted by a touch or vision.

Merleau-Ponty gives this gap, this openness between the seer and the seen, the tactile connotations of flesh. But this flesh is always latency, a virtual, pure potentiality. As such, flesh constitutes reversibility itself, of matter with a view to mind as it may be awakened in the present political tenses of viewing. Visual artifacts can be read as the metonymic representation of an instant of flesh. Perhaps in excess of himself, Merleau-Ponty was suggesting a politics of the flesh that is at the heart of aesthetics and theoretical issues at stake in some of the Latina representations and art making I've addressed briefly in these pages, one that provides strategies for looking back at the archives of prior forms of visual representation. Second visibilities are those valuations that by comparative glance are capable of making historically determined renderings foreign to themselves. If urgency and immediacy impose a force and shape not only on the visual nature of desire but on the kinds of visual culture we desire, we can begin to think of an art and politics not only in terms of identity but in terms of a metaphorics yielding the potential of a body to effect change. The Boystown photographs submit that bodies are an insufficient guarantee of knowledge and history: the gap they introduce between what a body says and means is mirrored in the dispute over bodies whereby the negligent bureaucratic state doubles as a national archive. If photographs successfully question preexisting subjectivities and the status of received images informing our image environment, then we can move strategically from figure to flesh at mutual purposes. If discontent and pleasure are only as tenable or untenable as the representations we make of them, we can explore the lines on both sides of the national camera as body politics—a double world of latency and excess on various sides of any social or sexualized assertion, that is, between represented subject positions, the image environment, and its various economies and manifold interpretive communities, both those foreseen and unsuspected.

The Boystown pictures point to the potentiality of indiscretion. Because an archive is a cultural category provisional in nature—the part tenuously standing for a protracted totality—we might consider some of the seemingly fixed oppositions of dominant to defiant, particular to universal, and self to other, as metonymic of that archival place of intertwining alliances and associations. There, an exchange between the identical and different can enter into temporary creative reversibility. In that image environment, power relations between dominant and subaltern subjects are never clear-cut and settled but dispersed, multiple, and perplexing, such that radical effects might be gained from the negative mirror of desire and frustration haunting the conditions of contact and exchange.

Acknowledgments

This book is indebted to individuals and communities too many to properly thank. Its conception was in Mexico City where, from 1987 to 1997, a range of intellectual formations and art scenes (some official, others improvised or makeshift) provided tough training ground for the critical inquiry that led to the present pages. That itinerary included magazines and journals such as *Vuelta, Artes de México, La jornada,* and *Luna córnea,* and such focal points for debate as *Curare, Centro de la Imagen,* and *FITAC,* as well as *Los viernes* organized by Fernando Leal Audirac; *Mel's Studio* hosted by Melanie Smith; and *La dalia negra* convoked by Cuauhtémoc Medina, Ernesto Priani, and Manuel Hernández. Foundational exchange was enabled by Jan William; so, too, the conversations owing to the boundless hospitality of friends Graciela Iturbide and Magali Lara.

A section of chapter 1 that was published in *CR: The New Centennial Review* benefited from communication with Margaret Archuleta, Audra Simpson, Darren Ranco, and Esther Gabara; Charles Briggs of the Center for Iberian and Latin American Studies (CILAS) at the University of California, San Diego, later provided the earliest opportunity to rehearse some of these claims. The first inflections of chapter 2 began as a talk delivered in light of "Modotti and Weston: Mexicanidad," an exhibition held in 1998 at the Austin Museum of Art, whose director, Elizabeth Ferrer, prompted me to further engage this material. Ramón Gutiérrez, of the Center for the Study of Race and Ethnicity at the University of California, San Diego, extended a more recent occasion to present this research at a symposium. Chapter 3 owes its existence above all to the dazzling generosity of Rose Shoshana, and then to my collaborations with Weston Naef and Mikka Gee Conway; this led to the exhibition "Optical Parables: Manuel Álvarez Bravo" and to an accompanying book. Some of the chapter's closer readings trace back to curatorial entries I authored for those joint undertakings; they survive here to form a palimpsest that honors those neglected art historical genres—the object description and wall text—so often lost to the archive. Another configuration of this research had the privilege of far finer phrasing in the excellent Spanish-language translation of Jaime Soler Frost for a Mexico City exhibition catalog.

Other venues to further develop my claims were afforded by a lecture delivered at the J. Paul Getty Museum and an essay I wrote for *Miradas convergentes,* a book published parallel to an exhibition of the same name organized by the late Mercedes Iturbe, director of Mexico City's Palacio de Bellas Artes. Chapter 4 owes to early articulations with, and the enduring patience of, Amanda Yorke Focke, Kathryn Calloway, E. Cameron Scott, Hoa Nguyen, and Dale Smith. I had the opportunity to share some of its later arguments and images in lectures at Drake University and James Madison University, thanks to the kindness and hospitality of Graham Foust and Maureen G. Shanahan, respectively; my colleague John Welchman at the University of California, San Diego, encouraged me to present consequent research in a seminar composed of MFA and PhD students. Richard Morrison at the University of Minnesota Press patiently walked me through the predicament and fortunes of formal constraints; these conversations thus led to a renewed engagement with the visual archive discussed therein. Earlier at the University of Minnesota Press, Andrea Kleinhuber helped me gain view of the inroads that traveling inquiries can properly map, and along the way Adam Brunner and Paula Dragosh lent a caring eye for detail that brought the landscape into view.

Triangulating with Southern California and Mexico's Distrito Federal, I call home yet another place—Buffalo, New York, a city that lays claim to long-standing venues for debate and innovative art making. Thanks to practitioners, scholars, and art professionals, its urban culture offers a vibrant, welcoming community, with institutions that include the State University of New York at Buffalo, the Albright-Knox Art Gallery, Big Orbit, CEPA Gallery, and Hallwalls. Accommodating various research needs were Lawrence Brose, executive director of CEPA Gallery; Susana Tejada, head of research resources at the Albright-Knox Art Gallery; and various departments and academic centers at SUNY-Buffalo. All members of my immediate family live as fortunate residents of Greater Buffalo—mother, father, sister, and brother—following migrations that first led my parents from Colombia to Los Angeles, a short tenure in Texas, and finally to the town of Kenmore, New York. All their support cannot be measured in a lifetime. I reserve particular appreciation for the scholars at SUNY-Buffalo whose friendship and generosity of mind had the most impact on these pages: Joan Copjec, Elizabeth Grosz, Nathan Grant, Carine Mardorossian, and David Johnson.

A year at Dartmouth College, under the aegis of the César E. Chávez Fellowship (2002–3), provided purpose and kindhearted company. Marysa Navarro, Silvia Spitta, and Derrick Cartwright, respectively, offered intellectual impetus through the Latin American, Latino, and Caribbean Studies program (LALACS), the Department of Spanish and Portuguese, and the Hood Museum of Art. During this time, Melissa Harris of *Aperture,* David Levi-Strauss for a special issue of *SF Camerawork,* Karen van Meenen of *Afterimage,* and Alan Gilbert of *NYFA Quarterly* presented opportunities to connect critically with camera-generated images. Abigail Solomon-Godeau, Andrea Noble, Grant Kester, and an anonymous reader at the University of Minnesota Press offered excellent suggestions in terms of structure and cadence that allowed me to better rehearse the claims of this book; any residual infelicity remains the sole responsibility of its author.

The University of California, San Diego, provided significant support during the final stages of this book's writing. UCSD's Senior Vice Chancellor of Academic Affairs and the Academic Senate Committee on Affirmative Action and Diversity awarded a Hellman Fellowship and release time through the Faculty Career Development Program; this assistance gave me the invaluable chance to focus on scholarship and interrelated curatorial projects. I'm grateful to UCSD's Visual Arts Department, a stimulating image-community of artists, theorists, and art historians, for frameworks of knowledge and thoughtfulness from which I have learned incalculably. Special thanks are due to Steve Fagin, Rubén Ortiz-Torres, and Yóshua Okón for the opportunity to collaboratively stage a conference in 2005 on the varieties of art world experience in Mexico City during the 1990s, and to Lesley Stern and Jack Greenstein, who remind me of the manifold ways in which camera-based media studies and critical art histories can matter. I extend secret hand signs to my fellow travelers in literature, ethnic studies, communication, anthropology, and critical gender studies. Also at UCSD, Leslie Abrams, Karen Linvall-Larson, and Lynda Classen confirm the degree to which so much scholarship is indebted to library professionals who share real stakes in the production of knowledge. I owe special thanks to David Pellow of UCSD's California Cultures in Comparative Perspective and to its cluster of scholars who challenge and validate the objective of interdisciplinary research so as to enliven our social constituencies.

The poet Robert Creeley applauded the company of friends and associates whose amity can comprise no adequate name. Likewise, no pitch can perfectly convey the gratitude I owe a joyful company that includes a handful of constant companions and interlocutors; the day-to-day metaphors they offer to enthuse and defy are styles of allegiance imperative for any sustained commitment to meaning. On the travels that led to this book—if only by name—they are Rosa Alcalá, Laura Armstrong, Joel Bettridge, Susan Briante, Derrick Cartwright, Mary Coffey, Richard Deming, Kristen Dykstra, Alan Gilbert, Ramón Gutiérrez, Nancy Kuhl, Natalia Molina, Peter Ramos, Reed Rudy, Nayan Shah, Meg Wesling, and Elana Zilberg.

The enduring syllables are for Michael Bryan.

Notes

Itinerary

1. Casasola, *Historia gráfica de la Revolución mexicana,* 138–40.

2. Haley, *Revolution and Intervention,* 14.

3. Echoing Walter Benjamin, W. J. T. Mitchell has usefully christened our period the "age of biocybernetic reproduction" ("Art in the Age of Biocybernetic Reproduction").

4. This image is inspired by the collaborative artist team of Margaret Crane and Jon Winet, and their political Web project "Democracy: The Last Campaign," dtlc.walkerart .org. See also the artist collective known as @rt-mark, www.rtmark.com.

5. Benjamin, "Goethe's Elective Affinities," 352.

6. Goethe, *Elective Affinities,* 232. "He occupied himself the greater part of the day in capturing the picturesque views of the park in a portable *camera obscura* and then drawing them, thus preserving for himself the fruit of his travels."

7. The citation in full is as follows: "For in jokes, too, in invective, in misunderstanding, in all cases where action puts forth its own image and exists, absorbing and consuming it, where nearness looks with its own eyes, the long-sought image sphere is opened, the world of universal and integral actualities, where the 'best room' is missing—the sphere, in a word in which political materialism and physical nature share the inner man, the psyche, the individual, or whatever else we wish to throw them, with dialectical justice, so that no limb remains unrent. Nevertheless—indeed, precisely after such dialectical annihilation—this will still be a sphere of images and more concretely, of bodies. . . . There is a residue. The collective is a body, too. And the *physis* that is being organized for it in technology can, through all its political and factual reality, only be produced in that image sphere to which profane illumination initiates us. Only when in technology body and image so interpenetrate that all revolutionary tension becomes bodily collective innervation, and all the bodily innervations of the collective become revolutionary discharge, has reality transcended itself to the extent demanded by the Communist Manifesto. For the moment, only the Surrealists have understood its present commands. They exchange,

to a man, the play of human features for the face of an alarm clock that in each minute rings for sixty seconds" (Benjamin, "Surrealism," 191–92).

8. Strauss, *Between Dog and Wolf*, 112.

9. Harrison and Wood, *Art in Theory*, 967.

10. Berger writes: "If one moment of that process is isolated, its image will seem banal and its banality, instead of serving as a bridge between two intense imaginative states, will be chilling. This is one reason why expressive photographs of the naked are even rarer than paintings. The easy solution for the photographer is to turn the figure into a nude which, by generalizing both sight and viewer and making sexuality unspecific, turns desire into fantasy" (*Ways of Seeing*, 58–59).

11. Harrison and Wood, *Art in Theory*, 1105, emphasis added.

12. Solomon-Godeau, *Photography at the Dock*, 258.

13. Limón, *American Encounters*, 23.

14. Bourdieu, *Photography*.

15. Ibid., 27.

16. Batchen, *Burning with Desire*, 12.

17. Bhabha, *Location of Culture*, 155.

18. Williams and Pinkney, *Politics of Modernism*, 37–48.

19. Grundberg, *Crisis of the Real*.

20. Spivak, *Critique of Postcolonial Reason*, 175.

1. Tenures of Land and Light

1. Brenner and Leighton, *Wind That Swept Mexico*, 8.

2. Rosenthal, "Spectacle Fear, and Protest," 42.

3. Krauze, *Porfirio Díaz*, 10.

4. Haley, *Revolution and Intervention*, 11.

5. Brenner and Leighton, *Wind That Swept Mexico*, caption 40.

6. For an excellent discussion of communal forms of land ownership, and the historiographic account of it, see Kourí, "Interpreting the Expropriation of Indio Pueblo Lands."

7. Compare Casasola and King, *Tierra y Libertad!* with Morales, Maawad, Assad, Palma, and Fototeca del INAH, *Los inicios del México contemporáneo (The beginnings of contemporary Mexico)*.

8. See Bartra, *El salvaje en el espejo*.

9. Bhabha, *Location of Culture*, 140.

10. Ibid., 142.

11. Ibid., 146.

12. Ibid., 150.

13. "I have waited with patience for the day in which the Mexican populace was prepared to select and adjust its government at each election without fear of armed revolutions, without jeopardizing the national credit and without encumbering the country's progress. I believe that day has come. I gladly welcome an opposition party in the Republic if it takes shape. I'd see it as a blessing, and not as a curse. . . . I have no desire to continue in the Presidency; this nation is ready for a definitive life of liberty" (Casasola, *Historia gráfica*, xv).

14. Casasola, *Historia gráfica*, 99.

15. Kourí, "Interpreting the Expropriation of Indio Pueblo Lands," 87.

16. Bhabha, *Location of Culture*, 142.

17. Deleuze, *Cinema 1*, 195. Deleuze employs the phrase in discussing Mizoguchi's classic film *Ugetsu*—the source material for the Mexican writer Carlos Fuentes and his novella *Aura*.

18. The first include the authors Anita Brenner and John Mason Hart; the second category is represented by a line that runs from Frank Tannenbaum to Alan Knight; and a third tendency includes François-Xavier Guerra. For an overview of this debate, see Meyer and Beezley, *Oxford History of Mexico*.

19. A difficult passage by Bhabha is suggestive of this: "In the metaphor of the national community as the 'many as one' the one is now both the tendency to totalize the social in a homogenous empty time, and the repetition of that minus in the origin, the less-than-one that intervenes with a metonymic, iterative temporality" (*Location of Culture*, 155).

20. A handful of these image makers can be identified. These include Eduardo Melhado, José María Lupercio and his younger brother Abraham; Samuel Tinoco, Gerónimo Hernández, Víctor León, Luis Santamaría, Manuel Ramos, and Hugo Brehme, as well as H. J. Gutiérrez, and C. B. Waite. See Debroise, *Mexican Suite*, and Casasola, *World of Agustín Víctor Casasola*.

21. Debroise, *Mexican Suite*, 186.

22. Lara Klahr, "Agustín Víctor Casasola," 7.

23. Ibid.

24. Sekula writes: "Taken literally, this traffic involves the social production, circulation and reception of photographs in a society based on commodity production and exchange. Taken metaphorically, the notion of traffic suggests the peculiar way in which photographic meaning—and the very discourse of photography—is characterized by an incessant oscillation between what Lukács termed the 'antinomies of bourgeois thought.' This is always a movement between objectivism and subjectivism" (Sekula and Ohio State University, Gallery of Fine Art, *Photography against the Grain*, xv).

25. Monsiváis writes: "The Casasola Archive is history waiting patiently and with serene expectancy for the first shot to be fired. . . . we see one thing time and again: without intending to, but also without intending otherwise, the Casasola Archive . . . becomes—and this is what makes it so immensely valuable—a sequential and purposeful progression of a limited number of images, of a limited number of themes: Power, the People, Defeat, Glory (perhaps), and the demise of a Social Order" (quoted in Casasola, *World of Agustín Víctor Casasola*, 38).

26. Ibid.

27. "Published in book form as *Álbum histórico gráfico* (1921), the photographs that Casasola gathered in the previous two decades comprised a particular body of work that early on was imbued with forceful historic and ideological connotations: as 'collective memory' they reaffirmed the ecumenical nature of the Mexican Revolution. The *Álbum histórico gráfico* was not an immediate success however: it was published during the period of national reconstruction during the Álvaro Obregón regime when Mexico preferred to leave behind the preceding years of gory struggle. Only a first volume (comprised of five albums) was published of the projected sixteen. By comparison, the 1942 edition of the *Historia gráfica de la Revolución mexicana*, published by Ismael Casasola, Agustín's eldest son, proved a resounding success" (Debroise and Fuentes Rojas, *Fuga mexicana*).

28. Debroise is of the following opinion: "It takes but one stride to go from the aesthetization of content (the Revolution) to the aesthetization of the container (the photographic vehicle), and it was Monsiváis who took that step at the end of the 1970s, when he wrote the prologue to a two-volume set of images selected from the Casasola Archive,

edited in Mexico by Larousse and the Librería Francesa, with the backing of the photographer's family descendants. As of that moment, the photographs attributed to Casasola, and until then sloppily printed, make a passage into the limited edition art book. Thereafter they serve to elaborate commercials for official propaganda in films and television, to decorate tourist restaurants of no uncertain 'Mexican ambience.' The Archive is acquired by the State and on this foundation is erected the first center in the country devoted solely to housing photographic material" (Debroise and Fuentes Rojas, *Fuga mexicana*).

29. Brenner and Leighton, *Wind That Swept Mexico,* 78.

30. Monsiváis, quoted in Casasola, *World of Agustín Víctor Casasola,* 45–46.

31. Beezley, Martin, and French, *Rituals of Rule, Rituals of Resistance.*

32. Nietzsche, *Beyond Good and Evil,* 134.

33. Ibid., 135.

34. In a different context, Jacques Derrida refers to this outcome in *Archive Fever.* In that book—in large part a discussion of the history of psychoanalysis in terms of its own annals, and hence about the concept of preservation—Derrida posits a series of hypotheses that have a common attribute: "They concern," he writes "the *impression* left . . . by the *Freudian signature* on its own archive and of archivization, that is to say also, inversely and as an indirect consequence, on historiography. Not only on historiography in general, not only on the history of the archive, but also on the history of a *concept in general*" (*Archive Fever,* 5).

35. Derrida, *Archive Fever,* 5.

36. The following two publications served also as exhibition catalogs: Casasola and King, *Tierra y Libertad!* and Casasola, *World of Agustín Víctor Casasola.*

37. Bergson, *Matter and Memory,* 38.

38. Ibid.

39. Bergson writes that "the body is changing form at every moment; or rather, there is no form, since form is immobile and the reality is movement. What is real is the continual *change of* form: *form is only a snapshot view of a transition.* Therefore, here again, our perception manages to solidify into discontinuous images the fluid continuity of the real (Bergson, *Creative Evolution,* 302).

40. This in-itself of the image is matter: not something hidden behind the image but, on the contrary, the absolute identity of the image and movement: "You may say that my body is matter or that it is an image." The movement-image and *flowing*-matter are strictly the same thing (Deleuze, *Cinema 1,* 58–59).

41. "By virtue of the cerebral interval, in effect, a being can retain from a material object and the actions issuing from it only those elements that interest him. So that perception is not the object plus something, but the object minus something, minus everything that does not interest us. . . . the present is not; rather, it is pure becoming, always outside itself. . . . At the limit, the ordinary determinations are reversed: of the present, we must say at every instant that it 'was,' and of the past, that it 'is,' that is eternally, for all time. This is the difference in kind between the past and the present" (Deleuze, *Bergsonism,* 24–25, 55).

42. Roget, "Explanation of an Optical Deception."

43. Benjamin and Arendt, *Illuminations,* 157.

44. Arendt, "Walter Benjamin: 1892–1940," 38.

45. Bergson, *Mind-Energy,* 22.

46. Deleuze, *Cinema 1,* 11.

47. Benjamin, "On Language as Such," 325.

48. "La filosofía de M. Bergson [propone] la corrección sistemática del intelectualismo por un llamamiento constante a la intuición. Esta combinación de los procedimientos puramente racionales y analíticos con la intuición directa y viva que reproduce la realidad y la esclarece con la ciencia, penetrando a la singularidad de los seres concretos irreducibles y no nada más a las definiciones abstractas que suministra la inteligencia, es el método exclusivo o privativo de la filosofía" (Caso, *Problemas filosóficos,* 108).

49. Krauze de Kolteniuk, *La filosofía de Antonio Caso,* 17.

50. Ibid.

51. Ibid., 18.

52. Comte, quoted in Harrison, Wood, and Gaiger, *Art in Theory,* 152, emphasis added.

53. Ibid.

54. Ibid.

55. Caso writes: "No physicist today believes Descartes was right in affirming as he did that without recourse to a prior knowledge of light, optics would be impossible. Optics is a science fulfilled: it has been possible to reduce the phenomenon of light to the precision of algebra and geometry and, nevertheless, the intrinsic nature of light is as mysterious for modern hypotheses, or somewhat less, than it was in the time that Descartes wrote his meditations on optics. But Descartes was not entirely wrong: insofar as the nature of light remains unknown, relative science will not be able reach its perfect development" ["Hoy día nadie entre los físicos cree que Descartes estuviera en lo justo al afirmar, como afirmaba, que sin el conocimiento previo de la naturaleza de la luz, la óptica sería imposible. La óptica está hecha: ha sido posible reducir a la precisión del álgebra y de la geometría el fenómeno luminoso, y, sin embargo, la intrínseca naturaleza de la luz es tan misteriosa para las hipótesis modernas, o poco menos, que lo era en la época en que Descartes hacía sus meditaciones sobre la óptica. Pero Descartes no carecía absolutamente de razón: mientras la naturaleza de la luz no se conozca, la ciencia relativa no podrá alcanzar su desarrollo perfecto"] (Caso, *Problemas filosóficos,* 63, my translation).

56. "Hay algo superior al *sentido espectacular* de los estetas y es el *sentido vital* de los moralistas que saben que el mundo no se ha acabado de hacer todavía, y que en hacerlo estamos y en perfeccionarlo debemos gastar nuestra fe y nuestro aliento" (Caso, *Problemas filosóficos,* 262–63).

57. "La filosofía no es ya un sistema *á prendre où á laisser,* como dice Bergson; es una obra esencialmente social y compleja, en la que el pensamiento filosófico y las ciencias se unifican en un movimiento de constante enlace, de circulación concomitante, de asidua y mutua colaboración" (Caso, *Problemas filosóficos,* 262–63).

58. "Es, por ende, un naturalismo ingenuo, tan ingenuo como el naturalismo estético: consiste en explicar el movimiento por el número y el espacio, el hecho físico-químico por la mecánica, las reacciones biológicas por virtud de las leyes de la química, y por la biología animal el espíritu" (Caso, *Problemas filosóficos,* 279–80).

59. "El naturalismo estético es un positivismo del arte; doctrina que carece de significación crítica, como su congénere filosófica. Cuando el naturalista piensa en reproducir la vida ordinaria con sus repeticiones absurdas, sus irregularidades numerosas, sus vacilaciones inestéticas y su inconexidad fenomenal característica, es hacer que copia la naturaleza profunda de las cosas, olvida que la realidad de las cosas no estriba en su desordenada manifestación utilitaria: olvida que la realidad es siempre ideal, que se necesita deshacer el convencionalismo de la experiencia diaria para elevarse a la contemplación estética, verdadera, y que, finalmente, un ser, un alma, una cosa, son más reales y más

precisos en el limbo etéreo de la inspiración idealista que en la reproducción fotográfica de la acción" (Caso, *Problemas filosóficos,* 281, emphasis added).

60. De Zayas, *How, When, and Why Modern Art Came to New York.*

61. Ibid., vii.

62. Stieglitz, "Photography," 17–20; Stieglitz, "Photography and Artistic Photography," 13–14.

63. Ibid.

64. Bergson, *Matter and Memory,* 186.

65. Ibid., 82.

66. Deleuze, *Bergsonism,* 37.

67. Benjamin, "Theses on the Philosophy of History," 262.

68. Benjamin, "The Work of Art in the Age of Mechanical Reproduction," 237.

2. Experiment in Related Form

1. Albers, *Shadows, Fire, Snow,* 119.

2. Ibid.

3. Ibid. The "R." after Modotti is a veiled or abbreviated reference to her married name. Her recently deceased husband, Roubaix (Robo) de l'Abrie Richey, had died earlier that year in Mexico City.

4. Eastman House curator Therese Mulligan writes: "For many photographers, the importance of place, whether home or country, contributes to a defining expression of life and art. Mexico was such a place for Tina Modotti and Edward Weston, who traveled from California to Mexico City in the late summer of 1923. They found a country that was reverberating with the modernizing effects of recent revolution: political and social reform coupled with cultural initiatives and new industries prompted a momentous revitalization of Mexican society" (Mulligan, quoted in George Eastman House, International Museum of Art, and Fundación Pedro Barrié de la Maza, *Modotti y Weston,* 75).

5. Weston's and Modotti's photographic styles, the exhibition press material tells us, "developed in different manners." It continues: "Weston began to focus on a formal aesthetic, which would later become highly influential in American photography. In search of what he called the 'quintessence of the thing itself,' he used the camera to emphasize the power of pure form, whether it be of architecture, the landscape, people, or simple folk art objects. Modotti, in contrast, merged her photographic ambitions with a deepening involvement in social reform and revolutionary politics. . . . Indeed, her intricately composed pictures present a bold language based on political conviction" ("Modotti and Weston: Mexicanidad" [press material], Austin Museum of Art, Austin, Texas, August 29–October 25, 1998).

6. For exhibitions, see Mulvey and Wollen, *Frida Kahlo and Tina Modotti*; Lowe, *Tina Modotti*; Modotti, Stoughton, Albers, Verdicchio, and University of California, San Diego, University Art Gallery, *Dear Vocio*; Casanova, Pastor, and Clapshaw, *Mexicana*; George Eastman House, International Museum of Art, and Fundación Pedro Barrié de la Maza, *Modotti y Weston*; Modotti, Albers, Cordero, Moderna museet, Rencontres internationales de la photographie d'Arles (Association), and Helsingin kaupungin taidemuseo, *Tina Modotti.* For biographies, see Hooks, *Tina Modotti*; Cacucci, *Tina Modotti*; Albers, *Shadows, Fire, Snow*; and Argenteri, *Tina Modotti.* For critical research, see Mulvey and Wollen, *Frida Kahlo and Tina Modotti*; Higgins and Arizona State University, School of Art, *Truth, Myth, and Erasure*; Lowe, *Tina Modotti*; and Noble, *Tina Modotti.*

7. Noble, *Tina Modotti.*

8. One of the values of Noble's study is the way it moves between Modotti's art historical contribution and present-day commodity-value as promoted by a ravenous market. One chapter of the book is a discussion of the photograph *Roses* and its recent sale at auction for the exorbitant price of $164,000. Noble examines the relationship between the ambitions of Sotheby's, the world of fashion (embodied by the person who purchased the photograph: Susie Tomkins, of the San Francisco women's apparel company Esprit) and the appeal of celebrity (in the persona of Madonna, who was outbid by Tomkins); together they collaborated in the production of a manufactured image-product: "This commodification of Modotti is a form of colonization that makes it difficult to plot either Modotti or Mexico onto the cultural map as anything other than paradigms of exotic otherness" (Noble, *Tina Modotti,* 29). Although Weston's nudes of Modotti have conflated her nude figure and Mexico as a body-landscape—therefore contributing to the too-easy identification of Modotti as "Mexican"—it is untenable to read any feminist gesture, Noble argues, by reifying the signature "Modotti," which comes to signify nothing so much as radical chic.

9. The reference here is to the panels "La tierra dormida" and "La tierra oprimida" of Rivera's murals at Chilpancingo. There is debate as to whether Modotti posed for Rivera or whether he rendered her nude body from a Weston photograph.

10. Noble, *Tina Modotti,* 24.

11. Ibid., 25, emphasis added.

12. Copjec, *Imagine There's No Woman,* 222.

13. Nieto Sotelo, Álvarez, and Centro de la Imagen, *Tina Modotti,* 126, emphasis added.

14. Many of her contemporary commentators inflected the twofold nature of Modotti's photography. Manuel Álvarez Bravo, whose work is discussed in the following chapter, was influenced by Modotti and had this to say of her images: "Tina's work was suddenly cut short, not so much by death as by the fact that her life had taken another course, but during the short period when she was working in photography she succeeded in leaving a lesson of which the main and most general significance consists in the understanding and affection felt for the resources and methods of the craft. When she came to Mexico she was still in her Romantic period, but soon after arriving, through the influence of artists in a state of aesthetic revolution who were fighting for a form of modernity wrested from tradition, together with Weston she found the meaning of photography now, the roots of which are bound up with early photography; this was the beginning of the exaltation of material and form in abstractions with a slight touch of poetry, and they began to blend with human documents, work of technical maturity, plastic solidity, and mastery of resources, which is now brought together in this exhibition as a stimulus and as a recollection (quoted in Casanova, Pastor, and Clapshaw, *Mexicana,* 247).

15. Armstrong, "This Photography Which Is Not One," 45.

16. Friedman, *Mappings,* 3.

17. Ibid., 6.

18. Center for Creative Photography, *Letters from Tina Modotti to Edward Weston,* 39–40.

19. To this effect, Homi Bhabha writes: "The 'beyond' is neither a new horizon, nor a leaving behind of the past. . . . [It is] the moment of transit where space and time cross to produce complex figures of difference and identity, past and present, inside and outside, inclusion and exclusion. For there is a sense of disorientation, a disturbance of direction,

in the 'beyond': exploratory, restless movement caught so well in the French rendition of the words *au-delà*—here and there, on all sides, fort/da, hither and thither, back and forth (*Location of Culture,* 1).

20. Armstrong suggests the following: "Modotti's photography was determining for Weston's as much as his was determining for hers, and at the same time [see] how divergent each one was from the other in their photographies. It proposes, finally, to find Modotti's celebrated otherness in her photographs, rather than in her person, and to locate her sedition in the subliminality of her formal strategies rather than in the politics that she consciously avowed" (Armstrong, "This Photography Which Is Not One," 23).

21. Armstrong, "This Photography Which Is Not One," 21.

22. Armstrong looks to Freud for the haptic foundations of visual desire, which in the case of Weston is rendered in aggressively invasive terms. In her literal and figural dissection of *Nautilus Shell,* Armstrong writes: "Sliced by the knife before it is cut by the camera shutter, the nautilus is simultaneously halved and centered, so that its bisection and its singularity seem to be one and the same, a natural fact surrendered up to the incisive eye of the photographer who pierces the outer shell and sees to the very core of the thing . . . an utterly autonomous, perfectly interiorized, chambered shape, almost architectural in sectioning, and like the photograph itself a consummate blend of auto-generated optical surface and self-spawned inner structure, of the sensuous and the rational. . . . It is thus, finally, that the *Nautilus Shell* harvested reactions that it did, whereby others were struck dumb by its sensuality while its author insisted on its sublimity" (Armstrong, "This Photography Which Is Not One," 24).

23. Armstrong, "This Photography Which Is Not One," 29.

24. Ibid., 42–43.

25. Solomon-Godeau, *Photography at the Dock,* 258.

26. Armstrong, "This Photography Which Is Not One," 45.

27. Ibid., 37.

28. Hooks, *Tina Modotti,* 69. "Tina and Edward were amicably received by most of the Mexicans they met. Xenophobia was not so prevalent then and, as a close friend recalled, 'There wasn't yet such a hatred of gringos and Mexicans didn't have such an inferiority complex about the United States . . .' In addition, men in post-revolutionary Mexico had become more willing to listen to women, as women began making inroads into areas previously closed to them. Tina's role as Weston's *interpreter* and the *organizer of his studio* seems to have been accepted without question" (emphasis added).

29. Center for Creative Photography, *Letters from Tina Modotti to Edward Weston,* 39.

30. González Cruz Manjarrez, Modotti, and Instituto de Investigaciones Estéticas, Universidad Nacional Autónoma de México, *Tina Modotti y el muralismo mexicano,* 13.

31. List Arzubide, *El movimiento estridentista,* 32. "Oh tierna geografía / de nuestro México, / sus paisajes aviónicos, / Alturas inefables de la economía política; / perdidas en la niebla / del tiempo, / y en los rumores eclécticos / de los levantamientos" (my translation).

32. Ibid., 14.

33. Balderston, "Poetry, Revolution, Homophobia," 59. "Ser estridentista es ser hombre. Sólo los eunucos no estarán con nosotros."

34. List Arzubide, *El movimiento estridentista,* 47. "El Estridentismo anclaba el triunfo: ellas se derretían en sus frases. . . . Los verseros consuetudinarios habían sido descubiertos en la Alameda, en juntas con probabilidades femeninas y habían sido obligados por la Inspección General de Policía a declarar su sexo y comprobarlo, acusados de un chantage *[sic]* de virilidades en caída" (emphasis added).

35. Grosz, *Space, Time, and Perversion,* 226. Also, in "Poetry, Revolution, Homophobia: Polemics from the Mexican Revolution," Balderston reminds us that for several decades two men in particular would bear the brunt of these attacks, Salvador Novo and Xavier Villaurrutia: "Despite the attacks—or perhaps because of them—Villaurrutia and Novo published a number of homoerotic texts . . . [but] this is not a homosexual poetry that specifies the gender of the beloved; instead, the gender of the beloved is carefully not specified, and the love is associated with danger, silence, and self-censorship" (64).

36. Hooks, *Tina Modotti,* 186.

37. "Los Contemporáneos / Ulises Rey de Itaca / y de Sodoma / también se forman del caballo de Troya (James Joyce)."

38. Ortega y Gasset, *Dehumanization of Art,* 36.

39. Spivak, *Critique of Postcolonial Reason,* 173.

40. Ibid., 238.

41. "Margarethe has been Weston's almost constant companion since 1912, but their relationship was complicated by the fact that she was 'mostly, though not wholly, a lesbian,' which was why presumably she resisted Weston's persistent sexual advances for years" (quoted in Hooks, *Tina Modotti,* 57). It is beyond the scope of this chapter to address the equally complex collaboration and partnership of Mather, whose own achievements and influence on Weston has been largely underestimated. For a recent estimation, see Warren, *Margrethe Mather and Edward Weston.*

42. Grosz, *Space, Time, and Perversion,* 227.

43. Weston and Newhall, *Daybooks of Edward Weston,* 10.

44. Argenteri, *Tina Modotti,* 30.

45. Ibid., 235n40.

46. Weston and Newhall, *Daybooks of Edward Weston,* 23.

47. Ibid., 30. Of the conversation at the home of Tomás Braniff, Weston writes: "There was brilliant repartee at the dinner table set under the garden trees, the conversation veering, as usual among intellectuals, to sex. Lupe, discussing the homosexuals in Guadalajara, 'A group of men there,' she said, 'actually wore high-heeled shoes and lace frills.' 'Every other man in Mexico is homosexual,' added Nahui Ollín."

48. Weston and Newhall, *Daybooks of Edward Weston,* 55. To witness: March 9 [1924].

49. Armstrong, "This Photography Which Is Not One," 26n8. "Throughout his *Daybooks*—the entries are too frequent to cite here—Weston himself linked sexual to photographic conquest, repeatedly following comments about "scoring" with one woman or another with remarks about getting one object or another properly on film, or vice versa."

50. Copjec, *Imagine There's No Woman,* 180.

51. Ibid., 38–39.

52. Lacan, *Four Fundamental Concepts of Psycho-Analysis,* 67–78.

53. Grosz further elaborates that this is "a space in which [a subject's] position is attained only relative to the position of the other, yet where the position of the other is reciprocally defined by the position of the subject" (*Volatile Bodies,* 48).

54. Weston and Newhall, *Daybooks of Edward Weston,* 55.

55. Copjec further argues: "Because I do not expose myself to the look of a determinate other, I do not receive a message back regarding my determinate identity. The reflexive circuit of the scopic drive does not produce a knowable object; it produces a transgression of the principle of pleasure, by forcing a hole in it. The scopic drive produces an exorbitant pleasure that disrupts the ego identity formed by the first circuit. Or: in the drive, the subject does not see itself by looking at itself through the Other, but rather, in

Freud's words *"Selbst ein Sexualglied beschauen"* [the self is seen in its sexual member]. It is this "seeing oneself in one's sexual member," in the exorbitant pleasure of the drive that occasions the feeling of shame, of being seen by others as such" (*Imagine There's No Woman,* 213–14).

56. Lacey, *Dictionary of Philosophy,* 163.

57. Copjec, *Imagine There's No Woman,* 192.

58. Ortega y Gasset, *Dehumanization of Art,* 35.

59. Drucker, *Theorizing Modernism,* 3.

60. Nieto Sotelo, Lozano Alvarez, and Centro de la Imagen, *Tina Modotti,* 118.

61. In its publication in the October–December issue of *Mexican Folkways,* edited by Frances Toor, the statement appeared stripped of the Trotsky epigraph.

62. Nieto Sotelo, Alvarez, and Centro de la Imagen, *Tina Modotti,* 60, emphasis added. Incidentally, no translation credit is given in any of the sources consulted. Having been published in the October–December 1929 issue of *Mexican Folkways,* edited by American Frances Toor, it is safe to assume the short essay appeared in English, but whether Modotti wrote it originally in English or whether Toor translated it from Modotti's presumably sophisticated Spanish awaits archival research in order to be ascertained.

63. Nieto Sotelo, Alvarez, and Centro de la Imagen, *Tina Modotti,* 60, emphasis added.

64. Was it this discourse on concealment and shame that led Villaurrutia to write what follows in the opening paragraph of his review of Modotti's exhibition? "It is seldom we are able to attend an exhibition, much less a photography exhibition, without having to leave out of boredom or disappointment. It is no small coincidence that in Spanish the word for *exhibit [exposición]* has two dissimilar meanings. It so happens that with hasty artists who seek to *display [exponer]* their work to viewers and to critics (to put it on show), they take one step further and *expose it* instead *[la exponen]* (that is, in jeopardy). Clearly, once they complete a series, painters are entitled to display their works, but this right is not always an obligation, and I believe that painters and artists should refrain from doing so until the moment they feel that such a right has been *converted* into a liability. In essence, this is a question of decorum. At brazen exhibitions there is a clear-cut remedy that entails shutting one's eyes. Except that there is also a category of painters who, upon seeing our eyes closed, try to command us to regard the canvas in a descriptive appeal to our ears, *inversely* to those poets who, at an exhibition of mural poems implored the viewer, by means of a sign, to read the poems" (quoted in Nieto Sotelo, Alvarez, and Centro de la Imagen, *Tina Modotti,* 60, my translation).

65. Copjec, *Imagine There's No Woman,* 222–23.

66. Cacucci, *Tina Modotti,* 52. Cacucci quotes the American poet Kenneth Rexroth in one of his less-inspired moments, when he wrote: "There was a café where they all hung out with heavily armed politicians, bullfighters, criminals, prostitutes, and burlesque girls. The most spectacular person of all was a photographer, artist's model, high-class courtesan, and Mata Hari for the Comintern, Tina Modotti."

67. Ortega y Gasset, *Dehumanization of Art,* 36.

68. Copjec, *Imagine There's No Woman,* 39.

69. Ortega y Gasset, *Dehumanization of Art,* 37.

70. Albers, *Shadows, Fire, Snow,* 56.

71. Drucker, *Theorizing Modernism,* 62.

72. Nietzsche, *Beyond Good and Evil,* 47.

73. Nietzsche, *Philosophy and Truth,* 96.

74. Nobel elaborates further: "We can also make out the suffix ending of two words 'ción' and 'ón,' which—Noble reminds us—are distinctive of Spanish abstract nouns. She resumes: "Two further tropes of reciprocity are articulated in the image. Namely, the writer and photographer are aligned, insofar as they both operate a piece of mechanical apparatus, so too, therefore are the photograph and the written text. Consequently, it is no exaggeration that the photograph figures itself in a gesture of self-referentiality, in the written text in the top right-hand corner. In *Mella's Typewriter* the text and the words written upon it symbolize the photograph and the image imprinted upon its surface, by virtue of a complex play on the visual and the textual whereby the visual becomes textual and the textual becomes visual" (*Tina Modotti,* 81).

75. Noble, *Tina Modotti,* 85. "La técnica se convertirá en una inspiración mucho más poderosa de la producción artística; más tarde encontrará su solución en una síntesis más elevada, el contraste que existe entre la técnica y la naturaleza."

76. Nieto Sotelo, Alvarez, and Centro de la Imagen, *Tina Modotti,* 60.

77. Cadava, *Words of Light,* 15.

78. Deleuze, *Logic of Sense,* 258.

79. Lacan, *Four Fundamental Concepts of Psycho-Analysis,* 71.

80. Cadava, *Words of Light,* 63.

81. Nieto Sotelo, Alvarez, and Centro de la Imagen, *Tina Modotti,* 147.

82. Johnston, quoted in Kittler and Johnston, *Literature, Media, Information Systems,* 14.

83. This is in keeping with the way sexual difference may be viewed as unattainable on one-to-one visual terms, as when Grosz writes: "Sexual difference is the horizon that cannot appear in its own terms, but is implied in the very possibility of an entity, an identity, a subject, an other and their relations. . . . The framework or terrain of sexual difference entails . . . the simultaneous recognition and effacement of the spacings, the intervals, the irreducible if unspecifiable positioning, the fissures and ruptures, that bind each 'thing' to every other and to the 'whole' of existence without, however, linking them into an organic or metaphysical wholeness or unity" (*Volatile Bodies,* 209).

84. These pertain to the collection at the George Eastman House in Rochester, New York, and they are herein listed by corresponding accession number: 74:0061:0168, *Woman Carrying Basket on Head,* ca. 1929; 74:0061:0169, *Market Scene,* ca. 1929; 74:0061:0170, *Market Scene,* 1929; 74:0061:0159, *Woman of Tehuantepec,* ca. 1929; 74:0061:0160, *Children Bathing in River,* ca. 1929; 74:0061:0162, *Woman Carrying Child,* ca. 1929; 74:0061:0163, *Market Scene,* ca. 1929; 74:0061:0173, *Two Women in Market,* ca. 1929; 74:0061:0176, *Women of Tehuantepec,* ca. 1929.

85. Michel de Certeau asserts as well that everyday practices "produce without capitalizing, that is, without taking control over time" (*Practice of Everyday Life,* xx).

86. Certeau, *Practice of Everyday Life,* xxi.

87. Clark, "Jackson Pollock's Abstraction," 179.

88. Spivak, *Critique of Postcolonial Reason,* 144.

89. Clark, *Farewell to an Idea,* 2, 7.

90. Certeau, *Practice of Everyday Life,* xiii.

3. Metropolitan Matters

1. Rosenthal, "Spectacle, Fear, and Protest," 33–73.

2. Williams and Pinkney, *Politics of Modernism,* 37–48.

3. Brenner, *Wind That Swept Mexico.*

4. A photograph (no. 180) depicts a group of men gathered under the arched entrance to the Cine Morelos in Cuernavaca. Posters and the theater marquee announce the showing of a film titled "Mil estudiantes y una muchacha." The caption below it reads: "On June 1, 1942, the Mexican government declared war against the Axis. Most Mexicans were thunderstruck. In towns they gathered in front of movie houses and stores to listen to the loud speakers announcing that President Manuel Ávila Camacho had taken them into the war. What were they doing, fighting on the same side as the United States . . . pointing their guns with the Yanquis and not at them? Was any good going to come of this?" (Brenner, *Wind That Swept Mexico*).

5. Monsiváis, *Amor perdido,* 19, my translation. "Durante tres décadas de armonía decretada y concentrada, esa entidad polifacética, la República Mexicana, conoció (formalmente) un solo estilo: el porfirismo."

6. Attributed to Paul Thompson of the European Picture Service, no. 36 (Brenner, *Wind That Swept Mexico*).

7. Monsiváis, "Alto contraste (a manera de foto fija)," in *Amor perdido,* 19.

8. Brenner, *Wind That Swept Mexico,* fig. 36 caption.

9. Of incidental interest is the fact that all the images were rephotographed for the book publication by Walker Evans.

10. Foucault, *Power/Knowledge,* 152. Relevant as well is the following passage: "This enclosed, segmented space, observed at every point, in which the individuals are inserted in a fixed place, in which the slightest movements are supervised, in which all events are recorded, in which an uninterrupted work of writing links the center and periphery, in which power is exercised without division, according to a continuous hierarchical figure, in which each individual is constantly located, examined and distributed among the living beings, the sick and the dead—all this constitutes a compact model of the disciplinary mechanism" (197).

11. "En 1910, con la gran excepción de núcleos liberales en provincia (ver la novela de Azuela *Los fracasados,* de 1909) y de formas de vida burguesas y bohemias en la capital, la moral feudal impera, con su ecuación 'defensa del derecho natural de posesión sobre la mujer, la tierra, los trabajadores y la patria = fortaleza de espíritu = pilar de la sociedad = represión sexual'. . . . Es el México a la vez ideal y trágico, sombrio y reprimido, ferozmente cruel y amortiguado . . . Esplendor y miseria, rituales y crímenes: los contrastes son obvios, pero sin la obviedad de los contrastes no hubiese habido revolución" (Monsiváis, *Amor perdido,* 20–22, my translation).

12. Brenner, *Wind That Swept Mexico,* 64.

13. For a compelling analysis of Gamio's complex desire to balance national unity with internal and external differences, see Limón, "Nation, Love, and Labor Lost," 35–71. Citing Gamio and the anthropologist Guillermo de la Peña, Limón writes: "Gamio held to the idea of nation as 'a superior kind of spiritual unity,' but also to the principle that in achieving this national unity, 'development should not be forced upon the different culture areas which constitute the nation; on the contrary each of them has to modernize on the basis of its own strengths.' Nevertheless, as de la Peña acknowledges, built into Gamio's nationalism 'was the "incorporation" of indigenous cultures into modernity.'"

14. "Los barrios nuevos de la capital, entregados antes al culto del *hotel* afrancesado y del *chalet* suizo, están llenos de edificios en que la antigua arquitectura del país reaparece adaptándose a fines nuevos: edificios fáciles de reconocer, no sólo por el interesante barroquismo de sus líneas, sino por sus materiales mexicanos, el tezontle rojo oscuro y la chiluca

gris, o a veces, además, el azulejo: ellos devuelven a la ciudad su carácter propio, sumándose a los suntuosos palacios de los barrios viejos" (Henríquez Ureña, "La influencia de la revolución en la vida intelectual de México," 615, my translation).

15. Williams and Pinkney, *Politics of Modernism,* 45.

16. Cultural difference is the imperative to think image making and representation as "presence" and "proxy" in the sense established by Homi Bhabha in *The Location of Culture*: "In the metaphor of the national community as the 'many as one' the one is now both the tendency to totalize the social in a homogenous empty time, and the repetition of that minus in the origin, the less-than-one that intervenes with a metonymic, iterative temporality" (155).

17. Williams and Pinkney, *Politics of Modernism,* 45.

18. Building for the Estridentista Movement (Edificio del movimiento Estridentista), unattributed, quoted in List Arzubide, *El movimiento estridentista,* 71. "Maples Arce, mira su imagen en el agua estancada del espejo, y la encuentra exacta a su deseo; luego me asegura que ha resuelto las ecuaciones del abstraccionismo y desarolla la teoría de imágenes logradas gracias a ecuaciones de cálculo infinitesimal y controladas por medio de la geometría en el espacio. Es el momento de las afirmaciones centrípetas sostenidas por gravitación en el planisferio de las letras de molde" (14, my translation).

19. Balderston, "Poetry, Revolution, Homophobia," 57–75.

20. For a superb discussion of the complex relationship of muralist practice to the Mexican state and pedagogical distributions of a viewer-centered citizenship, see Coffey, "Muralism and the People."

21. Toor, *Treasury of Mexican Folkways.*

22. "Álvarez Bravo, en cambio, se diría que cristaliza el estado de vaguedad en que el subconciente se apodera de los objetos exteriores y los hace vivir una vida inmaterial y embrionaria, diluidos casi, en el caudal de las ideas abstractas" (Leal, *El arte y los monstuos,* 137, my translation).

23. Williams and Pinkney, *Politics of Modernism,* 45.

24. Ibid.

25. "Con limpia sobriedad de elementos, sin violencias de línea, sombra o luz; sin gestos de miembros o visajes, dentro del entrañable envoltorio de hilachos que cubren la vida, expresa toda la lucha y las tragedias de clase de los años y los días" (Rivera, "Manuel Álvarez Bravo: Tercera exposición," 18).

26. Hughes, "Pictures More Than Pictures."

27. Marx, "German Ideology," 199.

28. Rosenthal, "Spectacle, Fear, and Protest," 34.

29. Ibid.

30. Brenner, *Wind That Swept Mexico,* caption 64.

31. "Ya es rutina la aceptación masiva del nuevo significado de la Revolución: el enriquecimiento súbito. La moral pública se seculariza y se emancipa de sanciones religiosas. Cumple ahora crearle las sanciones civiles y sociales. Éstas son el ostracismo, el repudio, la agobiante sensasión de falta. Los puntos claves de tales empresas punitivas son inevitables: el machismo y el respeto idolátrico a la propiedad privada. . . . Ser nacionalista es hacer el bien para con la patria, fundirse solidariamente con los compatriotas. Al descubrirse los contenidos y las formas del país, se dilucidan y despejan los pactos primordiales de una colectividad. El nacionalismo es la moral social que el Estado y los sectores progresistas aceptan y pregonan" (Monsiváis, *Amor perdido,* 19, my translation).

32. Rosenthal, "Spectacle, Fear, and Protest," emphasis added.

33. Kofman, *Camera Obscura,* 1.

34. Krauss, "Corpus Delicti," 39.

35. Ibid., 34.

36. Ibid., 53.

37. Krauss stages a rhetorical doubling herself in relation to the writing of Roger Caillois. Using his essay "Mimicry and Legendary Psychasthenia," Krauss describes a set of photographic practices—whereby the praying mantis serves as the ghost of human sexuality insofar as it resembles an automaton gesticulating in the mechanical imitation of life, but when decapitated it submits a convincing replica of life—a simulation of death. For Krauss, mimicry and surrealist doubling (in terms of structure and subject, at the level of form and content) is the invasion of a body by space.

38. Manuel Álvarez Bravo, interviewed by the artist Francisco Toledo, Mexico City, 1983. Transcript provided thanks to the generosity of Francisco Toledo and Graciela Iturbide.

39. Be it in the form of a nation to foreign economic interests, of a national subject to the state, or of differing sexual subject to each other, these questions of self-government were central to the political arena of Mexico in 1938, and they coalesce in *The Good Reputation Sleeping.* I began with Brenner's photo-historical account of Mexico as a national space instituted by images, and I return to her narrative conclusion. In tones that lionize the historical terminus of her description, President Lázaro Cárdenas (1934–40) appears as a legitimate figure—albeit "a dark horse whom nobody much knew about"—risen from the insurgent factions of the revolutionary, later governor of Michoacán, to the executive office where he is portrayed as a listener receptive to indigenous delegations, a tireless campaigner, sympathetic to the desperation of the landless: "In October 1936, President Cárdenas went in person to divide the land in the Laguna cotton district in Coahuila and Durango. In 1930 there were 130 holdings in this district, mainly owned by Spanish, British, German, and North American companies. The Cárdenas division distributed 220,000 acres to 31,000 families numbering more than 150,000 persons." In an increasing stand-off between foreign oil companies and the Mexican government, the overseas industries had terminated negotiations with labor unions on the renewal of their contract. In Mexico, Brenner writes, "subsoil wealth had been declared the property of the nation. It might be leased, but never sold outright." On March 18, 1938, the state of affairs around the issue of oil had reached such a breaking point as for Cárdenas to declare a "national emergency" and expropriate all wells and refineries within the Mexican territory. It is tempting to think the 1938 "national emergency" of the state with the "surrealist emergency" in Mexico by means of André Breton's proxy petition and the communication technology of the telephone.

40. Benjamin, "Surrealism," 181.

41. Kofman, *Camera Obscura,* 42.

42. Rivera, "Manuel Álvarez Bravo," 122.

43. Breton, "Souvenir du Mexique," 224–25.

44. Kofman, *Camera Obscura*, 42–43.

45. Álvarez Bravo, letter.

46. This section is indebted to the work of Ingrid Schaffner and Lisa Jacob in their fine institutional history and source book, *Julien Levy: Portrait of an Art Gallery.* I am especially grateful for the generous time spent in conversation with these scholar-curators who shared with me so much of their invaluable research and archival material.

47. In an estimation of Levy's cultural significance, Dorothea Tanning wrote: "Far stronger than the art dealer's temporal sponsorship of a new trend in painting was Julien's

commitment to what he saw as an irresistible blue-print for psychic adventure. With his avid research, his translations from the French, and especially his own writing, he ranged himself on the side of ideas rather than that of commercialism, and thus was only a part-time dealer" (quoted in Schaffner and Jacobs, *Julien Levy,* 19).

48. Burke, "Loy-alism," 61–79. See also Burke, *Becoming Modern,* 37–71, 376–81, 400–402.

49. Despite his promotion and support of Stieglitz's work, in his memoir, Levy wrote: "Not having the humility to be a true believer in anyone, including myself, I was never a disciple of Stieglitz, unconvinced, certainly of his mystique as an art dealer, which, at any rate, I did not entirely understand" (Levy, *Memoir of an Art Gallery,* 52).

50. Ibid., 90.

51. He and his colleagues at Harvard eventually formed an influential generation of cultural promoters or stewards of avant-garde institutions. These include Alfred Barr Jr. at the Museum of Modern Art and Arthur Everett Austin Jr. at the Wadsworth Athaneum.

52. Levy, *Memoir of an Art Gallery,* 7.

53. January 9–29, with works by Atget, Herbert Bayer, Jacques-André Boiffard, Jean Cocteau, Joseph Cornell, Salvador Dalí, Max Ernst, Charles Howard, Lynes, Ray, László Moholy-Nagy, Roger Parry, Pablo Picasso, Pierre Roy, Maurice Tabard, Umbo, Unknown Master, Jean Violier. The announcement cover was designed by Joseph Cornell.

54. Photographers included Herbert Bayer, Ilse Bing, Brassaï (credited as "Halesz"), André Kertész, Eli Lotar, Lee Miller, and Moholy-Nagy (February 20–March 11, 1932).

55. "Exhibition of Portrait Photography, Old and New," October 15–November 5, 1932. Other photographers included Abbott, Brady, Ray, Lee Miller, Lucia Moholy, Steichen, Stieglitz, and Clarence White.

56. Schaffner writes: "This bricolage of bric-a-brac seems closer to the marché aux puces than to the Leo Castelli Gallery. But for Julien Levy in the 1930s and 1940s, such a display was evidently surreal. And although he may not have gone so far as to deal in bijoux and bibelots, he did show the work of Joseph Cornell, whose collage boxes are filled, like miniature Wunderkammern, with such a world of 'strange and curious' things" (Schaffner and Jacobs, *Julien Levy,* 23).

57. Frizot, *New History of Photography,* 454.

58. Levy, *Memoir of an Art Gallery,* 48.

59. Ibid., 49.

60. Cartier-Bresson, Feyder, and Pieyre de Mandiargues, *Henri Cartier-Bresson,* 160. Pieyre de Mandiargues equates Cartier-Bresson's use of the camera—he was rarely without his Leica, from the very first camera, "with neither range finder nor interchangeable lenses"—to the Surrealists' use of automatic writing, "as a window that one leaves permanently open for visitations of the unconscious and the unpredictable."

61. Clifford and Marcus, *Writing Culture,* 121. Clifford writes: "The ethnographic label suggests a characteristic attitude of participant observation among the artifacts of a defamiliarized cultural reality. The surrealists were intensely interested in exotic worlds, among which they included a certain Paris. Their attitude, while comparable to that of the fieldworker who strives to render the unfamiliar comprehensible, tended to work in the reverse sense, making the familiar strange."

62. Leiris, "De Bataille el imposible a la impossible 'Documents,'" 264.

63. Research has failed to uncover any extant copy of the Palacio de Bellas Artes catalog. Reference to the piece by Hughes was provided by Colette Álvarez Urbajtel, the photographer's widow, in the form of a typewritten manuscript.

64. As for Cartier-Bresson, Hughes mentions the "tumble-down walls of demolished

dwellings in Spain where children are playing in a tumble down world; in others, the worn-bright gestures of prostitutes against doors that are also walls"—an image made on the Calle Cuauhtemoctzin in Mexico City. Regarding the work of Álvarez Bravo, Hughes discusses the photographs *Los Agachados, Escala de escalas,* and *Los obstáculos.*

65. Rosenheim, "'Cruel Radiance of What Is,'" 167.

66. Abbott, Kurt Baasch, Margaret Bourke-White, Maurice Brattner, Anton Bruehl, Arthur Gerlacj, Samuel Gottscho, Johnson, Lester, Lynes, Wendall McRae, Ira Martin, Mortimer Ottner, Thurman Rotan, Sherrill Schell, Stella Simon, Ralph Steiner.

67. Leiris, "Skyscraper," 72. By linking the skyscraper to Freud's oedipus complex, Leiris concludes that these American buildings constitute "one of the most powerful factors in evolution or, if one believes in it, of 'progress,' since it implies a desire not less for substitution than for joyful demolition."

68. Benjamin and Demetz, "Surrealism: The Last Snapshot of the European Intelligentsia," in *Reflections,* 190.

69. Ortega y Gasset, *Dehumanization of Art,* 35–36.

70. Read, *Art and Society,* 120.

71. Grundberg, "On the Dissection Table," 123–33. Grundburg sees an unsettled theoretical field in the various historical models fashioned for surrealism and its various appearances—as threads or pulses—throughout the last century. My point is simply that surrealism has various theories of itself, like the important efficacy of the documentary and the anti-graphic as they coalesced around the Levy Gallery in 1935. As a theory and a practice, the possibilities suggested by the mutual terms remain to be further explored today by photographers and cultural critics alike.

4. For History, Posterity, and Art

1. Southwest Texas State University (now Texas State University, San Marcos) was the institution of my employment, from 1998 to 1999. I remain indebted to my former colleagues among the staff and administration of the Alkek Library during my tenure at that research center. My involvement with the collections, including the Boystown archive, allowed me to formulate the ethical and photographic questions that compel the research in this essay.

2. Williams, *Long Revolution,* 65.

3. Hall, *Representation,* 274.

4. Pacheco, Hickey, Carter, Wittliff, Aperture Foundation, and Wittliff Gallery of Southwestern and Mexican Photography, *Boystown,* cover jacket.

5. Equally important is the aim to establish Wittliff's authority with Hollywood credentials: "Filmmaker, photographer, and book publisher Bill Wittliff was born in South Texas. In 1964, Wittliff and his wife Sally founded the Encino Press, an award-winning publishing company that focuses on regional material about Texas and the Southwest. Wittliff's photographs of the Mexican *vaquero* have been exhibited at the National Cowboy Hall of Fame, the Palacio de Bellas Artes in Mexico City, and the Texas Capitol. Wittliff has been a screenwriter for numerous films, including *The Black Stallion* (1979), *Honeysuckle Rose* (1980), *Country* (1984), *Lonesome Dove* (1989), *Legends of the Fall* (1994), and *The Perfect Storm* (2000)" (Pacheco, Hickey, Carter, Wittliff, Aperture Foundation, and Wittliff Gallery of Southwestern and Mexican Photography, *Boystown,* cover jacket).

6. Pacheco, Hickey, Carter, Wittliff, Aperture Foundation, and Wittliff Gallery of Southwestern and Mexican Photography, *Boystown.*

7. Nietzsche refers to this as "the metaphysical deployment of ideal significations and indefinite teleologies" (quoted in Foucault, *Language, Counter-Memory, Practice,* 140).

8. Pacheco, Hickey, Carter, Wittliff, Aperture Foundation, and Wittliff Gallery of Southwestern and Mexican Photography, *Boystown,* 106.

9. Ibid.

10. Sommer, *Proceed with Caution,* 37.

11. Pacheco, Hickey, Carter, Wittliff, Aperture Foundation, and Wittliff Gallery of Southwestern and Mexican Photography, *Boystown,* 106, emphasis added.

12. Wittliff, interview.

13. Pacheco, Hickey, Carter, Wittliff, Aperture Foundation, and Wittliff Gallery of Southwestern and Mexican Photography, *Boystown,* 107.

14. Pacheco, Hickey, Carter, Wittliff, Aperture Foundation, and Wittliff Gallery of Southwestern and Mexican Photography, *Boystown.*

15. "Fair Use: Overview and Meaning for Higher Education," http:www.cetus.org/fair5.html, November 10, 1999.

16. The text reads: "The Wittliff Gallery of Southwestern & Mexican Photography at Texas State University—San Marcos (formerly known as Southwest Texas State University), holds the copyright to the photographs contained in *BOYSTOWN: La Zona de Tolerancia,* published by the Aperture Foundation, Inc. Due to restrictions placed on this collection of photographs by the donor, the Wittliff Gallery of Southwestern & Mexican Photography at Texas State University—San Marcos is unable to grant permission to reproduce any photographs from the Boystown collection for use in the book tentatively titled: *Travels in the Image Environment: Camera Culture out of Mexico, 1900 and After,* by Roberto Tejada or excerpted articles" (Letter signed by Joan Heath, Assistant Vice President, University Library, October 26, 2005).

17. Instituto Nacional de Antropología e Historia, http://www.inah.gob.mx/ (accessed April 24, 2007).

18. Internet Movie Database, http://imdb.com/title/tt0410375 (April 24, 2007).

19. Wittliff, *Night in Old Mexico.*

20. Gutiérrez, "Erotic Zone," 261.

21. Ibid., 255.

22. Paz, *El ogro filantrópico,* 311, my translation.

23. By associating the right to abortion, birth control, machismo, and population growth, Paz turns to Max Weber, to submit that "sexual austerity" was a determining factor for the modern period, just as the economy of accumulation was for the capitalist system.

24. Paz, *El ogro filantrópico,* 53, my translation.

25. In literary references, Paz draws two limits: "A childlike and degenerate image: the child-devouring ogre of Perrault and that of De Sade, Minsk, in whose orgies libertines sup on steaming plates of human flesh over the charred bodies that serve as tables and chairs" ("Un grandulón generoso y un poco simple, un ingenuo que ignora su fuerza y al que se puede engañar pero cuya cólera puede destruirnos. A la imagen del gigante bueno y bobalicón se yuxtapone la del cíclope astuto y sanguinario. Imagen infantil y licenciosa: el ogro devorador de niños de Perrault y el ogro de Sade, Minsk, en cuyas orgiás los libertinos comen humeantes platos de carne humana sobre los cuerpos chamuscados que les sirven de mesas y sillas") (Paz, *El ogro filantrópico,* 53, my translation).

26. Paz, *El ogro filantrópico,* 53, my translation. "Personas de irreprochable conducta privada, espejos de moralidad en su casa y en su barrio, no tienen escrúpulos en disponer

de los bienes públicos como si fuesen propios. Se trata no tanto de una inmoralidad como de la vigencia inconsciente de otra moral: en el régimen patriomonial son más bien vagas y fluctuantes las fronteras entre la esfera pública y la privada, la familia y el Estado."

27. Paz continues: "Now, I believe that, much as our civilization needs equal rights for men and women, it also needs a feminization, like the one that courtly love brought about in the outlook of medieval Europe. Or like the feminine irradiation that the Virgin of Guadalupe casts on the imagination and sensibility of us Mexicans. Because of the Mexican woman's Hispano-Arabic and Indian heritage, her social situation is deplorable, but what I want to emphasize here is not so much the nature of the relation between men and women as the intimate relationship of woman with those elusive symbols, which we call femininity and masculinity. For the reasons I noted earlier, Mexican women have a very lively awareness of the body. For them, the body, woman's and man's, is a concrete, palpable reality. Not an abstraction or a function but an ambiguous magnetic force, in which pleasure and pain, fertility and death are inextricably intertwined" ("Reflections: Mexico and the United States," 408–9).

28. Paz, *El ogro filantrópico,* 279, my translation.

29. Zea, *La filosofía americana como filosofía sin más.*

30. Cited in Larsen, "Latin America as a Historico-Philosophical Relation," 58, trans. Neil Larsen.

31. Merleau-Ponty and Lefort, *Visible and the Invisible,* 132.

32. Ibid., 133.

33. Ibid., 130.

34. Ibid., 131.

35. "What there is then are not things first identical with themselves, which would then offer themselves to the seer, nor is there a seer who is first empty and who, afterward, would open himself to them—but something to which we could not be closer than by palpating it with our look, things we could not dream of seeing "all naked" because the gaze itself envelops them, clothes them with its own flesh" (Merleau-Ponty and Lefort, *Visible and the Invisible,* 131).

36. He writes: "A naked color, and in general a visible, is not a chunk of absolutely hard, indivisible being, offered all naked to a vision which could be only total or null, but is rather a sort of straits between exterior horizons and interior horizons ever gaping open, something that comes to touch lightly and makes diverse regions of the colored or visible world resound at the distances, a certain differentiation, an ephemeral modulation of this world—less a color or a thing, therefore, than a difference between things and colors, a momentary crystallization of colored being or of visibility" (Merleau-Ponty and Lefort, *Visible and the Invisible,* 132).

37. Merleau-Ponty and Lefort, *Visible and the Invisible,* 133.

38. Ibid., 135.

39. Ibid., 132.

40. "What we call a visible is, we said, a quality pregnant with texture, the surface of a depth, a cross section upon a massive being, a grain or corpuscle borne by a wave of Being. Since the total visible is always behind, or after, or between the aspects we see of it, there is access to it only through an experience which, like it, is wholly outside of itself" (Merleau-Ponty and Lefort, *Visible and the Invisible,* 136).

41. To the degree that flesh can be first-order, Merleau-Ponty claims: "If we can show that the flesh is an ultimate notion, that it is not the union or compound of two substances, but thinkable by itself, if there is a relation of the visible with itself that traverses

me and constitutes me as a seer, this circle which I do not form, which forms me, *this coiling over of the visible upon the visible, can traverse, animate other bodies as well as my own*" (Merleau-Ponty and Lefort, *Visible and the Invisible*, 140–41, emphasis added).

42. Merleau-Ponty and Lefort, *Visible and the Invisible*, 139.

43. Activating Irigaray's critique of Merleau-Ponty, Grosz writes: "If Irigaray's reading is appropriate, it is clear that [Merleau-Ponty's] work derives much from the implicit sexualization of ontology, the utilization of a whole series of metaphors embedded in and derived from relations between the sexes. These metaphors underlie and make possible his notion of the flesh and reversibility. In this sense, the feminine may be understood as the unspoken, disembodied underside of the flesh: the flesh, Irigaray argues, has a point-for-point congruence with the attributes of both femininity and maternity (*Volatile Bodies*, 103). His language relies heavily on an unacknowledged female body—with terms that encompass "invagination," "folding back," "cavity," "embryo," and, more violently, the suggested opening of an organ along a suture in a "dehiscence of the seeing into the visible and of the visible into the seeing." There is a duality that runs counter to the rhythm that sets the text in pointed motion: references to double meaning, facing mirrors, two-dimensional being, two laps (Irigaray's "two lips"?), two halves of an orange, two systems, two phases, things obverse and reverse.

44. The intimate language, as with a secret sharer, swells with erotic undertones: "Then, through the concordant operation of his body and my own, what I see passes into him, this individual green of the meadow under my eyes invades his vision without quitting my own, I recognize in my green his green, as the customs officer recognizes suddenly in a traveler the man whose description he had been given. There is here no problem of *alter ego* because it is not I who sees, not he who sees, because an anonymous visibility inhabits both of us, a vision in general, in virtue of that primordial property that belongs to the flesh, being here and now, of radiating everywhere and forever, being an individual, of being also a dimension and a universal" (Merleau-Ponty and Lefort, *Visible and the Invisible*, 142).

45. Merleau-Ponty's theorizing of the other side, finally, has implications in language to be further explored. The connective invisibilities of the world are "a second life and perception, which make the mathematician go straight to entities no one has yet to see, make and operative language and algorithm make use of a second visibility, and make ideas be the other side of language and calculus" (Merleau-Ponty and Lefort, *Visible and the Invisible*, 153). The chiasm is etymologically related to the chiasmus, the literary figure that is call and response, the inversion of the order of syntactical elements in the second of two juxtaposed and syntactically parallel phrases and clauses, as in Ralph Waldo Emerson's "If Fate follows and limits Power, Power attends and antagonizes Fate" (in his essay "Fate"). Can the question of sexual difference in viewing ultimately be equated with syntax? That is, with what vocabulary and grammar? In what order do subjects, predicates, and objects appear within the prepositional clauses of place and situation in time? Can phallocentrism be viewed as a system of hypotaxis (syntactic subordination) to be countered, in a chiasmus clause, by languages—including the visual—based on parataxis (as in a poetics of side by side, the placing of clauses or phrases one after the other without coordinating or subordinating connectives)?

46. Certeau, *Practice of Everyday Life*.

47. Ibid., xx.

48. One degree by which this can be measured is suggested in one of the few reviews of the Aperture publication *Boystown: La Zona de Tolerancia*. Written by the Mexican

American novelist Dagoberto Gilb, I quote an important part of his review at length: "Wittliff explains that after he bought a first stack of negatives, he made a deal to buy all of the photos these photographers took. And clearly the focus of these photographers changed, or their understanding. They thought they were taking 'art' photos, glam/carny shots of the women who make a living in this sordid business. They believed they were being appreciated for their art and photojournalism skills. . . . But instead it made me realize how I'd been trained to have shame. This 'puta' world is what so many Americans talk about when they discuss the other side. And it's this 'conversation' that makes so many of us feel like our blood is 'less than,' 'dirty.' And this kind of book only perpetuates that—a book not for Mexicans or Mexican Americans, this is certainly not one that is going to be collected in such a household. It's what Mexican Americans have to be taught, that this is a fundamental perception, according to them, of Mexican heritage and culture. All I could think was, 'What is this endless fascination for Mexican whores? Why do these guys obsess on this so much? If it were in their own poor neighborhood, if it were their poor junkie alcoholic aunts and cousins, would they be so intrigued?' And that's when a 'found art' thing kicked in for me. This book, the entirety of its black-and-white photos—grainy, cheap, mundanely composed—is the unconscious, subliminal: a dream, a fantasy, a phobia. These are the images of their Mexican border fetish, and it is depicted with such unawareness, with such a comfortable arrogance of historical power, it can seem to them, almost charmingly, like art" (*San Antonio Express-News,* "Books 'Found Art'—Maybe," June 2, 2001).

As it continues to stand now, neither the touring exhibition nor the Aperture publication have generated the necessary public discussions with the community most directly implicated. Indeed, given the sensitive legal and ethical issues involved, if the project to relocate a viewing of these images is a political one—and I believe it is—it is a further task to debate the legality of the archive itself, even as it forces potential viewers into an inescapable, troubled, but nonetheless ethical relationship. In effect, another important aspect about the Boystown Archive is that it is just as interesting for what it conceals as for what it proposes to make visible.

What I hope to suggest with Gilb's critique is that—even despite the questionable sexual politics often attributed to Gilb's own narrative work, and its representation of women, as is true of other masculinist (Chicano/Latino) writers and scholars—we can render productive existing subject positions that in turn compel us to make available our own. Are the particulars of one's own sexed position—queer, U.S., Latino—enough to read these photographs through an optimistic lens no matter how aligned to feminist perspectives of varying kinds?

49. Carroll, "'Accidental Allegories' Meet 'The Performative Documentary,'" 367.

50. Crowther, "Against Curatorial Imperialism," 477, 479.

51. Tatiana Parcero writes: "*Interior Cartography* is a series of black and white photographs on acetate, and color prints of anatomical diagrams and pre-Columbian codices. The central idea was to redefine the inside of the body, to explore interior space from the outside as a process of self-knowledge, and to open up the possibility of depicting what eludes simple sight. In the first part of this project, I used antique anatomy-diagrams and later, in the second stage, I deployed images derived from Maya, Aztec, and Mixtec codices. In this way, my research gave way to further associations with features related to identity, memory, history, territory, and time. The technique I developed to undertake this work, a method I continue to employ, consists of juxtaposing acetates and color photographs. This has allowed me to obtain transparencies and to achieve an "x-ray" glimpse

into the body, even as I activate various levels of scale and get close to the microscopic. These images are a way of constructing visual metaphors and of exploring the body as a map; of showing the inside from the outside, and what cannot be seen at first instance" (pers. comm., June 5, 2007).

52. Alarcón, "This Bridge Called My Back and Anglo-American Feminism," 39.

53. Fusco, *English Is Broken Here,* 33.

54. Mitchell, "Word and Image," 49.

55. Butler, "Sexual Ideology and Phenomenological Description," in Allen and Young, *Thinking Muse,* 98–99.

56. Merleau-Ponty and Lefort, *Visible and the Invisible,* 132.

Bibliography

Alarcón, Norma. "This Bridge Called My Back and Anglo-American Feminism." In *Criticism in the Borderlands: Studies in Chicano Literature, Culture, and Ideology, Post-Contemporary Interventions,* ed. Héctor Calderón and José Saldívar. Durham, N.C.: Duke University Press, 1991.

Albers, Patricia. *Shadows, Fire, Snow: The Life of Tina Modotti.* New York: Clarkson Potter, 1999.

Allen, Jeffner, and Iris Marion Young, eds. *The Thinking Muse: Feminism and Modern French Philosophy.* Bloomington: Indiana University Press, 1989.

Álvarez Bravo, Manuel. Letter to David Travis (assistant curator of photography, Art Institute of Chicago), September 20, 1976, Julien Levy Archive, Art Institute of Chicago, transcribed by Lisa Jacobs.

———. *Manuel Álvarez Bravo: Cien años, cien días.* [Mexico City]: Consejo Nacional para la Cultura y las Artes: Instituto Nacional de Bellas Artes: Fundación Televisa: Fomento Cultural Banamex; Madrid: Turner Publicaciones, 2001.

Álvarez Bravo, Manuel, and Centro de la Imagen. *Variaciones, 1995–1997.* Mexico City: Centro de la Imagen, 1997.

Álvarez Bravo, Manuel, and A. D. Coleman. *Manuel Álvarez Bravo.* Aperture Masters of Photography No. 3. New York: Aperture, 1987.

Álvarez Bravo, Manuel, and Teresa del Conde. *Mucho Sol.* Mexico City: Fondo de Cultura Económica, 1989.

Álvarez Bravo, Manuel, and Instituto Nacional de Bellas Artes. *Manuel Álvarez Bravo: 400 Fotografías.* Mexico City: Instituto Nacional de Bellas Artes, 1972.

Álvarez Bravo, Manuel, and Museum of Photographic Arts. *Revelaciones: The Art of Manuel Álvarez Bravo.* San Diego, Calif.: Museum of Photographic Arts, 1990.

Álvarez Bravo, Manuel, Victoria Blasco, and J. Paul Getty Museum. *Recuerdo de unos años.* [Malibu, Calif.]: J. Paul Getty Museum, 1992.

Álvarez Bravo, Manuel, Ana Laura Delgado, and Casa Lamm Centro de Cultura.

Manuel Álvarez Bravo: Fotografías: Colección fotográfica de la Fundación Televisa. Mexico City: Centro de Cultura Casa Lamm, 2001.

Álvarez Bravo, Manuel, Carlos Fuentes, and Ariadne Kimberly Huque. *Nudes: The Blue House: The Photographs of Manuel Álvarez Bravo Desnudos: Las Casa Azul.* New York: Distributed Art Publishers, 2002.

Álvarez Bravo, Manuel, Museo Nacional de Arte, and J. Paul Getty Museum. *Parábolas ópticas.* Mexico City: Museo Nacional de Arte: Patronato del Museo Nacional de Arte: Fundación Televisa: CONACULTA INBA, 2002.

Álvarez Bravo, Manuel, Roberto Tejada, and Gallery of Contemporary Photography. *Manuel Álvarez Bravo at Ninety-Five: An Exhibition of Rare Platinum Prints; Manuel Álvarez Bravo en sus 95 años: Una muestra de impresiones exclusivas en platino.* Santa Monica, Calif.: Gallery of Contemporary Photography Bergamot Station Arts Center, 1997.

Álvarez Bravo, Manuel, Sandra Benito, Victoria Blasco, and Fundación Cultural Televisa. *Luz y tiempo: Colección fotográfica formada por Manuel Álvarez Bravo para la Fundación Cultural Televisa, A.C., Julio 1995.* Mexico City: Centro Cultural/Arte Contemporáneo, 1995.

Álvarez Bravo, Manuel, Jane Livingston, Alex Castro, and Corcoran Gallery of Art. *M Álvarez Bravo.* Boston: D. R. Godine, 1978.

Álvarez Bravo, Manuel, Nissan Perez, Ian Jeffrey, and Muzeon Yisrael. *Dreams, Visions, Metaphors: The Photographs of Manuel Álvarez Bravo.* Jerusalem: Israel Museum, 1983.

Álvarez Bravo, Manuel, José Gorostiza, Salas Pablo Ruiz Picasso, and Dirección General de Bellas Artes y Archivos. *Manuel Álvarez Bravo.* [Madrid]: Ministerio de Cultura Dirección General de Bellas Artes y Archivos, 1985.

Arendt, Hannah. "Walter Benjamin: 1892–1940." In *Illuminations,* ed. Walter Benjamin and Hannah Arendt. New York: Schocken Books, 1988.

Argenteri, Letizia. *Tina Modotti: Between Art and Revolution.* New Haven, Conn.: Yale University Press, 2003.

Armstrong, Carol. "This Photography Which Is Not One: In the Gray Zone with Tina Modotti." *October,* no. 101 (Summer 2002): 19–52.

Balderston, Daniel. "Poetry, Revolution, Homophobia: Polemics from the Mexican Revolution." In *Hispanisms and Homosexualities,* edited by Sylvia Molloy and Robert McKee Irwin. Durham, N.C.: Duke University Press, 1998.

Barthes, Roland. *Camera Lucida: Reflections on Photography.* New York: Hill and Wang, 1981.

Bartra, Roger. *El salvaje en el espejo.* Mexico City: Coordinación de Difusión Cultural Universidad Nacional Autónoma de México, 1992.

Bataille, Georges, Robert Lebel, Isabelle Waldberg, and Alastair Brotchie. *Encyclopaedia Acéphalica: Comprising the Critical Dictionary and Related Texts.* London: Atlas, 1995.

Batchen, Geoffrey. *Burning with Desire: The Conception of Photography.* Cambridge Mass.: MIT Press, 1997.

Baudrillard, Jean. *Simulations.* Foreign Agents Series. New York: Semiotext(e), 1983.

Beezley, William H., Cheryl English Martin, and William E. French, eds. *Rituals of Rule, Rituals of Resistance: Public Celebrations and Popular Culture in Mexico.* Wilmington, Del.: SR Books, 1994.

Benjamin, Walter. "Goethe's Elective Affinities." In *Selected Writings, Volume 1: 1913–1926.* Cambridge, Mass.: Belknap Press of Harvard University Press, 1996.

———. "On Language as Such and on the Language of Man." In *Reflections: Essays,*

Aphorisms, Autobiographical Writings, ed. Walter Benjamin and Peter Demetz. New York: Harcourt Brace Jovanovich, 1978.

———. "Surrealism: The Last Snapshot of the European Intelligentsia." In *Reflections,* trans. Edmund Jephcott. New York: Schocken Books, 1978.

———. "Theses on the Philosophy of History." In *Illuminations,* ed. Walter Benjamin and Hannah Arendt. New York: Schocken Books, 1988.

———. "The Work of Art in the Age of Mechanical Reproduction." In *Illuminations,* trans. Harry Zohn. New York: Schocken Books, 1968.

Benjamin, Walter, and Hannah Arendt, eds. *Illuminations.* New York: Schocken Books, 1988.

Benjamin, Walter, and Peter Demetz, eds. *Reflections: Essays, Aphorisms, Autobiographical Writings.* New York: Harcourt Brace Jovanovich, 1978.

Benjamin, Walter, Marcus Paul Bullock, and Michael William Jennings. *Selected Writings.* Cambridge, Mass.: Belknap Press, 1996.

Berger, John. *Ways of Seeing.* London: British Broadcasting Corporation, 1972.

Bergson, Henri. *The Creative Mind.* New York: Philosophical library, 1946.

———. *Matter and Memory.* New York: Zone Books, 1988.

———. *Mind-Energy: Lectures and Essays.* New York: H. Holt, 1920.

Bergson, Henri, and Arthur Mitchell. *Creative Evolution.* New York: H. Holt, 1911.

Bhabha, Homi K. *The Location of Culture.* London: Routledge, 1994.

Bolton, Richard, ed. *The Contest of Meaning: Critical Histories of Photography.* Cambridge, Mass.: MIT Press, 1989.

Bourdieu, Pierre. *Photography: A Middle-Brow Art.* Stanford, Calif.: Stanford University Press, 1990.

Bowden, Charles. *Juárez: The Laboratory of Our Future.* New York: Aperture, 1998.

Brenner, Anita. *The Wind That Swept Mexico: The History of the Mexican Revolution, 1910–1942.* New York: Harper and Brothers, 1943.

Brenner, Anita, and George Ross Leighton. *The Wind That Swept Mexico: The History of the Mexican Revolution, 1910–1942.* Texas Pan American Series. Austin: University of Texas Press, 1996.

Breton, André. "Souvenir du Mexique," trans. Agustín Lazo. In *Manuel Álvarez Bravo: Cien años, cien días.* Mexico City: CONACULTA, 2001.

Burke, Carolyn. *Becoming Modern: The Life of Mina Loy.* New York: Farrar Straus and Giroux, 1996.

———. "Loy-alism: Julien Levy's Kinship with Mina Loy." In *Julien Levy: Portrait of an Art Gallery,* ed. Ingrid Schaffner and Lisa Jacobs. Cambridge, Mass.: MIT Press, 1998.

Butler, Judith. "Sexual Ideology and Phenomenological Description: A Feminist Critique of Merleau Ponty's *Phenomenology of Perception.*" In *The Thinking Muse: Feminism and Modern French Philosophy,* ed. Jeffner Allen and Iris Marion Young. Bloomington: Indiana University Press, 1989.

Cacucci, Pino. *Tina Modotti: A Life.* New York: St. Martin's, 1999.

Cadava, Eduardo. *Words of Light: Theses on the Photography of History.* Princeton, N.J.: Princeton University Press, 1997.

Camera Work: A Photographic Quarterly. 50 vols. in 24. New York: Alfred Stieglitz.

Carroll, Amy. "'Accidental Allegories' Meet 'The Performative Documentary': Boystown, Señorita Extraviada, and the Border-Brothel-Maquiladora Paradigm," *Signs: Journal of Women in Culture and Society* 31, no. 21 (2006): 357–96.

Cartier-Bresson, Henri, Vera Feyder, and André Pieyre de Mandiargues. *Henri Cartier-Bresson: À propos de Paris.* Boston: Little Brown, 1994.

Casanova, María, Nuria Pastor, and Karel Clapshaw. *Mexicana: Fotografía moderna en México, 1923–1940.* [Valencia]: Generalitat Valenciana, 1998.
Casasola, Agustín Víctor. *The World of Agustín Víctor Casasola: Mexico, 1900–1938; El mundo de Agustín Víctor Casasola.* Washington, D.C.: Fondo del Sol Visual Arts and Media Center, 1984.
Casasola, Agustín Víctor, and David King, eds. *Tierra y Libertad! Photographs of Mexico, 1900–1935, from the Casasola Archive.* Oxford: Museum of Modern Art, 1985.
Casasola, Gustavo. *Historia gráfica de la Revolución mexicana, 1900–1960.* Mexico City: Editorial F. Trillas, 1960.
Caso, Antonio. *El concepto de la historia universal y la filosofía de los valores.* Mexico City: Ediciones Botas, 1923.
———. *Discursos a la nación mexicana, por Antonio Caso.* Mexico City: Porrúa hermanos, 1922.
———. *Ensayos críticos y polémicos.* Mexico City, 1922.
———. *Principios de estética.* Mexico City: Publicaciones de la Sria. de Educación, 1925.
———. *Problemas filosóficos.* Mexico City: Porrúa hermanos, 1915.
Center for Creative Photography. *The Letters from Tina Modotti to Edward Weston,* vol. 22 of *The Archive.* Tucson: Center for Creative Photography, University of Arizona, 1986.
Certeau, Michel de. *The Practice of Everyday Life.* Berkeley: University of California Press, 1984.
Clark, T. J. *Farewell to an Idea: Episodes from a History of Modernism.* New Haven, Conn.: Yale University Press, 1999.
———. "Jackson Pollock's Abstraction." In *Reconstructing Modernism: Art in New York, Paris, and Montreal, 1945–1964,* ed. Serge Guilbaut. Cambridge, Mass.: MIT Press, 1990.
Clifford, James. *Routes: Travel and Translation in the Late Twentieth Century.* Cambridge, Mass.: Harvard University Press, 1997.
Clifford, James, and George E. Marcus, eds. *Writing Culture: The Poetics and Politics of Ethnography: A School of American Research Advanced Seminar.* Berkeley: University of California Press, 1986.
Coffey, Mary. "Muralism and the People: Culture, Popular Citizenship, and Government in Post-Revolutionary Mexico." *Communication Review* 5 (2002): 7–38.
Conferencias del Ateneo de la Juventud. 2nd ed. Mexico City: Instituto de Investigaciones Filosóficas Universidad Nacional Autónoma de México, 1984.
Copjec, Joan. *Imagine There's No Woman: Ethics and Sublimation.* Cambridge, Mass.: MIT Press, 2002.
———. *Read My Desire: Lacan against the Historicists.* Cambridge, Mass.: MIT Press, 1994.
Crowther, Paul. "Against Curatorial Imperialism: Merleau-Ponty and the Historicity of Art." In *A Companion to Art Theory,* ed. Paul Smith and Carolyn Wilde. Oxford: Blackwell, 2002.
Danto, Arthur Coleman. *Beyond the Brillo Box: The Visual Arts in Post-Historical Perspective.* New York: Farrar Straus Giroux, 1992.
———. *The Transfiguration of the Commonplace: A Philosophy of Art.* Cambridge, Mass.: Harvard University Press, 1981.
Debroise, Olivier. *Mexican Suite: A History of Photography in Mexico.* Austin: University of Texas Press, 2001.
Debroise, Olivier, and Elizabeth Fuentes Rojas. *Fuga mexicana: Un recorrido por la fotografía en México.* Mexico City: Consejo Nacional para la Cultura y las Artes, 1994.

Deleuze, Gilles. *Bergsonism.* New York: Zone Books, 1988.
———. *Cinema 1: The Movement-Image.* Minneapolis: University of Minnesota Press, 1986.
———. *Cinema 2: The Time-Image.* Minneapolis: University of Minnesota, 1991.
———. *The Logic of Sense.* European Perspectives. New York: Columbia University Press, 1990.
Derrida, Jacques. *Archive Fever: A Freudian Impression.* Chicago: University of Chicago Press, 1998.
De Zayas, Marius. *How, When, and Why Modern Art Came to New York.* Cambridge, Mass.: MIT Press, 1996.
———. *A Study of the Modern Evolution of Plastic Expression.* New York: "291," 1913.
Drucker, Johanna. *Theorizing Modernism: Visual Art and the Critical Tradition.* New York: Columbia University Press, 1994.
Elkins, James. *The Object Stares Back: On the Nature of Seeing.* New York: Simon and Schuster, 1996.
Evans, Walker. *Walker Evans.* New York: Metropolitan Museum of Art in association with Princeton University Press, 2000.
Foucault, Michel. *Discipline and Punish: The Birth of the Prison.* New York: Pantheon Books, 1977.
———. *The History of Sexuality.* New York: Pantheon Books, 1978.
———. *Language, Counter-Memory, Practice: Selected Essays and Interviews.* Ithaca, N.Y.: Cornell University Press, 1977.
———. *Power/Knowledge: Selected Interviews and Other Writings, 1972–1977.* New York: Pantheon Books, 1980.
Freud, Sigmund, Joyce Crick, and Ritchie Robertson. *The Interpretation of Dreams.* Oxford: Oxford University Press, 1999.
Friedman, Susan Stanford. *Mappings: Feminism and the Cultural Geographies of Encounter.* Princeton, N.J.: Princeton University Press, 1998.
Frizot, Michel, ed. *A New History of Photography.* Cologne: Könemann, 1998.
Fusco, Coco. *English Is Broken Here: Notes on Cultural Fusion in the Americas.* New York: New Press, 1995.
George Eastman House, International Museum of Art, and Fundación Pedro Barrié de la Maza. *Modotti y Weston: Mexicanidad.* Trans. Alejandro Piñón Freire. Coruña, Spain: Fundación Pedro Barrié de la Maza, 1999.
Glissant, Edouard. *Poetics of Relation.* Ann Arbor: University of Michigan Press, 1997.
Goethe, Johann Wolfgang von. *Elective Affinities.* Trans. R. J. Hollingdale. London: Penguin Books, 1971.
González Cruz Manjarrez, Maricela, Tina Modotti, and Instituto de Investigaciones Estéticas, Universidad Nacional Autónoma de México. *Tina Modotti y el muralismo mexicano.* Mexico City: Instituto de Investigaciones Estéticas, Universidad Nacional Autónoma de México, 1999.
González Echevarría, Roberto. *Myth and Archive: A Theory of Latin American Narrative.* Cambridge: Cambridge University Press, 1990.
Grosz, Elizabeth A. *Space, Time, and Perversion: Essays on the Politics of Bodies.* New York: Routledge, 1995.
———. *Volatile Bodies: Toward a Corporeal Feminism.* Bloomington: Indiana University Press, 1994.
Grundberg, Andy. *Crisis of the Real: Writings on Photography, 1974–1989.* New York: Aperture, 1990.

———. "On the Dissection Table: The Unnatural Coupling of Surrealism and Photography." In *Over Exposed: Essays on Contemporary Photography,* ed. Carol Squiers. New York: New Press, 1999.

Gunn, Giles B. *Thinking across the American Grain: Ideology, Intellect, and the New Pragmatism.* Chicago: University of Chicago Press, 1992.

Gutiérrez, Ramón. "The Erotic Zone: Sexual Transgression on the US-Mexican Border." In *Mapping Multiculturalism,* ed. Avery F. Gordon and Christopher Newfield. Minneapolis: University of Minnesota Press, 1996.

Haley, P. Edward. *Revolution and Intervention: The Diplomacy of Taft and Wilson with Mexico, 1910–1917.* Cambridge, Mass.: MIT Press, 1970.

Hall, Stuart, ed. *Representation: Cultural Representations and Signifying Practices, Culture, Media and Identities.* London: Sage, 1997.

Hall, Stuart, and Paul Du Gay, eds. *Questions of Cultural Identity.* London: Sage, 1996.

Hall, Stuart, Sut Jhally, and Media Education Foundation. *Representation and the Media.* Video recording. Northampton, Mass.: Media Education Foundation, 1997.

Hall, Stuart, David Morley, and Kuan-Hsing Chen, eds. *Stuart Hall: Critical Dialogues in Cultural Studies.* London: Routledge, 1996.

Harrison, Charles. "Modernism." In *Critical Terms for Art History,* edited by Robert S. Nelson and Richard Shiff. Chicago: University of Chicago Press, 1996.

Harrison, Charles, and Paul Wood, eds. *Art in Theory, 1900–1990: An Anthology of Changing Ideas.* Oxford: Blackwell, 1993.

Harrison, Charles, Paul Wood, and Jason Gaiger, eds. *Art in Theory, 1815–1900: An Anthology of Changing Ideas.* Malden, Mass.: Blackwell, 1998.

Henríquez Ureña, Pedro. *Obra crítica.* Mexico City: Fondo de Cultura Económica, 1960.

Higgins, Gary, and Arizona State University, School of Art. *Truth, Myth, and Erasure: Tina Modotti and Edward Weston.* Tempe: School of Art, Arizona State University, 1991.

Hooks, Margaret. *Tina Modotti.* London: Phaidon, 2002.

———. *Tina Modotti: Photographer and Revolutionary.* London: Pandora, 1993.

Hughes, Langston. "Pictures More Than Pictures: The Work of Manuel Álvarez Bravo and Cartier-Bresson." Mexico City: Galería de Exposiciones del Palacio de Bellas Artes, 1935.

Irigaray, Luce. *This Sex Which Is Not One.* Ithaca, N.Y.: Cornell University Press, 1985.

J. Paul Getty Museum, and Manuel Álvarez Bravo. *Manuel Álvarez Bravo: Photographs from the J. Paul Getty Museum.* Los Angeles: J. Paul Getty Museum, 2001.

Jones, Jonathan. "Portrait of the Week, No. 145: Men Reading El Machete, Tina Modotti (1924)." *Guardian Unlimited,* February 15, 2003.

Kaplan, Caren. *Questions of Travel: Postmodern Discourses of Displacement.* Durham, N.C.: Duke University Press, 1996.

Kawash, Samira. *Dislocating the Color Line: Identity, Hybridity, and Singularity in African-American Narrative.* Stanford, Calif.: Stanford University Press, 1997.

Kismaric, Susan, Manuel Álvarez Bravo, and Museum of Modern Art. *Manuel Álvarez Bravo.* New York: Museum of Modern Art, 1997.

Kittler, Friedrich A. *Gramophone, Film, Typewriter,* trans. Geoffrey Winthrop-Young and Michael Wutz. Stanford, Calif.: Stanford University Press, 1999.

Kittler, Friedrich A., and John Johnston. *Literature, Media, Information Systems: Essays, Critical Voices in Art, Theory and Culture.* Amsterdam: G+B Arts International, 1997.

Kofman, Sarah. *The Camera Obscura of Ideology.* Ithaca, N.Y.: Cornell University Press, 1999.

Kourí, Emilio. "Interpreting the Expropriation of Indio Pueblo Lands in Porfirian Mexico: The Unexamined Legacies of Andrés Molina Enríquez." *Hispanic American Historical Review* 82, no. 1 (2002): 69–117.

Krauss, Rosalind E. "Corpus Delicti," *October* 33 (Summer 1985): 31–72.

———. *The Originality of the Avant-Garde and Other Modernist Myths.* Cambridge, Mass.: MIT Press, 1985.

Krauze, Enrique. *Porfirio Díaz: Místico de la autoridad.* Mexico City: Fondo de Cultura Económica, 1987.

Krauze de Kolteniuk, Rosa. *La filosofía de Antonio Caso.* 3rd ed. Mexico City: Universidad Nacional Autónoma de México Imprenta Universitaria, 1985.

Lacan, Jacques. *The Four Fundamental Concepts of Psycho-Analysis.* New York: Norton, 1978.

Lacey, A. R. *A Dictionary of Philosophy.* 3rd ed. London: Routledge, 1996.

Lara Klahr, Flora. "Agustín Víctor Casasola: Photographer and Collector." In *Tierra y Libertad! Photographs of Mexico, 1900–1935, from the Casasola Archive,* ed. Agustín Víctor Casasola and David King. Oxford: Museum of Modern Art, 1985.

Larsen, Neil. "Latin America as a Historico-Philosophical Relation." *CR: The New Centennial Review* 3, no. 1 (2003): 55–66.

Leal, Fernando. *El arte y los monstruos.* Mexico City: Instituto Politécnico Nacional, 1990.

Leiris, Michel. "De Bataille el imposible a la imposible 'Documents.'" In *Huellas.* Mexico City: Fondo de Cultura Económica, 1988.

———. "Skyscraper." In *Encyclopaedia Acéphalica: Comprising the Critical Dictionary and Related Texts,* Georges Bataille, Robert Lebel, Isabelle Waldberg, and Alastair Brotchie. London: Atlas, 1995.

Levy, Julien. *Memoir of an Art Gallery.* New York: Putnam, 1977.

Levy, Julien, Gardner Colby Walworth, and Black Sun Press. *Surrealism.* New York: Black Sun Press, 1936.

Limón, José Eduardo. *American Encounters: Greater Mexico, the United States, and the Erotics of Culture.* Boston: Beacon, 1998.

Lingis, Alphonso. *The Community of Those Who Have Nothing in Common.* Bloomington: Indiana University Press, 1994.

———. *The Imperative.* Bloomington: Indiana University Press, 1998.

List Arzubide, Germán. *El movimiento estridentista.* Jalapa, Mexico: Ediciones de Horizonte, 1927.

Lowe, Sarah M. *Tina Modotti: Photographs.* New York: H. N. Abrams in association with the Philadelphia Museum of Art, 1995.

———. *Tina Modotti and Edward Weston: The Mexico Years.* London: Merrell, 2004.

Manuel Álvarez Bravo: Photographs and Memories, Aperture, no. 147. New York: Aperture Foundation Inc., 1997.

Marx, Karl. "The German Ideology." In *The Marx-Engel Reader,* ed. Robert C. Tucker. New York: Norton, 1972.

Merleau-Ponty, Maurice. *Phenomenology of Perception.* New York: Humanities, 1962.

Merleau-Ponty, Maurice, and Claude Lefort, eds. *The Visible and the Invisible,* Evanston, Ill.: Northwestern University Press, 1968.

Meyer, Michael C., and William H. Beezley, eds. *The Oxford History of Mexico.* Oxford: Oxford University Press, 2000.

Mitchell, W. J. T. "Art in the Age of Biocybernetic Reproduction." Lecture, Dartmouth College, Hanover, N.H., November 17, 2002.

———. *Iconology: Image, Text, Ideology.*

———. "Word and Image." In *Critical Terms for Art History,* ed. Robert S. Nelson and Richard Shiff. Chicago: University of Chicago Press, 1996.

Mitchell, W. J. Thomas. *Picture Theory: Essays on Verbal and Visual Representation.* Chicago: University of Chicago Press, 1994.

Mitchell, W. J. T., Christine Wiesenthal, and Brad Bucknell. "Essays into the Imagetext: An Interview with W. J. T. Mitchell." *Mosaic* 33, no. 2 (2000): 1–23.

Modotti, Tina. *Una mujer sin país: Las cartas a Edward Weston y otros papeles personales.* 2nd. ed. Mexico City: Cal y Arena, 2001.

Modotti, Tina, and Amy Stark. *The Letters from Tina Modotti to Edward Weston.* Tucson, Ariz.: Center for Creative Photography, University of Arizona, 1986.

Modotti, Tina, Kathleen Stoughton, Patricia Albers, Pasquale Verdicchio, and University of California, San Diego, University Art Gallery. *Dear Vocio: Photographs by Tina Modotti.* Exhibition, November 8, 1996–January 11, 1997. La Jolla, Calif.: University Art Gallery, University of California, San Diego, 1997.

Modotti, Tina, Patricia Albers, Karen Cordero, Moderna museet, Rencontres internationales de la photographie d'Arles (Association), and Helsingin kaupungin taidemuseo. *Tina Modotti: The Mexican Renaissance.* Paris: Jean-Michel Place éditions, 2000.

Monsiváis, Carlos. *Amor perdido.* Mexico City: Biblioteca Era, 1977.

———. *Días de guardar.* Mexico City: Biblioteca Era, 1970.

Morales, Alfonso, David Maawad, Carlos R. Martínez Assad, Francisco Reyes Palma, and Fototeca del INAH. *Los inicios del México contemporáneo.* Mexico City: Consejo Nacional para la Cultura y las Artes, 1997.

Mulvey, Laura. *Visual and Other Pleasures.* Bloomington: Indiana University Press, 1989.

Mulvey, Laura, and Peter Wollen. *Frida Kahlo and Tina Modotti.* 2nd ed. London: Whitechapel Art Gallery, 1982.

Nelson, Robert S., and Richard Shiff, eds. *Critical Terms for Art History.* Chicago: University of Chicago Press, 1996.

Nieto Sotelo, Jesús, Elisa Lozano Alvarez, and Centro de la Imagen. *Tina Modotti: Una nueva mirada, 1929 (Tina Modotti: A New Vision, 1929).* [Mexico City]: CNCA/ Centro de la Imagen, 2000.

Nietzsche, Friedrich. *Beyond Good and Evil: Prelude to a Philosophy of the Future.* Trans. J. R. Hollingdale. Middlesex, U.K.: Penguin Books, 1973.

———. *Philosophy and Truth: Selections from Nietzsche's Notebooks of the Early 1870's.* Atlantic Highlands, N.J.: Humanities, 1979.

Noble, Andrea. *Tina Modotti: Image, Texture, Photography.* Albuquerque: University of New Mexico Press, 2000.

Ortega y Gasset, José. *The Dehumanization of Art; and Other Essays on Art, Culture, and Literature.* Princeton, N.J.: Princeton University Press, 1972.

Pacheco, Cristina, Dave Hickey, Keith Carter, William D. Wittliff, Aperture Foundation, and Wittliff Gallery of Southwestern and Mexican Photography. *Boystown: La Zona de Tolerancia.* New York: Aperture, in association with the Wittliff Gallery of Southwestern and Mexican Photography, 2000.

Paz, Octavio. *El ogro filantrópico: Historia y política (1971–1978).* Madrid: Seix Barral, 1979.

———. "Reflections: Mexico and the United States," trans. Rachel Phillips. *History Teacher* 13, no. 3 (1980): 408–9.

Paz, Octavio, and Manuel Álvarez Bravo. *Instante y revelación.* Mexico City: Editado por A. Muñoz [para el] Círculo editorial, 1982.

Platt, Susan Noyes. *Art and Politics in the 1930s: Modernism, Marxism, Americanism:*

A History of Cultural Activism During the Depression Years. New York: Midmarch Arts Press, 1999.
———. *Modernism in the 1920s: Interpretations of Modern Art in New York from Expressionism to Constructivism.* Ann Arbor: UMI Research Press, 1985.
Poniatowska, Elena, and Manuel Álvarez Bravo. *Manuel Álvarez Bravo: El artista, su obra, sus tiempos.* Mexico City: Banco Nacional de México, 1991.
Read, Herbert Edward. *Art and Society.* London: Heinemann, 1937.
Rivera, Diego. "Manuel Álvarez Bravo." In *Manuel Álvarez Bravo: Cien años, cien días.* Mexico City: CONACULTA, 2001.
———. "Manuel Álvarez Bravo: Tercera exposición de la sociedad de arte moderno." In *Manuel Álvarez Bravo: Fotografías.* Mexico City: Sociedad de Arte Moderno, 1945.
Roget, P. M. "Explanation of an Optical Deception in the Appearance of the Spokes of a Wheel Seen through Vertical Apertures." *Philosophical Transactions of the Royal Society of London* (1825): 131–40.
Rosenheim, Jeff L. "'The Cruel Radiance of What Is': Walker Evans and the South." In *Walker Evans.* New York: Metropolitan Museum of Art in association with Princeton University Press, 2000.
Rosenthal, Anton. "Spectacle, Fear, and Protest: A Guide to the History of Urban Public Space in Latin America." *Social Science History* 24, no. 1 (2000): 33–73.
Schaffner, Ingrid, and Lisa Jacobs. *Julien Levy: Portrait of an Art Gallery.* Cambridge, Mass.: MIT Press, 1998.
Schulte, Rainer, and John Biguenet, eds. *Theories of Translation: An Anthology of Essays from Dryden to Derrida.* Chicago: University of Chicago Press, 1992.
Sedgwick, Eve Kosofsky. *Epistemology of the Closet.* Berkeley: University of California Press, 1990.
Sekula, Allan, and Ohio State University, Gallery of Fine Art. *Photography against the Grain: Essays and Photo Works, 1973–1983.* Halifax, N.S.: Press of the Nova Scotia College of Art and Design, 1984.
Solomon-Godeau, Abigail. *Photography at the Dock: Essays on Photographic History, Institutions, and Practices.* Minneapolis: University of Minnesota Press, 1991.
Sommer, Doris. *Proceed with Caution, When Engaged by Minority Writing in the Americas.* Cambridge, Mass.: Harvard University Press, 1999.
Spivak, Gayatri Chakravorty. "Can the Subaltern Speak?" In *Colonial Discourse and Post-Colonial Theory: A Reader,* ed. Patrick Williams and Laura Chrisman. New York: Columbia University Press, 1994.
———. "Can the Subaltern Speak?" In *Marxism and the Interpretation of Culture,* ed. Cary Nelson and Lawrence Grossberg. Urbana: University of Illinois Press, 1988.
———. *A Critique of Postcolonial Reason: Toward a History of the Vanishing Present.* Cambridge, Mass.: Harvard University Press, 1999.
———. *In Other Worlds: Essays in Cultural Politics.* New York: Routledge, 1988.
Squiers, Carol. *Over Exposed: Essays on Contemporary Photography.* New York: New Press, 1999.
Stieglitz, Alfred. "Photography." *Camera Work: A Photographic Quarterly* 41 (1913): 17–20.
———. "Photography and Artistic Photography." *Camera Work: A Photographic Quarterly* 42–43 (1913): 13–14.
Strauss, David Levi. *Between Dog and Wolf: Essays on Art and Politics in the Twilight of the Millennium.* New York: Autonomedia, 1999.
Tibol, Raquel. *Episodios fotográficos.* Mexico City: Libros de Proceso, 1989.

Toor, Frances. *A Treasury of Mexican Folkways.* New York: Crown, 1947.
Unruh, Vicky. *Latin American Vanguards: The Art of Contentious Encounters.* Berkeley: University of California Press, 1994.
Wallis, Brian, ed. *Art after Modernism: Rethinking Representation.* New York: New Museum of Contemporary Art, 1984.
Warren, Beth Gates. *Margrethe Mather and Edward Weston: A Passionate Collaboration.* [Santa Barbara, Calif.]: Santa Barbara Museum of Art in association with W. W. Norton, 2001.
Weston, Edward, and Nancy Wynne Newhall, eds. *The Daybooks of Edward Weston.* 2nd ed. New York: Aperture, 1990.
Williams, Raymond. *The Long Revolution.* New York: Columbia University Press, 1961.
Williams, Raymond, and Tony Pinkney, eds. *The Politics of Modernism: Against the New Conformists.* London: Verso, 1989.
Wittliff, Bill. 1998. Interview and discussion conducted by Keith Carter, Connie Todd, and Roberto Tejada, August 15, 1998. Tape recording, Accession no. 99-174, Special Collections, Albert A. Alkek Library, Southwest Texas State University, San Marcos.
———. *A Night in Old Mexico (Tattoo).* Final draft, 1974–88, Wittliff Papers, Accession no. 89-034, Special Collections, Albert A. Alkek Library, Southwest Texas State University, San Marcos.
Zea, Leopoldo. *La filosofía americana como filosofía sin más.* Mexico City: Siglo Veintiuno editores, 1977.

Index

Roberto Tejada is an art historian, curator, literary translator, and poet. He is associate professor in the art and art history department at the University of Texas, Austin. His monograph on the artist Celia Álvarez Muñoz for the series A Ver: Revisioning Art History is also published by the University of Minnesota Press.